# Reminiscences of a Highland Parish.

## D.D. Norman Macleod

## GUIDE TO FOLD-OUTS, MAPS and OVERSIZED IMAGES

In an online database, page images do not need to conform to the size restrictions found in a printed book. When converting these images back into a printed bound book, the page sizes are standardized in ways that maintain the detail of the original. For large images, such as fold-out maps, the original page image is split into two or more pages.

Guidelines used to determine the split of oversize pages:

• Some images are split vertically; large images require vertical and horizontal splits.
• For horizontal splits, the content is split left to right.
• For vertical splits, the content is split from top to bottom.
• For both vertical and horizontal splits, the image is processed from top left to bottom right.

*REMINISCENCES OF*

# A HIGHLAND PARISH

*REMINISCENCES OF*

# A HIGHLAND PARISH

By NORMAN MACLEOD, D.D.
ONE OF HER MAJESTY'S CHAPLAINS

ALEXANDER STRAHAN, PUBLISHER
56 LUDGATE HILL, LONDON
1867

# CONTENTS.

# A HIGHLAND PARISH.

## PREAMBLE.

THE Highlands of Scotland, like many greater things in the world, may be said to be unknown, yet well-known. Thousands of summer tourists every year, and from every part of the civilised world, gaze on the romantic beauties of the Trosachs and Loch Lomond, skirt the Hebrides from the Firth of Clyde to Oban, trundle through the wild gorge of Glencoe, chatter among the ruins of Iona, scramble over the wonders of Staffa, sail along the magnificent line of lakes to Inverness, reach the sombre Coolins, or disturb the silence of Coruisg. Pedestrains also, with stick and knapsack, search the more solitary wildernesses and glens of the main-

A

land, from the Grampians to Ross-shire and Caithness. Sportsmen, too, have their summer quarters dotted over the moors, or scattered on the hill-sides and beside clear streams, with all the irregularity of the boulders of the great northern drift, but furnished with most of the luxuries of an English home. All these, it must be admitted, know something of the Highlands.

Tourists know the names of steamers, coaches, and hotels; and how they were cheated by boat-men, porters, and guides. They have a vague impression of misty mountains, stormy seas, heavy rains, difficult roads, crowded inns, unpronounce-able Gaelic names, with brighter remembrances of landscapes whose grandeur they have probably never seen surpassed.

Pedestrians can recall lonely and unfrequented paths across broken moorlands undulating far away, like brown shoreless seas, through unploughed and untrodden valleys, where the bark of a shepherd's dog, and much more the sight of a shepherd's hut, were dearly welcomed. They can also recall panoramas from hill-tops or from rocky promontories, of lake and river, moor and forest, sea and island, of lonely keeps and ruined homesteads, and of infinite sheep-walks and silent glens which seemed to end in chaos. And these remembrances will flit before them like holy days of youth, and "hang about the beatings of the heart," refreshing and sanctifying it, amidst the din and worry of a city life.

Sportsmen, when they visit old shootings, hail from afar the well-known hill-sides and familiar "ground." They can tell twenty miles off where the birds are scarce, or where, according to the state of the weather, they can be found. They have waded up to the shoulders in Highland lakes, nothing visible but hat swathed with flies, and hand wielding the lithe rod and line. They have trodden the banks and tried the pools of every famous stream, until the very salmon that are left know their features and their flies, and tremble for their cunning temptations. The whole scenery is associated in their memory with the braces that have been bagged, the stags which have been killed, or—oh, horrid memory !—missed, "when the herd was coming right towards us, and all from that blockhead Charlie, who *would* look if they were within shot." * The keepers, and gillies, and beaters, and the whole tribe of ex- pectants, are also well-known, as such ; and every furrowed face is to these sportsmen a very poem, an epic, a heroic ballad, a history of the past season of happiness, as well as a prophecy of the morrow, hoped for with a beating heart, which blames the night and urges on the morn.

There are others, too, who may be expected to know something of the Highlands. Low-country sheep-farmers, redolent of wool ; English proprie- tors, who, as summer visitants, occupy the old castle of some extinct feudal chief ; Highland

---

* The following are two authentic anecdotes of the manner in which such *misses* are sometimes brought about. A young English gentleman was very recently stationed on a good pass, while a crowd of gillies, with the usual unnatural shouting and screaming, "beat" the wood for his special benefit. An antlered monarch soon made for the pass. The young gentleman, by way of being very cool, lighted a cigar. The stag soon snuffed the tainted gale, and retreated to his cavern—as a certain excellent Dean would do to his deanery—whence he refused again to issue forth.

Another, a Highlander, a keen, perhaps a too keen sportsman, was stationed on a pass; a stag was speeding towards him, when a friend on the opposite edge of the corrie, wishing to give him due warning, shouted out, "There he is near you !" "Where ? where ?" roared out the sportsman, in greatest excitement. Of course, while echo answered "where," he saw no more of the stag.

lairds, who are absentees save during the grouse season; geologists, who have explored the physical features of the land; and antiquaries, who have dipped into, or even studied profoundly, its civil and ecclesiastical antiquities.

Nevertheless, to all such, the Highlands may be as unknown in their real life and spirit as the scent of the wild bog-myrtle is to the accomplished gentleman who has no sense of smell; or as a Gaelic boat-song is to a Hindoo pundit.

Some readers may very naturally be disposed to ask, with a sneer of contempt, what precise loss any human being incurs from want of this knowledge? The opinion may be most reasonably held and expressed that the summer tourist, the wandering pedestrian, or the autumnal sportsman, have probably taken out of the Northern wilderness all that was worth bringing into the Southern Canaan of civilised life; and that as much gratitude, at least, is due for what is forgotten as for what is remembered.

Perhaps those readers may be right. And if so, then, for their own comfort as well as for mine, I warn them that if they have been foolish enough to accompany me thus far, they should pity me, bid me farewell, and wish me a safe deliverance from the mountains.

Is there any one, let me ask, who reads these lines, and yet dislikes peat-reek? any one who puts his fingers in his ears when he hears the bagpipe—the real war-pipe—begin a réal pibroch? any one who dislikes the kilt, the Gaelic, the clans, and who does not believe in Ossian? any one who has a prejudice to the Mac, or who cannot comprehend why one Mac should prefer a Mac of his own clan to the Mac of any other clan? any one who smiles at the ignorance of a Highland parson who never reads a London review, who never heard about one in ten of the "schools of modern thought," and who believes, without any mental suffering, that two and two make four? any one who puts his glass to his eye during prayer in a Highland church, and looks at his fellow-traveller with a sneer while the peasants sing their psalms? any one who, when gazing on a Highland landscape, descants to his local admirers upon some hackneyed Swiss scene *they* never saw, or enumerates a dozen Swiss Horns, the Wetter Horn,

Schreckhorn, or any other horn which has penetrated into his brain? Forbid that any such
terribly clever and well-informed cosmopolitans
should "lose ten tickings of their watch" in reading these reminiscences!

One other class sometimes found in society,
I would especially beseech to depart; I mean
Highlanders ashamed of their country. Cockneys
are bad enough, but they are sincere and honest
in their idolatry of the Great Babylon. Young
Oxonians or young barristers, even when they become slashing London critics, are more harmless
than they themselves imagine, and after all inspire
less awe than Ben Nevis, or than the celebrated
agriculturist who proposed to decompose the
mountain with acids, and scatter the debris as
a fertiliser over the Lochaber moss. But a
Highlander, who was nurtured on oatmeal porridge and oatmeal cakes; who in his youth wore
home-spun cloth, and was innocent of shoes and
stockings; who blushed in his first attempts to
speak the English language; who never saw a
nobler building for years than the little kirk in
the glen; and who owes all that makes him toler-

able in society to the Celtic blood which flows in spite of him through his veins;—for this man to be proud of his English accent, to sneer at the everlasting hills, the old kirk and its simple worship, and to despise the race which has never disgraced him—faugh! Peat-reek is frankincense in comparison with him; let him not be distracted by any of my reminiscences of the old country; leave them, I beseech of thee!

I ask not how old or how young those are who remain; I care not what their theory of political economy or their school of modern philosophy may be; I am indifferent as to their evening employment, whether it be darning stockings, sitting idle round the winter fire in the enjoyment of repose, or occupying, as invalids, their bed or their chair. If only they are charitable souls, who hope all things, and are not easily provoked; who would like to get a peep into forms of society, and to hear about customs differing greatly from what they have hitherto been acquainted with; or to have an easy chat about a country less known, perhaps, than any other in Europe,—then shall I gladly

unfold to them my reminiscences of a people
worth knowing about and loving, and of a period
in history that is passing, if, indeed, it has not
already passed away.

And now, by way of further preamble to my
reminiscences, let me take a bird's-eye view of
the parish. It is not included, by Highland
ecclesiastical statists, among what are called the
large parishes. I have no correct knowledge of
the number of square miles, of arable acres, or
of waste land, which it contains; but science and
the trigonometrical survey will, it is presumed,
give those details in due time. When viewed,
as passing tourists view it, from the sea, it has
nothing remarkable about it; and if it is pronounced by these same tourists to be uninterest-
ing, and "just the sort of scenery one would
like to pass when dining or sleeping," I won't
censure the judgment. A castled promontory, a
range of dark precipices supporting the upland
pastures, and streaked with white waterfalls, which
are lost in the copse at their base, form a picture
not very imposing when compared with " what one

sees everywhere." A long ridge of hill rising some two thousand feet above the sea, its brown sides, up to a certain height, chequered with green stripes and patches of cultivation; brown heather-thatched cottages, with white walls; here and there a mansion, whose chimneys are seen above the trees which shelter it:—these are the chief features along its seaboard of many miles. But how different is the whole scene when one lands! New beauties reveal themselves, and every object seems to change its size, appearance, and relative position. A rocky wall of wondrous beauty, the rampart of the old upraised beach which girdles Scotland, runs along the shore; the natural wild wood of ash, oak, and birch, with the hazel copse, clothes the lower hills and shelters the herds of wandering cattle; lonely sequestered bays are everywhere scooped out into beautiful harbours; points and promontories seem to grow out of the land, and huge dykes of whinstone fashion to themselves the most picturesque outlines; clear streams everywhere hasten on to the sea; small glens, perfect gems of beauty, open up entrances into deep dark pools, hemmed in by steep banks hanging with ivy, honeysuckle, rowan-trees, and ferns; while on the hill-sides scattered cottages, small farms, and shepherds' huts, the signs of culture and industry, give life to the whole scene. Ruins there are too, which show us that whatever faults belonged to the Church before the Reformation, she excelled the Church of the present day in the greater number and the greater beauty of her parish churches.* There are few sights which more rebuke the vulgar Church parsimony of these later days, or which imbue us with more grateful and generous feelings towards the missionaries of an earlier and more difficult time, than the faith and love which reared so many chapels on distant islands, and so many beautiful and costly fabrics

---

* Since writing the above I have been struck by a sarcastic and pithy remark in Dr Johnson's tour :—" It has been, for many years, popular to talk of the lazy devotion of the Romish clergy, and the sleepy laziness of men that erected churches. We may indulge our superiority with a new triumph by comparing it with the fervid activity of those who suffer them to fall." A great change has happily come over the Highlands since the time when these words were written—a period when, as the doctor informs us, there were some parishes in the far north without churches, and the people had to assemble in private houses for worship, owing to the selfish greed of those who appropriated the lands belonging to the old Church, and cared nothing for the new. No such cases can now be found.

in savage wildernesses, among a people who were too rude to appreciate such works, or the spirit which originated them. These old Highland Church extensionists were not stimulated by party rivalry, public meetings, or newspaper articles. Their praise could not have been from men. How they got the means and money we know not, but this we believe, that

> " They dreamt not of a perishable home
> Who thus could build ! "

But to view the parish in all its outward aspect, we must ascend to the top of—

> " I name not its name, lest inquisitive tourist
> Hunt it, and make it a lion, and get it at last into guide-books."

The upward path soon leaves the cultivated settlements, passes several streams, winds across tracks of moorland, and at last reaches the shielings of Corrie Borodale. One cannot imagine a sweeter spot than this in which to repose before attempting the ascent of the hill proper. A stream, clear as a diamond, and singing its hill-song, takes a sweep, and folds within its embrace a bay of emerald grass, surrounded with blooming heather.

Here and there appear small groups of ruins, mere gatherings of stones, to mark where man once built his temporary home. Before sheep-farming was introduced generally into the Highlands, about seventy or eighty years ago, the young cattle ranged at large over the hills, clambering as far up as any grass grew, and at mid-summer the milch-cows also were removed to the upland pastures, as is still the habit in Norway, and probably in other mountainous countries. The greenest, grassiest, and most sheltered nooks were always chosen for these summer residences, or shielings, as they were called. Bothies, rude but substantial, were built for the family, and various enclosures for calves, lambs, and kids surrounded them. Each family had such a number of sheep as sufficed for their own need as to food and clothing. The whole household flitted to the shieling with great glee. The men, however, remained there only for a few days, to see that bothy and pen were all right and tight. They returned to the strath, or homestead, to attend to the crops and to the peats, to thatch the houses, to set matters generally in order for the winter

season.   The women and the young folks remained at the shieling for a period of twelve or
fourteen weeks, their chief care being to gather
as much butter and cheese as could be effected
without starving the calfs or lambs; and the
housewife who succeeded in combining the "filling of the milk-pail" with the "rearing of the
calf," was celebrated in song and story.   The
never-failing distaff filled up the intervals of un-
employed time with the aged; but the young had
abundant leisure, which they seem to have bestowed on mirth and enjoyment; and among the
comparatively few songs of the Gaelic Muse which
are truly blithe and joyous — for generally she
is in sad and sombre mood—the shieling songs
occupy a prominent place.   They depict a life
of simple and genuine happiness.   Thus it is
that when one rests in such a green oasis, his
fancy again peoples the waste with the herd-lads
"calling the cattle home," and with the blithe
girls at the milking; he sees again the life among
the huts, and hears the milking songs and innocent glee; and when awakened from his reverie
by bleating sheep—the only living tenants of the

pastures—he is not disposed to admit the present time to be an improvement on the past.

But let us up to that green spot beside the ravine; then to the left along the rocks, then to the right till past the deep "peat-bogs," and finally straight up to the Cairn. When we have taken breath, let us look around. This is the very high altar of the parish, and I maintain that all the glories which can be seen from a parish rightfully belong to the parish itself, and are a part of its own rich inheritance.

Let us first look northward. Almost at our feet is a chain of small lakes, round whose green shores, unseen from the Cairn, because immediately beneath it, a prosperous tenantry once lived, of whom no trace remains, except those patches of ruins which mark their once happy homesteads.

Opposite to the spectator, and rising abruptly from the valley, is a range of hills, broken into wild scaurs and clothed with copse; while beyond these, ridge on ridge rise, like a mighty ocean sea, heaving in gigantic billows onward towards Ben Reshiepol, until lost to sight beyond the head of Loch Shiel and among the braes of Lochaber.

Sweeping the eye from the north to the west what a glorious spectacle! The chain of lakes beneath ends in the lovely Loch Sunart, with its beauteous bays and wooded islets. Over its farther shore, and above picturesque hills, the more distant Hebrides rear their heads out of the ocean.

Along the horizon northwards are seen the Scur of Eigg lifting its gigantic pillar, and the dark lines of Rum; westwards the islands of Coll and Tiree, with gleams of the ocean between. The long dark moorland ascent by which we have reached the hill-top, now carries the eye down to the sea; that sea is a strait, worming itself for more than twenty miles between the mainland where we stand, and the island of Mull, which gathers up its hills into a cluster of noble peaks about its centre, with Bentealbh (Bentalve) and Benmore towering over all. A low isthmus right opposite, opens up an arm of the sea beyond Mull, with noble headlands, beneath which the man who would see Staffa aright should himself sail out to the ocean with only a Highland crew; for not from crowded steamer can he fully

understand that pillared island and its cathedral
cave.

Let us glance to the east—the eye following the
Sound of Mull, and our panorama is completed.
How nobly the Sound, dotted with vessels, opens
up past Ardtornish and Duart Castles, ere it
mingles with the broader waters that sweep in
eddying tides past the Slate Isles, past Jura,
Scarba, on to Islay, until they finally spread
out into the roll and roar of the shoreless
Atlantic! In that eastern distance may be
seen some white smoke that marks Oban, and
over it Ben Cruachan, the most beautiful of
our west Highland mountains, accompanied by
its gray companions, "the shepherds of Etive
Glen."

I back this view from the highest hill in the
parish, for extent and varied beauty, against any
view in Europe! It is the Righi of Argyle-shire;
and, given only—what, alas! is not easily obtained—a good day, good with "gorgeous cloudland," good with lights and shadows, the bright
blue of the northern sky; (more intense than

B

that of the Italian,) mingling with the sombre dark of the northern hills, dark even when relieved in autumn by the glow of the purple heather—given all this, and I know not where to find a more magnificent outlook over God's fair earth. No reminiscences of the outer world so haunt my memory as those so often treasured up from that gray cairn; and however frequently I have returned from beholding other and more famous scenes, this one has ever appeared like a first love, more beautiful than them all.

As we descend from the hill, the minister—how oft has he gone with me there!—tells us stories worth hearing, and as he alone can tell them; stories of a pastor's life, "from perils in the wilderness, and perils of waters, and perils of the sea;" stories of character, such as the lonely hills and misty moors alone can mould; stories of combats among the wild and primitive inhabitants of the olden time; and stories, too, of the early invaders of the land from Denmark and Norway, sea-kings, or pirates rather, whose names yet linger where they fell in battle, as at Corrie *Borrodale*, Corrie *Lundie*, and Eas *Stangadale*.

But we have reached "the manse;" and from thence I must start with my "Reminiscences of a Highland Parish."

## THE MANSE.

THERE lived in the Island of Skye, more than a century ago, a small farmer or "gentleman tacksman." Some of his admirably-written letters are now before me; but I know little of his history beyond the fact revealed in his correspondence, and preserved in the affectionate traditions of his descendants, that he was "a good man," and among the first, if not the very first, in the district where he lived who introduced the worship of God in his family.

One great object of his ambition was to give his sons the best education that could be obtained for them, and in particular to train his first-born for the ministry of the Established Church of Scotland. His wishes were fully realised, for that noble institution, the parochial school, provided in the remotest districts teaching of a very high order, and produced admirable classical scholars— such as even Dr Johnson talks of with respect.

And in addition to the school teaching there was an excellent custom then existing among the tenantry in Skye, of associating themselves to obtain a tutor for their sons. The tutor resided alternately at different farms, and the boys from the other farms in the neighbourhood came daily to him. In this way the burden of supporting the teacher, and the difficulties of travelling on the part of the boys, were divided among the several families in the district. In autumn the tutor, accompanied by his more advanced pupils, journeyed on foot to Aberdeen to attend the University. He superintended their studies during the winter, and returned in spring with them to their Highland homes to pursue the same routine. The then Chief of Macleod was one who took a pride in being surrounded by a tenantry who possessed so much culture. It was his custom to introduce all the sons of his tenants who were studying at Aberdeen to their respective professors, and to entertain both professors and students at his hotel. On one such occasion, when a professor remarked with surprise, "Why, sir, these are all gentlemen!" Macleod replied, "Gentlemen I found them, as gentlemen I wish to see them educated, and as gentlemen I hope to leave them behind me." *

The "gentleman tacksman's" eldest son acted as a tutor for some time, then as parochial teacher, and finally became minister of "the Highland Parish." It was said of him that "a prettier man never left his native island." He was upwards of six feet in height, with a noble countenance which age only made nobler.

He was accompanied from Skye by a servant-lad, whom he had known from his boyhood, called "Ruari Beg," or Little Rory. Rory was rather a

* "At dinner I expressed to Macleod the joy which I had in seeing him on such cordial feelings with his clan. 'Government,' said he, 'has deprived us of our ancient power; but it cannot deprive us of our domestic satisfactions. I would rather drink punch in one of their houses, (meaning the houses of the people,) than be enabled by their hardships to have claret in my own.'"—Boswell's "Life of Johnson," vol. iv., p. 275.

contrast to his master in outward appearance.
One of his eyes was blind, but the other seemed
to have stolen the sight from its extinguished
neighbour to intensify its own. That gray eye
gleamed and scintillated with the peculiar saga-
city and reflection which one sees in the eye of
a Skye terrier, but with such intervals of feeling as human love of the most genuine kind
could alone have expressed. One leg, too, was
slightly shorter than the other, and the manner
in which he rose on the longer or sunk on the
shorter, and the frequency or rapidity with
which the alternate ups and downs in his life
were practised, became a telegraph of his
thoughts when words, out of respect to his master, were withheld. "So you don't agree with
me, Rory?" "What's wrong?" "You think
it dangerous to put to sea to-day?" "Yes;
the mountain-pass also would be dangerous?"
"Exactly so. Then we must consider what is to be
done." Such were the remarks which a series of
slow or rapid movements of Rory's limbs would
draw forth from his master, though no other
token were afforded of his inner doubt or opposi-

tion. A better boatman, a truer genius at the helm, never took a tiller in his hand; a more enduring traveller never trod the heather; a better singer of a boat-song never cheered the rowers, nor kept them as one man to their stroke; a more devoted, loyal, and affectionate "minister's man" and friend never lived than Rory—first called "Little Rory," but as long as I can remember, "Old Rory." More of him anon, however. The minister and his servant arrived in the Highland parish nearly ninety years ago, almost total strangers to its inhabitants, and alone they entered the manse to see what it was like.

I ought to inform my readers in the south, some of whom—can they pardon the suspicion if it be unjust?—are more ignorant of Scotland and its Church than they are of France or Italy and the Church of Rome,—I ought to inform them that the Presbyterian Church is established in Scotland, and that the landed proprietors in each parish are bound by law to build and keep in repair a church, suitable school, and parsonage or "manse," and also to secure a portion of land, or "glebe,"

for the minister. Both manses and churches
have of late years improved immensely in Scotland, so that in many cases they are now far
superior to those in some of the rural parishes of
England. But much still remains to be accomplished in this department of architecture and taste.
Yet even at the time I speak of, the manse was in
its structure rather above than below the houses
occupied by the ordinary gentry, with the exception of " the big house " of the Laird. It has been
replaced by one more worthy of the times; but
it was nevertheless respectable, as the sketch of
it on the title-page showeth.

The glebe was the glory of the manse! It was
among the largest in the county, consisting of
about sixty acres, and containing a wonderful
combination of Highland beauty. It was bounded
on one side by a " burn," whose torrent rushed
far down between lofty steep banks clothed with
natural wood, ash, birch, hazel, oak, and rowan-
tree, and which poured its dark moss-water over
a series of falls, and through deep pools, " with
beaded bubbles winking at the brim." It was
never tracked along its margin by any human

being, except herd-boys and their companions, who swam the pools and clambered up the banks, holding by the roots of trees, starting the kingfisher from his rock, or the wild cat from his den. On the other side of the glebe was the sea, with here a sandy beach, and there steep rocks and deep water, and small gray islets beyond ; while many birds, curlews, cranes, divers, and gulls of all sorts, gave life to the rocks and shore. Along the margin of the sea there stretched a flat of green grass which suggested the name it bore, namely, " the Duke of Argyle's walk." And pacing along that green margin at evening, what sounds and wild cries were heard of piping sea-birds, chafing waves, the roll of oars, and the song from fishing-boats, telling of their return home. The green terrace-walk which fringed the sea, was but the outer border of a flat that was hemmed in by the low precipice of the old upraised beach of Scotland. Higher still was a second story of green fields and emerald pastures, broken by a lovely rocky knoll, called Fingal's hill, whose gray head, rising out of green grass, bent towards the burn, and looked down into its own image reflected in the deep pools which slept at its feet. On that upper table-land, and beside a clear stream, stood the manse and garden sheltered by trees. Beyond the glebe began the dark moor, which swept higher and higher, until crowned by the mountain-top looking away to the Western Islands and the peaks of Skye.

The minister, like most of his brethren, soon took to himself a wife, the daughter of a neighbouring "gentleman tacksman," and the granddaughter of a minister, well born and well bred ; and never did man find a help more meet for him. In that manse they lived for nearly fifty years, and there were born to them sixteen children; yet neither father nor mother could ever lay their hand on a child of theirs and say, "We wish this one had not been." They were all a source of unmingled joy.

A small farm was added to the glebe, for it was found that the plant required to work sixty acres of arable and pasture land could work more without additional expense. Besides, John, Duke of Argyle, made it a rule at that time to give farms at less than their value to the ministers on his

estates ; and why, therefore, should not our minister, with his sensible, active, thrifty wife, and
growing sons and daughters, have a small one, and
thus secure for his large household abundance of
food, including milk and butter, cheese, potatoes,
and meal, with the excellent addition of mutton,
and sometimes beef too?   And the good man did
not attend to his parish worse that his living was
thus bettered ; nor was he less cheerful or earnest
in duty because in his house "there was bread
enough and to spare."

The manse and glebe of that Highland parish
were a colony which ever preached sermons, on
week days as well as Sundays, of industry and
frugality, of courteous hospitality and bountiful
charity, and of the domestic peace, contentment,
and cheerfulness of a holy Christian home.

Several cottages were built by the minister
in sheltered nooks near his dwelling.   One or
two were inhabited by labourers and shepherds ;
another by the weaver, who made all the carpets, blankets, plaids, and finer webs of linen
and woollen cloths required for the household ;
and another by old Jenny, the henwife, herself

an old hen, waddling about and *chucking* among her numerous family of poultry. Old Rory, with his wife and family, was located near the shore, to attend at spare hours to fishing, as well as to be ready with the boat for the use of the minister in his pastoral work. Two or three cottages besides were inhabited by objects of charity, whose claims upon the family it was difficult to trace. An old sailor—Serrasnan Long, "George of the Ships," was his sole designation—had settled down in one, but no person could tell anything about him, except that he had been born in Skye, had served in the navy, had fought at the Nile, had no end of stories for winter evenings, and span yarns about the wars and "foreign parts." He had come long ago in distress to the manse, from whence he had passed after a time into the cottage, and there lived—very much as a dependent on the family—until he died twenty years afterwards. A poor decayed gentle-woman, connected with one of the old families of the county, and a tenth cousin of the minister's wife, had also cast herself in her utter loneliness, on the glebe. She had only intended to remain

a few days—she did not like to be troublesome
—but she knew she could rely on a blood relation, and she found it hard to leave, for whither
could she go? And those who had taken her
in never thought of bidding this sister "depart
in peace, saying, Be ye clothed;" and so she
became a neighbour to the sailor, and was always
called "Mrs" Stewart, and was treated with the
utmost delicacy and respect, being fed, clothed,
and warmed in her cottage with the best which
the manse could afford. And when she died, she
was dressed in a shroud fit for a lady, while tall
candles, made for the occasion according to the old
custom, were kept lighted round her body. Her
funeral was becoming the gentle blood that flowed
in her veins; and no one was glad in their heart
when she departed, but all sincerely wept, and
thanked God she had lived in plenty and died
in peace.

Within the manse the large family of sons and
daughters managed, somehow or other, to find
accommodation not only for themselves, but
also for a tutor and governess. And such a
thing as turning any one away for want of room

was never dreamt of. When hospitality demanded such a small sacrifice, the boys would all go to the barn, and the girls to the chairs and sofas of parlour and dining-room, with fun and laughter, joke and song, rather than not make the friend or stranger welcome. And seldom was the house without either. The " kitchen-end," or lower house, with all its indoor crannies of closets and lofts, and outdoor additions of cottages, barns, and stables, was a little world of its own, to which wandering pipers, parish fools, and beggars, with all sorts of odd-and-end characters came, and where they ate, drank, and rested. As a matter of course, the "upper house" had its own set of guests to attend to. The traveller by sea, whom adverse winds and tides drove into the harbour for refuge ; or the traveller by land ; or any minister passing that way ; or friends on a visit ; or, lastly and but rarely, some foreign " Sassanach " from the Lowlands of Scotland or England, who dared then to explore the unknown and remote Highlands as one now does Montenegro or the Ural Mountains—all these found a hearty reception.

One of the most welcome visitors was the packman. His arrival was eagerly longed for by all, except the minister, who trembled for his small purse in presence of the prolific pack. For this same pack often required a horse for its conveyance. It contained a choice selection of everything which a family was likely to require from the lowland shops. The haberdasher and linendraper, the watchmaker and jeweller, the cutler and hairdresser, with sundry other crafts in the useful and fancy line, were all fully represented in the endless repositories of the pack. What a solemn affair was the opening up of that peripatetic warehouse! It took a few days to gratify the inhabitants of manse and glebe, and to enable them to decide how their money should be invested. The boys held sundry councils about knives, and the men about razors, silk handkerchiefs, or, it may be, about the final choice of a silver watch. The female servants were in nervous agitation about some bit of dress. Ribbons, like rainbows, were unrolled ; prints held up in graceful folds before the light ; cheap shawls were displayed on the back of some handsome lass, who served as a model. There never was seen such new fashions or such cheap bargains! And then how "dear papa" was coaxed by mamma; and mamma again by her daughters. Each thing was so beautiful, so tempting, and was discovered to be so necessary! All this time the packman was treated as a friend. He almost always carried pipe or violin, with which he set the youngsters a-dancing, and was generally of the stamp of him whom Wordsworth has made illustrious. The news gathered on his travels was as welcome to the minister as his goods were to the minister's family. No one in the upper house was so vulgar as to screw him down, but felt it due to his respectability to give him his own price, which, in justice to those worthy old merchants, I should state was generally reasonable.

The manse was the grand centre to which all the inhabitants of the parish gravitated for help and comfort. Medicines for the sick were weighed out from the chest yearly replenished in Edinburgh or Glasgow. They were not given in homœopathic doses, for Highlanders, accustomed to things on a large scale, would have had no faith in globules, and faith was half their cure. Common sense and common medicines were found helpful to health. The poor, as a matter of course, visited the manse, not for an order on public charity, but for aid from private charity, and it was never refused in *kind*, such as meal, wool, or potatoes. There being no lawyers in the parish, lawsuits were adjusted in the manse; and so were marriages not a few. The distressed came there for comfort, and the perplexed for advice; and there was always something material as well as spiritual to share with them all. No one went away empty in body or soul. Yet the barrel of meal was never empty, nor the cruise of oil extinguished. A "wise" neighbour once remarked, "That minister with his large family will ruin himself, and if he dies they will be beggars." Yet there has never been a beggar among them to the fourth generation. No saying was more common in the mouth of this servant than the saying of his Master, "It is more blessed to give than to receive."

A striking characteristic of the manse life was its constant cheerfulness. One cottager could play the bagpipe, another the fiddle. The minister was an excellent performer on the violin, and to have his children dancing in the evening was his delight. If strangers were present, so much the better. He had not an atom of that proud fanaticism which connects religion with suffering, as suffering, apart from its cause.*

Here is an extract from a letter written by the minister in his old age, some fifty years ago, which gives a very beautiful picture of the secluded manse and its ongoings. It is written at the beginning of a new year, in reply to one which he had received from his first-born son, then a minister in a distant parish :—

"What you say about the beginning of another year is quite true. But, after all, may not the same observations apply equally well to every new day? Ought not daily mercies to be acknowledged, and God's favour and protection asked for

---

* A minister in a remote island parish once informed me that, "on religious grounds," he had broken the only fiddle in the island! His notion of religion, I fear, is not rare among his brethren in the far west and north. We are informed by Mr Campbell, in his admirable volumes on the "Tales of the Highlands," that the old songs and tales are also being put under the clerical ban in some districts, as being too secular and profane for the pious inhabitants. What next? Are the singing-birds to be shot by the kirk-sessions?

every new day? and are we not as ignorant of what a new day as of what a new year may bring forth? There is nothing in nature to make this day in itself more worthy of attention than any other. The sun rises and sets on it as on other days, and the sea ebbs and flows. Some come into the world and some leave it, as they did yesterday and will do to-morrow. On what day may not one say, 'I am a year older than I was this day last year?' Still I must own that the first of the year speaks to me in a more commanding and serious language than any other common day; and the great clock of time, which announced the first hour of this year, did not strike unnoticed by us.

"The sound was too loud to be unheard, and too solemn to pass away unheeded. '*Non obtusa adeo gestamus pectora Poeni.*' We in the manse did not mark the day by any unreasonable merriment. We were alone, and did eat and drink with our usual innocent and cheerful moderation. I began the year by gathering all in the house and on the glebe to prayer. Our souls were stirred up to bless and to praise the Lord: for what more reasonable, what more delightful duty than to show forth our gratitude and thankfulness to that great and bountiful God from whom we have our years, and days, and all our comforts and enjoyments? Our lives have been spared till now; our state and conditions in life have been blessed; our temporal concerns· have been favoured; the blessing of God has co-operated with our honest industry; our spiritual advantages have been great and numberless; we have had the means of grace and the hope of glory; in a word, we have had all that was requisite for the good of our body and soul; and shall not our souls and all that is within us, all our powers and faculties, be stirred up to bless and praise His name?

"But to return. This pleasant duty being gone through, refreshments were brought in, and had any of your clergy seen the crowd, (say thirty, great and small, besides the family of the manse,) they would pity the man who, under God, had to support them all! This little congregation being dismissed, they went to enjoy themselves. They entertained each other by turns. In the evening, I gave them one end of the house, where they danced and sang with great glee and good manners till near day. We enjoyed ourselves in a different manner in the other end. Had you popped in un- noticed, you would have seen us all grave, quiet, and studious. You would see your father reading ' The Seasons ;' your mother, ' Porteus' Lectures ;' your sister Anne, ' The Lady of the Lake ;' and Archy, ' Tom Thumb !'

"Your wee son was a new and great treat to you in those bonny days of rational mirth and joy, but not a whit more so than you were to me at his time of life, nor can he be more so during the years to come. May the young gentleman long live to bless and comfort you! May he be to you what you have been and are to me! I am the last that can honestly recommend to you not to allow him get too strong a hold of your heart, or rather not to allow yourself *doat too much* upon him. This was a peculiar weakness of my own, and of which I had cause more than once to repent with much grief and sore affliction. But your mother's creed always was, (*and truly she has acted up to it,*) to enjoy and delight in the blessings of the Almighty, while they were spared to her, with a thankful and grateful heart, and to part with them when it was the will of the gracious Giver to remove them, with humble submission and meek resignation."

I will have something more to say afterwards about this pastor and his work in the parish.

## THE BOYS OF THE MANSE, AND THEIR EDUCATION.

THE old minister having no money to leave his boys when he died, wisely determined to give them, while he lived, the best education in his power. The first thing necessary for the accomplishment of his object, was to obtain a good tutor, and a good tutor was not difficult to get.

James, as we shall call the tutor of the manse boys, was a laborious student, with a most creditable amount of knowledge of the elements of Greek and Latin. When at college he was obliged to live in the top story of a high house in a murky street, breathing an atmosphere of smoke, fog, and consumed tallow; cribbed in a hot, close room;

feeding on ill-cooked meat, (fortunately in small
quantities;) drinking coffee consisting of half
water and half chicory; sitting up long after
midnight writing essays or manufacturing exercises, until at last dyspepsia depressed his
spirits and blanched his visage except where it
was coloured by a hectic flush, which deepened
after a fit of coughing. When he returned home
after having carried off prizes in the Greek and
Latin classes, what cared his mother for all these
honours? No doubt she was "prood o' oor James,"
but yet she could hardly know her boy, he had become so pale, so haggard, and so "unlike himself."
What a blessing for James to get off to the Highlands! He there breathed such air, and drank
such water, as made him wonder at the untaxed
bounty of creation. He climbed the hills and
dived into the glens, and rolled himself on the
heather; he visited old castles, learned to fish, and
perhaps to shoot, shutting both eyes at first when
he pulled the trigger. He began to write verses,
and to fall in love with one or all of the young
ladies. That was the sort of life which Tom
Campbell the poet passed when sojourning in the

West Highlands ; ay, for a time in this very parish too, where a lovely spot is yet pointed out as the scene of his solitary musings. James had a great delight not only in imparting the rudiments of language, but also in opening up various high roads and outlying fields of knowledge. The intellectual exercise braced himself, and delighted his pupils.

If ever "muscular Christianity" was taught to the rising generation, the Highland manse of those days was its gymnasium. After school hours, and on "play-days" and Saturdays, there was no want of employment calculated to develop physical energy. The glebe and farm made a constant demand for labour which it was joy to the boys to contribute. Every season brought its own appropriate and interesting work. But sheep-shearing, the reaping and ingathering of the crops, with now and then the extra glory of a country market for the purchase and sale of cattle, with tents, games, gingerbread, horse jockeys, and English cattle dealers,—these were their great annual feasts.

The grander branches of education were fishing, sailing, shooting—game-laws being then unknown

—and also what was called "hunting." The fishing I speak of was not with line and fly on river or lake, or the spearing of salmon in the pools, though both these kinds of sport were in abundance ; but sea-fishing, with rod and white fly, for "seath" and mackerel in their season. It was delightful towards evening to pull for miles to the fishing-ground in company with other boats. A race was sure to be kept up both going and returning, while songs arose from all hands and from every boat, intensifying the energy of the rowers. Then there was the excitement of getting among a great play of fish, which made the water foam for half a mile round, and attracted flocks of screaming birds who seemed mad with gluttony, while six or seven rods had all their lines tight, and their ends bent to cracking with the sport, keeping every fisher hard at work pulling in the fine lithe creatures, until the bottom of the boat was filled with scores. Sometimes the sport was so good as to induce a number of boats' crews to remain all night on a distant island, which had only a few sheep, and a tiny spring of water. The boats were made fast on the lee side, and their crews landed to wait

for daybreak. Then began the fun and frolic!—
"sky-larking," as the sailors call it, among the
rocks—pelting one another, amid shouts of laughter, with clods and wrack, or any harmless substance
which could be collected for the battle, until they
were wearied, and lay down to sleep in a sheltered
nook, and all was silent but the beating wave, the
"eerie" cries of birds, and the splash of some sea-
monster in pursuit of its prey. What glorious
reminiscences have I, too, of those scenes, and
especially of early morn, as watched from those
green islands! It seems to me as if I had never
beheld a true sunrise since; yet how many have
I witnessed! I left the sleeping crews, and
ascended the top of the rock, immediately before
daybreak, and what a sight it was, to behold the
golden crowns which the sun placed on the brows
of the mountain-monarchs who first did him hom-
age; what heavenly dawnings of light on peak
and scaur, contrasted with the darkness of the
lower valleys; what gems of glory in the eastern
sky, changing the cold, gray clouds of early morning into bars of gold and radiant gems of beauty;
and what a flood of light suddenly burst upon the

dancing waves, as the sun rose above the horizon, and revealed the silent sails of passing ships; and what delight to see and hear the first break of the fish on the waters! With what pleasure I descended, and gave the cheer which made every sleeper awake, and scramble to their boats, and in a few minutes resume the work of hauling in our dozens! Then home with a will for breakfast — each striving to be first on the sandy shore!

Fishing at night with the drag-net was a sport which cannot be omitted in recording the enjoyments of the manse boys. The spot selected was a rocky bay, or embouchure of a small stream. The night was generally dark and calm. The pleasure of the occupation was made up of the pull, often a long one, within the shadow of the rocky shore, with the calm sea dimly reflecting the stars in the sky, and then the slow approach, with gently-moving oars, towards the beach, in order not to disturb the fish; the wading up to the middle to draw in the net when it had encircled its prey; and the excitement as it was brought into shallow water, the fish shining with their phosphoric light; until, at last, a grand haul of salmon-trout, flounders, small cod, seath, and lythe, lay walloping in the folds of the net upon the sandy beach.

Those fishing excursions, full of incident as they were, did not fully test or develop the powers of the boys. But others were afforded capable of doing so. It was their delight to accompany their father on any boating journey which the discharge of his pastoral duties required. In favourable weather they had often to manage the boat themselves without any assistance. When the sky was gloomy, old Rory took the command. Such of my readers as have had the happiness, or the horror, as their respective tastes may determine, of sailing among the Hebrides in an open boat, will be disposed to admit that it is a rare school for disciplining its pupils to habits of endurance, foresight, courage, decision, and calm self-possession. The minister's boat was about eighteen feet keel, undecked, and rigged fore and aft. There were few days in which the little *Roe* would not venture out, with Rory at the helm; and with no other person would his master divide the honour of being the most famous steersman in those waters. But to navigate her across the wild seas of that stormy coast demanded "a fine hand," such as a rider for the Derby prides himself in, and which can only be acquired by years of constant practice. If Rory would have made a poor jockey, what jockey would have steered the *Roe* in a gale of wind? I can assure the reader it was a solemn business, and solemnly was it gone about! What care in seeing the ropes in order; the sails reefed; the boys in their right place at the fore and stern sheets; and everything made snug. And what a sight it was to see that old man when the storm was fiercest, with his one eye, under its shaggy gray brow, looking to windward, sharp, calm, and luminous as a spark; his hand clutching the tiller —never speaking a word, and displeased if any other broke the silence, except the minister, who sat beside him, assigning this post of honour as a great favour to Rory, during the trying hour. That hour was generally when wind and tide met, and "gurly grew the sea," whose green waves rose with crested heads, hanging against the cloud-rack,

and sometimes concealing the land : while black
sudden squalls, rushing down from the glens struck
the foaming billows in fury, and smote the boat,
threatening, with a sharp scream, to tear the tiny
sail in tatters, break the mast, or blow out of the
water the small dark speck that carried the manse
treasures. There was one moment of peculiar
difficulty and concentrated danger when the hand
of a master was needed to save them. The boat
has entered the worst part of the tideway. How
ugly it looks! Three seas higher than the rest
are coming; and you can see the squall blowing
their white crests into smoke. In a few minutes
they will be down on the *Roe.* " Look out,
Rory !" whispers the minister. " Stand by the
sheets !" cries Rory to the boys, who, seated on
the ballast, gaze on him like statues, watching his
face, and eagerly listening in silence. " Ready !"
is their only reply. Down came the seas rolling,
rising, breaking ; falling, rising again, and looking
higher and fiercer than ever. The tide is running
like a race-horse, and the gale meets it ; and the
three seas appear now to rise like huge pyramids
of green water, dashing their foam up into the sky.

The first may be encountered and overcome, for the boat has good way upon her; but the others will rapidly follow up the thundering shock, and a single false movement of the helm by even one hair's-breadth will bring down a cataract like Niagara that would shake a frigate, and sink the *Roe* into the depths like a stone. The boat meets the first wave, and rises dry over it. "Slack out the main sheet, quick, and hold hard; there—steady!" commands Rory in a low firm voice, and the huge back of the second wave is seen breaking to leeward. "Haul in, boys, and belay!" Quick as lightning the little craft, having again gathered way, is up in the teeth of the wind, and soon is spinning over the third topper, not a drop of water having come over the lee gunwale. "Nobly done, Rory!" exclaims the minister, as he looks back to the fierce tideway which they have passed. Rory smiles with satisfaction at his own skill, and quietly remarks of the big waves, "They have *their* road, and she has hers!" "Hurrah for the old boat!" exclaims one of the boys. Rory repeats his favourite aphorism—yet never taking his eye off the sea and sky—"Depend on it, my lads, it is not

D

boats that drown the men, but men the boats!"
I take it that the old *Roe* was no bad school
for boys who had to battle with the storms and
tides of life. I have heard one of these boys
tell, when old and grayheaded, and after having encountered many a life storm, how much
he owed to those habits of mind which had
been strengthened by his sea life with old
Rory.*

* For the sake of any genuine Celt who may be among my readers I print the following song, still sung by many a boatman in
the Western Isles, who knows nothing of either its subject or its
author. It was composed by the eldest son of the manse in
honour of Rory. The air is the same as that to which Sir W.
Scott composed the song in the *Lady of the Lake*, " Roderick Vic
Alpin Dhu " :—

### RUARAI BEAG SHABHARI, HO I HORO.

" Fàilt' air a' Ghille
    Le 'chaog-shùilibh biorach
    Le 'chòta, 's le 'bhrigiosan
    Gasda de 'n chlò !
    'S maith dh' aithn 'ear air d' aogas
    Gur Leòdach do Chinne
    Siòl Thormaid o 'n Eilein
    Air an luidheadh an ceo.
    O Aonghais 'Ic Ruarai,
    'S tu athair an deadh mhic,
    'S tu dh' fhaodadh 'bhi moitcil
    Na-m bitheadh tu beò ;
    'S nach 'eil neach anns au Sgìreachd

The "hunting" I have alluded to as affording another branch of out-door schooling, was very different from what goes under that term in the south. It was confined chiefly to wild cats and otters. The animals employed in this work were terriers. Two of the manse terriers which became famous were "Gaisgeach" or "Hero," and "Cuileag" or "Fly." They differed very considerably in character: Gaisgeach was a large terrier with wiry black and gray hair; Cuileag was of a dusky brown, and so small that she

Cho fharasda, fhìnealt'
Ri Ruarai beag Shabhari, Ho i horō.

" Cha n-eil Cléireach a' s dùthaich
A 's lùthmhoire shiùbhlas ;
Gu 'n toirt gu pùsadh
Bithidh tu dlùth air an toìr.
Cha n-eil Cléireach 's au t Seanadh
Co ro mhaith a stiùireas
A' Bhìrlinn troi chuaintibh
Nan stuaghannan mòr' ;
'N uaìr 'sheideas an doinionn
Na siùil o na crannaibh,
'S a chaillear gach cladach
Le sìoban, 's le ceò,
'S in éighidh gach maraich',
O 's ro mhaith do ghabhail
A Ruarai bhig Shabhari, Ho i horō.

could be carried in the pocket of a shooting jacket.
Gaisgeach presumed not to enter the parlour,
or to mingle with genteel society; Cuileag
always did so, and lay upon the hearth-rug, where
she basked and reposed in state. Gaisgeach was
a sagacious, prudent, honest police sergeant, who
watched the house day and night, and kept the
farm-dogs in awe, and at their respective posts.
He was also a wonderful detective of all beggars,
foumarts, wild cats, and vermin of every kind,
smelling afar off the battle with man or beast.
Cuileag was full of *reticence,* and seemed to think of
nothing or do nothing until *seriously* wanted; and

> " 'N uair sheinneadh tu 'n Iorram
> 'S tu 'dhùisgeadh an spiorad
> Ann an guaillibh nan gillean,
> 'S iad 'an glacan nan ràmh :
> 'N uair sheinneadh tu 'n duanag,
> 'N sin b' ait leam 'bhi suas riut
> 'Bhi 'm shuidhe ri 'd ghuallainn
> 'S an t searrag a' m làimh.
> Cha n-eil eadar so 's Rò-ag
> A sheirmeadh leat 'Mòrag'
> 'S tu 'g iomairt le furan
> Ràmh-bràghad an Rōe ;
> 'N sin their iad rī Ruarai,
> 'O piseach 'us buaidh ort
> A Ruarai bhig Shabhari, Ho i horō."

then indomitable courage bristled in every hair of her body. Both had seen constant service since their puppyhood, and were covered with honourable scars from the nose to the tip of the tail; each cut being the record of a battle, and the subject of a story by the boys.

The otters in the parish were numerous, large, and fierce. There was one famous den called "Clachòrain," or the otter's stone, composed of huge blocks, from which the sea wholly receded during spring-tides. Then was the time to search for its inhabitants. This was done by the terriers driving the otters out, that they might be shot while making their way across a few yards of stone and tangle to the sea. I have known nine killed in this one den during a single year. But sometimes the otter occupied a den a few hundred yards inland, where a desperate fight ensued between him and the dogs. Long before the den was reached, the dogs became nervous and impatient, whining, and glancing up to the face of their master, and, with anxious look, springing up and licking his hands. To let them off until quite close to the den was sure to destroy the sport, as the otter would, on hearing them bark, make at once for the sea. Gaisgeach could, without difficulty, be kept in the rear, but little Cuileag, conscious of her moral weakness to resist temptation, begged to be carried. Though she made no struggle to escape, yet she trembled with eagerness, as, with cocked ears and low cry, she looked out for the spot where she and Gaisgeach would be set at liberty. That spot reached—what a hurry-scurry, as off they rushed, and sprang in! Gaisgeach's short bark was a certain sign that the enemy was there; it was the first shot in the battle. If Cuileag followed, the fight had begun in earnest.

One of the last great battles fought by Cuileag was in that inland den. On gazing down between two rocks which met below at an angle, Cuileag's head and the head of a huge otter, amid loud barkings and the sound of a fierce combat, were seen alternately appearing, as each tried to seize the throat of the other. At last Cuileag made a spring, and caught the otter by the nose or lip. A shepherd who was present, fearing the dog would be cut to pieces, since the den was too narrow to

admit Gaisgeach, (who seemed half apoplectic with
passion and inability to force his way in,) managed,
by a great effort, to get hold of the otter's tail, and
to drag it upwards through a hole resembling a
chimney. He was terrified that the otter, when
it got its head out, would turn upon him and
bite him,—and what a bite those beautiful teeth
can give!—but to his astonishment, the brute appeared with Cuileag hanging to the upper lip. Both
being flung on the grass, Gaisgeach came to the
rescue, and very soon, with some aid from the
boys, the animal of fish and fur was killed and
brought in triumph to the manse.

There is another story about Cuileag which is
worth recording. The minister, accompanied by
her, went to visit a friend, who lived sixty miles
off in a direct line from the manse. To reach the
place he had to cross several wild hills, and five
arms of the sea or freshwater lochs stretching for
miles. On their arrival the dog took her place,
according to custom, on the friend's hearthrug,
from which, however, she was ignominiously
driven by a servant, and sent to the kitchen. She
disappeared, and left no trace of her whereabouts.

One evening, about a fortnight afterwards, little Cuileag entered the manse parlour, worn down to a skeleton, her paws cut and swollen, and hardly able to crawl to her master, or to express her joy at meeting all her dear old friends once more. Strange to say, she was accompanied into the room by Gaisgeach, who, after frolicking about, seemed to apologise for the liberty he took, and bolted out to bark over the glebe, and tell the other dogs which had gathered round what had happened. How did Cuileag discover the way home, since she had never visited that part of the country before? How did she go round the right ends of the lochs, which had been all crossed by boat on their onward journey, and then recover her track, traveling twice or thrice sixty miles? How did she live? These were questions which no one could answer, seeing Cuileag was silent. She never, however, recovered that two weeks' wilderness journey. Her speed was ever after less swift, and her grip less firm.

The games of the boys were all athletic,—throwing the hammer, putting the stone, leaping, wrestling, and the like. Perhaps the most favourite game was "shinty," called *hockey*, I believe, in England. This is played by any number of persons, as many as a hundred often engaging in it. Each has a club, or stick bent at the end, and made short or long, as it is to be used by one or both hands. The largest and smoothest field that can be found is selected for the game. The combat lies in the attempt of each party to knock a ball beyond a certain boundary in his opponent's ground. The ball is struck by any one on either side who can get at it. Few games are more exciting, or demand more physical exertion than a good shinty match.

I have said nothing regarding a matter of more importance than anything touched upon in this chapter, and that is the *religious* education of the manse boys. But there was nothing so peculiar about it as to demand special notice. It was very real and genuine; and perhaps its most distinguishing feature was, that instead of its being confined to "tasks," and hard, dry, starched Sunday lessons only, it was spread over all the week, and consisted chiefly in developing the religious and domestic affections by a frank, loving, sympathising intercourse between parents and children; by making home happy to the "bairns;" by training them up wisely and with *tact*, to reverence *truth*,—truth in word, deed, and manner; and to practise *unselfishness* and courteous considerateness towards the wants and feelings of others. These and many other minor lessons were never separated from Jesus Christ, the source of all life. They were taught to know Him as the Saviour, through whose atonement their sins were pardoned, and through whose grace alone, obtained daily in prayer, they could be made like Himself. The teaching was *real*, and was felt by the boys to be like sunshine on dew, warming, refreshing, and quickening their young hearts; and not like a something forced into the mind, with which it had no sympathy, as a leaden ball is rammed down into a gun-barrel. Once I heard an elderly Highland gentleman say that the first impression he ever received of the reality of religion was in connexion with the first death which occurred among the manse boys.

Need I add, in conclusion, that the manse was a perfect paradise for a boy during his holidays!

Oh, let no anxious mother interfere at such times with loving grandmother and loving aunts or uncles! In spite of the Latin or Greek lesson which his grandfather or the tutor delights to give him in the morning, his excellent parents write to say that "too much idleness may injure him." Not a bit! The boy is drinking in love with every drink of warm milk given him by the Highland dairymaid, and with every look, and kiss, and gentle hug given him by his dear grannie or aunts. Education, if it is worth anything, *draws out* as much as it puts in; and this sort of education will strengthen his brain and brace his nerves for the work of the town grammar-school, to which he must soon return. His parents further write, "It does not do to pamper him too much, it may make him selfish." Quite true as an educational axiom; but his grandmother denies—bless her for it, dear, good woman!—that giving him milk or cream *ad libitum*, with "scones" and cheese at all hours, is pampering him. And his aunts take him on their knees, and fondle him, and tell him stories, and sit beside him when he is in bed, and sing songs to him; and there is not a herd or shepherd but

wishes to make him happy; and old Rory has him
always beside him in the boat, and gives him the
helm, and, in spite of the old hand holding the
tiller behind the young one, persuades his "darling,"
as he calls him, that it is he, the boy, who steers
the boat.   Oh! sunshine of youth, let it shine on!
Let love flow out fresh and full, unchecked by any
rule but what love creates; pour thyself down
without stint into the young heart; make the days
of boyhood happy, for other days of labour and
sorrow must come, when the memory of those
dear eyes, and clasping hands, and sweet caress-
ings, will, next to the love of God from which
they flow, save the man from losing faith in the
human heart, help to deliver him from the curse of
selfishness, and be an Eden in his memory when
he is driven forth into the wilderness of life!

## THE MANSE BOY SENT TO COLLEGE.

IT is a great era in most Scotch manses when
one of the boys begins his college career.
There is first the question of money—the importance of which, over the whole world, and among
all races of men, is fully recognised. A large
family, and a small "stipend," are not rare phe-
nomena in the Highland manse — and how to
clothe, feed, and educate the "bairns," often seems
an insoluble problem. For they *do* grow so
rapidly out of their clothes, and their appetites
are *so* good, "puir things," as Betty the nurse
says. And the eldest girls are every day looking
bonnier, as the same unbiassed witness asserts,

and they require something nice, no doubt; and the younger ones are such romps, and with such high spirits, that they require something which will not easily wear out; and then the boys!— how they wear their shoes, and destroy their clothes, and never think how they can be supplied with new ones. But somehow that most wonderful and most blessed Angel in the house, the mother, manages to supply every want, without disturbing her husband at his sermon or in his sleep; and he, good man, seldom knows the genius of contrivance, and the wakeful hours, and the busy thoughts, and the alternate smiles and tears, and the personal self-denial by which, with little means, she accomplishes great ends. It has long been a part of my social creed that, as a rule, the wives are far greater than their husbands, one part of their greatness being that they never allow their husbands to suspect their own inferiority.

But to return to the old manse, and an older generation. When a boy had to go to college, the minister required to exercise all his faculties, and bring every power into play to raise the necessary funds. What calculations as to what could be spared from his stipend; or how much could be raised from his barley or potato crop, from his cattle, or from his pigs even! Ah! he is now disturbed in his study, and in his sleep; yet the matter of twenty pounds would make him feel like a king—for his boy's sake. And such a boy!—just look at those eyes, as his parents see them, pure and innocent as a mountain spring; and look at that head, like a granite rock, with yellow fern drooping over it; and that mouth—oh! that it were opened in the pulpit! The boy has the make of a grand man in him. "But twenty pounds!"—the minister mutters in his dream, about three in the morning, while his wife is staring at the moon then shining into the room. In spite of every difficulty the good man succeeds—God's strength is often perfected in his weakness—and he makes no complaint, and owes no man anything.

The night before the boy goes is a night to be remembered by the family. What a packing of the few clothes! they are very few, but good home-spun, durable, and blessed, for every thread has the mark of love in it! What a numbering

of shirts and stockings;—what directions about
the tender and wise usage of them;—what quiet
confidential talk about the Bible, rolled up in a
white handkerchief, and put into a corner of the
trunk;—what an extra sobriety about the family
devotions, during which smothered sobs are heard,
and a universal blowing of noses, from young
brothers and sisters. And then on the morning
of departure there is not only the new trunk to be
seen to, with an address upon it which might do
for a sign-board, but a cheese, a "crock" of
butter, a mutton ham, kippered salmon, and other
provisions for use in the lodgings, with a few
pots of jam and jelly for sore throat—his mother
says. And then the parting with all, not forget-
ting the dogs, which follow to the water's edge,
and with their low whine strike a note in harmony with the sorrow which all feel, though it
is kept down by forced words of cheer till the
last moment. Soon the old manse is out of
sight, and an old world has departed with it,
and a new world for good or evil begun to the
boy.

Our Scottish college system is as unlike that of

England as the Presbyterian Church system to the Episcopalian. Each is best suited, as things are and have been, to their respective countries. The buildings in Glasgow College—soon to be swept away—are unchanged from a period long antecedent to that in which the manse boy first entered them. There is still the same old gate, in the dingy yet solemn-looking walls, entering into the quiet courts, out of the bustle of the High Street, with its filthy crowds of squalid men and women, its ragged children, and besotted drunken creatures with their idiotic looks, and whatever else combines to give to it a look of vice and poverty, unsurpassed by any street in Europe. But once within the college gate, there are the same lecture rooms in which Adam Smith and Reid taught, and James Watt studied or experimented; and the same stone pavement, to me more sacred, from its peculiar associations with the long past, than the floor of almost any church in Europe.

The students attending our Scotch colleges live anywhere, and in any way they please, in so far as the college authorities are concerned.

E

The more respectable, yet certainly not very aristocratic, streets near the university have from time immemorial furnished lodgings to the students, from the flat over the shops up to the attics. A small room with fire, cooking, attendance, &c., could be obtained for a few shillings weekly ; and it was a common custom for the poorer students, for the sake of economy, to share both room and bed with a companion. The following extract from the college life of the eldest son of the manse, dictated, when he was fourscore years, to one of his daughters, as a portion of a domestic autobiography, will give a characteristic idea of the student life and its difficulties in those days, and such as was, and in some respects is still, familiar to not a few of those who have helped to make Scotland what she is :—

"In November I went to Glasgow College, and the mode of travelling at that time is a strange contrast to the present. On a Monday morning Sandy M'Intyre, with two horses, was ferried across to Mull. My father and I followed soon after, and we got to the ferry of Auchnacraig, near Duart, that night, where we had to remain for a couple of nights, the weather being too stormy for us to proceed. I have a very pleasing recollection of the kindness of our old host, who, on parting, put a five-shilling piece into my pocket, the kindly custom of the time, while he laid his hand on my head and gave me a fatherly blessing. We next crossed to Kerrara, rode to the next ferry, and arrived at Oban in the course of the afternoon, Sandy accompanying us on foot. A pair of saddle-bags on each of our horses carried all our luggage. At Oban the 'Gobhain Sassenach,' or English smith, a drunken wit and poet, was sent for to shoe our horses, which he promised to do immediately. But when the horses were expected to be in readiness the 'Gobhain Sassenach' was drunk, so that we were compelled to remain for that night in Oban. Next day we proceeded to Tynault, where the landlord met us at the door with a bottle of bitters. Sandy M'Intyre had arrived before us, having taken a short cut across the hill. After a short stay, we pushed on to Port Sonachan, from thence to Inverary. On Saturday afternoon

we came to Arrochar, and having left Sandy
and the horses at the inn, we walked to the
manse, then occupied by an old college friend
of my father's. We found the good man in his
study with his Concordance and Pulpit Bible
before him, which on recognising my father he
soon closed and put aside. Very hearty was the
welcome which we received. My father preached
there next day. On Monday morning we proceeded by Loch Long side and the Gair Loch
to Roseneath. At that time there was on the
shore of the Gair Loch, now studded with villas
on both shores, but one or two houses, and little
did I expect that I should ever possess a cottage
there. Leaving Sandy and the horses at Roseneath till my father's return, and, crossing over
to Greenock, we reached the house of my grand-
uncle, where we passed the night. We arrived
at Glasgow on Wednesday forenoon, having been
ten days on a journey that can now be accomplished in twice as many hours. I was next
morning enrolled as a student in the Latin class,
taught at the time by Mr Richardson, a most
amiable and accomplished man, whose memory

I shall ever revere. I was boarded in a respectable family in the High Street, opposite the Cross, at the rate of twenty pounds in six months, and where I had the advantage of having two amiable and delightful companions.

"My first session at college passed rapidly and most agreeably; and upon the evening of the 1st of May, I took my departure for home with twenty shillings in my pocket, and carrying two shirts and two pairs of stockings in a bundle on my back, and with a good oak stick in my hand. I walked to Dumbarton that night, and got drenched to the skin. I was glad to take my place opposite to a large fire in the kitchen, where I dried the contents of my bundle, and made myself as comfortable as circumstances would permit. Having got some slight refreshment I was shown to my room in the garret flat of the house tenanted by rats. The waiter removed my shoes lest they should be eaten up! As might be supposed my sleep was not very comfortable. I started at six next morning for Helensburgh. I was joined on the road by a man who was followed by a beautiful English terrier, which I agreed to purchase from him for half-a-crown. He gave me a cord by which I could lead him on, but he assured me that I might in a very short time give him his liberty, which I did. Scarcely had I done so when a loud and peculiar whistle, which the dog quickly recognised, announced to me that I had been swindled, for off set the terrier, and he and my half-crown were for ever lost! I walked on by the banks of the lovely Gair Loch, to the ferry on Loch Long, intending to proceed to Inverary by the Argyle bowling-green. I was joined by a young man who said that he was going the same way to Inverary. I was glad to have his company, as I had never before travelled across those hills. He ordered some refreshment for himself, but said that he had no change, and the landlord being unable to accommodate him, I paid for his refreshment, and for his share of the ferry. We got to Loch-Goilhead, and found a cart proceeding to St Catherine's, and for the sum of sixpence each, I still paying for my companion, we crossed to Inverary. This young man was a most amusing fellow. He asked me to come to tea, and to sleep at his mother's house, giving me her name and place of residence, recommending me, in the meantime, to go to a hotel near, till he should call for me. To this day I have neither seen nor heard of my friend or of his mother. The hotel-keeper informed me afterwards that there was no such family at Inverary!

"Early next morning I started for Port Sonachan, with eighteenpence still in my pocket. The inn and ferry at Port Sonachan was at that time kept by a man with whom I had been acquainted: he having at one time been a travelling packman, and in that capacity had made frequent visits to the manse. He received me most cordially, gave me breakfast, and ferried me across, refusing to accept of any payment. I certainly did not urge his acceptance in very strong terms. I walked on with a light heart and still lighter purse, till I reached Tynault, where my food cost me a shilling. On leaving Tynault for Oban, I was deluged by a torrent of rain. I overtook a cart within four miles of Oban, and the driver had compassion on me, giving me

a seat during the rest of my journey. He was
singing an old Gaelic song, but had not the
words correctly: fortunately, I was acquainted
with them, and I gave him one of the most beautiful of all the verses and one which he had never
heard before. On parting from him, I told him
that I was sorry I could not offer him anything
for the drive. He said, 'I would not take a
farthing though your pockets were full. I am
richly rewarded with the beautiful verse which
you have taught me.' At the hotel at Oban I
found young Maclean of Coll, with whom I was
well acquainted. He told me that he expected
his barge, and would land me at my father's,
meantime that I must be his guest. The barge
arrived, and after a couple of days we sailed
with fair wind and tide, and the old piper playing to us during the passage. Most joyful was I
when once more I reached the manse, and many
and affectionate were the salutations with which
I was welcomed by its dear and numerous occupants.

"Soon after my return, I joined the 'Volunteers,' and had great pleasure in attending drill.

"There existed at that time a most loyal and martial spirit in the Highlands, forming an extraordinary contrast to their present feelings as regards the army. There were then three regiments of 'fencibles' raised in the county of Argyle, who were considered the finest-looking men in the army sent to Ireland during the rebellion. Besides the company of volunteers in each parish, I have still in my possession the names and designation of *one hundred and ten* officers, who held commissions in the army, and with each of whom I was personally acquainted. Many of them were highly distinguished, and some attained to the rank of general officers; and, alas! very many of them perished during the war. I am not aware of a dozen from that country now in the army, and even some of these are on the retired list. I am unwilling to account for this melancholy change. I fear, however, that the clearances which, for years past, have most extensively taken place in these countries, has contributed in some degree to bring about this state of things; but also as likely the outlets afforded by commerce to young men, and the improved education of the country.

"It was during the harvest of this year that I became an ardent sportsman, as also an enthusiastic boatman; and I must confess that I spent much more of my time in wandering over the mountains in quest of game, or in sailing on the Sound of Mull with old Rory, than at my classics.

"I shall pass over the following sessions at college, as there were very few incidents worthy of remark. I generally lived in lodgings with some companion, having a small parlour and bed-room, and truly I must say that we lived most sparingly and moderately. The expense of a session, including professors' fees and some new clothes, cost me from twenty-five to thirty pounds. During two of my last sessions at college in Glasgow my cousin, Neil Campbell, a medical student, was my companion in lodgings, and during the last three months that we were in Glasgow we had another medical student from the Highlands of the name of M'Millan living with us. We were both much attached to this young man. He was obliged for want of funds to leave his lodgings, and had nearly starved himself before doing so. We insisted on his joining us in our room, which was then in the Stockwell; but this additional burden reduced us at times to great extremities, and had it not been for an excellent girl from Oban, who was serving in the house, I do not know what should have become of us. We often took a walk to the green, stating that we were to be out at dinner, and took some eggs and potatoes for supper when we returned. Macmillan was a young man of very superior talent and an ardent student. When the session closed, he was enabled, through the kindness of some Highland gentlemen in Glasgow to whom his case had been made known, to obtain his diploma as surgeon, and he agreed to accompany me home. He had not been with us above a week when his appointment as assistant-surgeon in the navy was announced to him. The letter which contained his appointment directed him, upon his passing his examination at the Surgeons' Hall, Edinburgh, to draw upon the treasury for a certain sum of money, and to proceed to Edinburgh immediately. But what was to be done in the meantime? He had not a farthing, and not a moment could be lost. I could not advance him a pound. We told all the circumstances of the case to a carpenter in the parish, and he, with great generosity, advanced upon our mere verbal promise, four pounds, with which we proceeded to Tobermory, where that very evening we found a vessel sailing for Greenock, in which he took his passage. He passed his examination in Edinburgh with *éclat*, remitted the money we had borrowed from the honest carpenter, and on his arrival in England was placed on board of a frigate, and the first letter I received from him was dated from Van Diemen's Land, of which we knew very little in those days. The ship was on a voyage of discovery, and absent for many years.

"Long after, when I was a parish minister, I remarked a stranger whose face interested me much, who waited for me at the door of the church, and addressed me in very mournful accents in Gaelic, saying that the last sermon he had heard was from my father many years before. I asked his name. He burst into tears and said, 'I came to see you.

I have lost almost every friend I had in the world. I buried my wife and only child not many days ago. Ask for me at the Inn, but you must pardon me in the meantime for concealing my name from the only person on earth from whom I expected sympathy.' He was greatly agitated. I assured him that I would go in the morning to see him, but all night I could think of little else than my interview with this mysterious stranger. On calling at the inn next morning, I found that this was my friend Macmillan. He had gone away by an early packet boat for Greenock, leaving a long and affectionate letter giving me a brief but painful account of his own history since we parted, and stating that he was about to retire to some quiet country town in England, from which he would again write to me. I never heard of him afterwards. He is most honourably mentioned in an account published of the voyage of discovery on which he had been.

" But to return to the story of my life at college. I recollect one Saturday night when we had not one halfpenny among us, I discovered at the bottom of my trunk an otter's skin, with which Neil Campbell and I proceeded to a well-known shop at the head of King Street, and offered it for sale. The person at the counter named for it a sum that we considered far below its value, upon which the good shopkeeper himself came in from the backshop and told him that the sum he offered was too little, and, speaking to us with great kindness, he gave us at least a half more than its value. This to us at such a time was a treasure.

"On one of those days we were asked to dine with old 'Barnicarry' at the 'Buck's Head.' This generous man was uncle to my companion, and my grand uncle. We received the message with great joy, as he usually gave us a donation of a guinea when he parted from us. In this hope we were not disappointed, and we returned home to poor Macmillan with great rejoicing, and had a comfortable supper. Neil had two brothers at sea. Both of them commanded fine West India-men. One of them was in the habit of sending us sea biscuits and other articles, especially *corned beef*, which we liked much. One evening a loud rap came to the door. Our Oban woman

went to open it, when we heard a half scream that
brought us to the lobby to see what the matter
was. The porter entered, having on his back a
pair of large canvas trousers filled with brown
sugar, a leg hanging down on each side of his
shoulder, which the poor girl supposed was a dead
'subject' for the medical students. This sugar
and a quantity of rice he brought along with it
was of great service to us. Our kind servant-maid
was permitted to take as much as she pleased for
her own tea, and we gave several bowlfuls to our
landlady. A poor student of the name of M'Gre-
gor, from Lismore, also got a share. This lad
was an excellent scholar, and very superior in
every way, but exceedingly poor. He lived in a
small apartment at the back of a place where
they baked oat cake. It was a very small room,
containing a bed, a small table and stool, but
without any fire-place. Here he contracted disease of the lungs, of which he soon after died.
I felt a deep interest in him, and the night I
parted from him he told me that he had been
much indebted to me for my kindness to him,
and that he wished to " treat " me as expressive

of his regard. He did not mention what "the treat" was to consist of, but knowing his inability, I objected to his putting himself to any expense on my account. He begged of me to wait for a few minutes, during which he purchased two halfpenny rolls, and handing me one, he took the other greedily himself! In the course of a year I visited his grave in the Island of Lismore, meditating with mournful reflections on the struggle that this most promising young man had made to obtain education enough to become a minister of the gospel. He was eminently pious, and much was I indebted to him for his kind guidance and Christian admonition."

## THE MANSE GIRLS AND THEIR EDUCATION.

THE manse girls were many. They formed a large family, a numerous flock, a considerable congregation; or, as the minister expressed it in less exaggerated terms, "a heavy handful." One part of their education, as I have already noticed, was conducted by a governess. The said governess was the daughter of a " governor," or commandant of one of the Highland forts—whether Fort-Augustus or Fort-William, I remember not— where he had for years reigned over a dozen rusty guns, and twice as many soldiers, with all the dignity of a man who was supposed to guard the great Southern land against the outbreaks and incursions

F

of the wild Highland clans, although, in truth, the
said Highland clans had been long asleep in the
old kirkyard "amang the heather," for, as the song
hath it,—

> " No more we'll see such deeds again ;
> Deserted is the Highland glen,
> And mossy cairns are o'er the men
> Who fought and died for Charlie."

The " major"—for the commandant had attained
that rank in the first American war—left an only
daughter who was small and dumpy in stature,
had no money, and but one leg.  Yet was she
most richly provided for otherwise, with every
womanly quality, and the power of training girls
in "all the branches" then considered most useful
for sensible well-to-do women and wives.  She
was not an outsider in the family, or a mere teaching machine, used and valued like a mill or plough
for the work done, but a member of the household,
loved and respected for her own sake.  She was
so dutiful and kind, that the beat of her wooden
leg on the wooden stair became musical—a very
beating of time with all that was best and happiest
in her pupils' hearts.  She remained for some years

educating the younger girls, until a batch of boys broke the line of feminine succession, and then she retired for a time to teach one or more families in the neighbourhood.   But no sooner was the equilibrium of the manse restored by another set of girls, than the little governess returned to her old quarters, and once more stumped through the schoolroom, with her happy face, wise tongue, and cunning hand.

The education of the manse girls was neither learned nor fashionable.  They were taught neither French nor German, music nor drawing, while dancing as an art was out of the question, with the wooden leg as the only artist to teach it.  The girls, however, were excellent readers, writers, and arithmeticians ; they could sew, knit, shape clothes, and patch to perfection, and give all needful directions for the kitchen, the dairy, the garden, or the poultry-yard.  I need hardly say that they were their own and their mother's only dressmakers, manifesting wonderful skill and taste in making old things look new, and in so changing the cut and fashion of the purchases made long ago from the packman, that Mary's

" everlasting silk," or Jane's merino, seemed capable
of endless transformations ; while their bonnets,
by judicious turning, trimming, and tasteful use
of a little bit of ribbon, looked always fresh
and new.

Contrasted with an expensive and fashionable
education, theirs will appear to have been poor and
vulgar.   Yet in the long course of years, I am not
sure that the manse girls had not the best of it.
For one often wonders what becomes of all this
fashionable education in the future life of the
young lady.   What French or German books does
she read as a maid or matron ?   With whom does
she, or can she, converse in these languages ?
Where is her drawing, beyond the Madonna's
heads and the Swiss landscape which she brought
from school, touched up by the master ?   What
music does she love and practise for the sake of
its own beauty, and not for the sake of adding to
the hum of the drawing-room after dinner ?   The
manse girls could read and speak two languages,
at least—Gaelic and English.   They could sing,
too, their own Highland ditties : wild, but yet as
musical as mountain streams and summer winds ;

sweet and melodious as song of thrush or black-
bird in spring, going right to the heart of the
listener, and from his heart to his brimming eyes.
And so I am ready to back the education of the
poor manse against that of many a rich and
fashionable mansion, not only as regards the ordinary "branches," but much more as developing the
mental powers of the girls. At all events they
acquired habits of reflective observation, with a
capacity of thoroughly relishing books, enjoying
Nature in all her varying scenes and moods, and
of expressing their own thoughts and sentiments
with such a freshness and force as made them
most delightful members of society. A fashionable education, on the other hand, is often a mere
tying on to a tree of a number of "branches" without life, instead of being a developing of the tree
itself, so that it shall bear its own branches loaded
with beautiful flowers and clustering fruit.

But the manse school included more rooms than
the little attic where the girls met around that
familiar knot of wood which projected from beneath the neat calico of the major's daughter.
The cheerful society of the house; the love of

kindred,—each heart being as a clear spring that sent forth its stream of affection with equable flow to refresh others; the innumerable requirements of the glebe and farm; the spinning and shearing; the work in the laundry, the kitchen, and the dairy; the glorious out-door exercise over field and moor, in the glens or by the shore; the ministrations of charity, not with its doled-out alms to beggars only, but with its "kind words and looks and tender greetings" to the many cottagers around,—these all were teachers in the Home School. And thus, partly from circumstances, partly, it must be acknowledged, from rare gifts bestowed upon them by God, they all grew up with a purity, a truthfulness, a love and gladness, which made the atmosphere of the manse one of constant sunshine. Each had her own strong individual character, like trees which grow free on the mountain side. They delighted in books, and read them with head and heart, undisturbed by the slang and one-sided judgments of hack critics. And it occasionally happened that some Southern friend, who in his wanderings through the Highlands enjoyed the hospitality of the manse, sent the girls a new volume of pleasant literature as a remembrance of his visit.  These gifts were much valued, and read as volumes are seldom read now-a-days.  Books of good poetry especially were so often conned by them that they became as portions of their own thoughts.

The manse girls did not look upon life as a vain show, aimless and purposeless; upon everything and every person as "a bore;" or upon themselves as an insupportable burden to parents and to brothers,—unless they got husbands!  Choice wives they would have made, for both their minds and persons had attractions not a few; and "good offers," as they were called, came to them as to others.  Young men had been "daft" about them, and they were too sensible and womanly not to wish for a home they could call their own; yet it never crossed their thoughts that they *must* marry, just as one must get a pair of shoes.  They never imagined that it was possible for any girl of principle and feeling to marry a man whom she did not love, merely because he had a number of sheep and cattle on a Highland farm; or had good prospects from selling tea and sugar in Glasgow; or

had a parish as a minister, or a property as a
"laird." Poor foolish creatures were they not to
think so? without one farthing they could call
their own; with no prospects from their father,
the minister; with no possessions save what he
had last purchased for them from the packman!
What on earth would come of them, or of their
mother, if the parson were drowned some stormy
night with Rory and the "Roe?" Were they
to be cast on the tender mercies of this or that
brother who had a home of his own? What? a
brother to afford shelter to a sister! Or could
they seriously intend to trust God's Providence for
the future, if they only did His will for the present?
Better far, surely, to accept the first good offer;
snatch at the woolly hand of the large sheep-
farmer, the sweet hand of the rich grocer, the
thin, sermon-writing hand of the preacher; nay,
let them take their chance even with James, the
tutor, who has been sighing over each of them in
turn! But no; like "fools," they took for granted
that it never could come wrong in the end to do
what was right at the time, and so they never
thought it to be absolutely incumbent on them

to "marry for marrying's sake." Neither father nor mother questioned the propriety of their conduct. And thus it came to pass that none of them, save one, who loved most heroically and most truly unto death, ever married. The others became what married ladies and young expectants of that life-climax call—Old Maids. But many a fireside, and many a nephew and niece, with the children of a second generation, blessed God for them as precious gifts.

I feel that no apology is required for quoting the following extract from a letter written by the pastor, more than sixty years ago, when some of the eldest of the manse girls left home for the first time. It will find, I doubt not, a response in the heart of many a pastor in similar circumstances:—

"It was, my dear, my very dear girls, at seven in the morning of Thursday, the 31st August, you took your departure from the old quay—that quay where often I landed in foul and fair weather, at night and by day; my heart always jumping before me, anticipating the happiness of joining the delightful group that formed my fireside,—a group I may never see collected again. How happy the

parents, the fewest in number, who can have their
families within their reach! happier still, when,
like you, their families are to them a delight and
comfort! You left the well-known shores of ——,
and your parents returned with heavy steps, the
weight of their thoughts making their ascent to
the manse much slower and harder to accomplish
than ever they found it before. We sat on the
hill-side bathed in tears, giving many a kind and
longing look to the wherry, which always went
further from us, till our dim eyes, wearied of their
exertions, could see nothing in its true state;
when, behold, cruel Castle Duart interrupted our
view, and took out of our sight the boat that
carried from us so much of our worldly treasure.
Our thousand blessings be with our dear ones, we
cried, and returned to the house,—to the manse
of ——; a housewhere much comfort and happiness were always to be found; where the friend
was friendly treated, and where the stranger found
himself at home; where the distressed and the
needy met with pity and kindness, and the beggar
never went off without being supplied; where the
story and the joke often cheered the well-pleased

guests, and were often accompanied with the dance and the song, and all with an uncommon degree of elegance, cheerfulness, and good humour. But with me these wonted scenes of merriment are now over. The violin and the song have no charms for me; the dance and the cheerful tale delight no more. But hold, minister! what mean you by these gloomy thoughts? Why disturb for a moment the happiness of the dear things you write to, and for whose happiness you so earnestly pray, by casting a damp upon their gay and merry hours? Cease, foolish, and tempt not Providence to afflict you! What! have you not many comforts to make you happy? Is not the friend of your bosom, the loving dutiful wife, and the loving dutiful mother, alive to bless and to comfort you? Is not your family, though somewhat scattered, all alive? Are they not all good and promising? None of them ever yet caused you to blush; and are not these great blessings? and are they not worthy of your most cheerful and grateful acknowledgments? They are, they are, and I bless God for His goodness. But the thought—I cannot provide for these! Take care, minister, that the anxiety of your affection does not unhinge that confidence with which the Christian ought to repose upon the wise and good providence of God! What though you are to leave your children poor and friendless? Is the arm of the Lord shortened that He cannot help? is His ear heavy that He cannot hear? You yourself have been no more than an instrument in the hand of His goodness; and is His goodness, pray, bound up in your feeble arm? Do you what you can; leave the rest to God. Let them be good, and fear the Lord, and keep His commandments, and He will provide for them in His own way and in His own time. Why, then, wilt thou be cast down, O my soul; why disquieted within me? Trust thou in the Lord! Under all the changes and the cares and the troubles of this life, may the consolations of religion support our spirits. In the multitude of the thoughts within me, thy comforts, O my God, delight my soul! But no more of this preaching-like harangue, of which, I doubt not, you wish to be relieved. Let me rather reply to your letter, and tell you my news."

It was after this period that he had to mourn

the loss of many of his family.  And then began for the manse girls the education within the school of sickness and death, whose door is shut against the intrusion of the noisy world, and into which no one can enter, except the Father of all, and " the Friend who sticketh closer than a brother."

The first break in a family is a solemn and affecting era in its history; most of all when that family is " all the world " to its own members. The very thought—so natural to others who have suffered—that this one who has been visited by disease can ever become *dangerously* ill—can ever die, is by them dismissed as a dreadful night-mare. Then follow "the hopes and fears that kindle hope, an undistinguishable throng;" the watchings which turn night into day, and day into night; the sympathy of sorrow which makes each mourner hide from others the grief that in secret is breaking the heart; the intense realisation, at last, of all that may be—ay, that must be—until the last hours come, and what these are they alone know who have loved and lost.  What a mighty change does this first death make in a family, when it is so united, that if one member suffers all suffer!  It

G

changes everything. The old haunts by rock or stream can never be as they were; old songs are hushed for years, and, if ever sung again, they are like wails for the dead; every room in the house seems, for a time, tenanted more by the dead than by the living; the books belong to the dead; the seat in church is not empty, but occupied by the dead; plans and purposes, family arrangements and prospects, all seem for a time so purposeless and useless. No one ever calculated on this possibility! The trial which has come verily seems "strange." Yet this is, under God, a holy and blessed education. Lessons are then taught, "though as by fire," which train all the scholars for a higher school. And if that old joyousness and hilarity pass away which belong to a world that seemed as if it could not change—like a very Eden before the fall—it is succeeded by a deeper life; a life of faith and hope which find rest in the unchanging rather than the changing present.

Such was a portion of the education which the pastor and his family received for many succeeding years in the old manse; but its memory was ever accompanied by thanksgiving for the true, genuine Christian life and death of those who had died.    I need hardly say that the girls, more than the other members of the family, shared these sorrows and this discipline ; for whatever men can do in the storm of ocean or of battle, women are the ministering angels in the room of sickness and of suffering.

Before I turn away from the manse girls, I must say something more of their little governess.    She lingered long about the manse, as a valued friend, when her services were no longer needed.    But she resolved at last to attempt a school in the low country, and to stamp some uneducated spot with the impress of the wooden knob.    Ere doing so, she confided to the minister a story told her by her father, the fort-commandant, about some link or other which bound him to the Argyle family. What that link precisely was, no history records. It may have been that her mother was a Campbell, or that the major had served in a regiment commanded by some member of that noble house, or had picked an Argyle out of the trenches of Ticonderoga.    Anyhow, the commandant fancied that his only daughter would find a crutch of support, like many others, in "the Duke," if he only knew the story. Never up to this time was the crutch needed; but needed it was now if she was to pursue her life-journey in peace. Why not tell the story then to the Duke? quoth the minister. Why not? thoughtfully ruminated the little governess. And so they both entered the manse study—a wonderful little sanctum of books and MSS., with a stuffed otter and wild-cat, a gun, compass, coil of new rope, the flag of the "Roe," a print of the Duke of Argyle, and of several old divines and re-formers, in wigs and ruffs. There the minister wrote out, with great care, a petition to the Duke for one of the very many kind charities, in the form of small annuities, which were dispensed by his Grace. The governess determined to present it in person at Inveraray. But the journey thither was then a very serious matter. To travel now-a-days from London to any capital on the Continent is nothing to what that journey was. For it could only be done on horseback, and by crossing stormy ferries, as wide as the Straits of Dover. The journey was at last, however, arranged in this way. There lived in one of the many cottages on

the glebe, a man called "old Archy," who had
been a servant in the family of the pastor's father-
in-law.   Archy had long ago accompanied, as
guide and servant, the minister's wife, when she
had gone to Edinburgh for her education.   Having
been thus trained to foreign travel, and his fame
established as a thoroughly qualified *courier*, he
was at once selected to accompany the governess
to Inveraray on horseback.   That excellent woman
did not, from nervous anxiety, go to bed the night
previous to her departure ; and she had worked
for a fortnight to produce a new dress in which to
appear worthily before the Duke.   She had daily
practised, moreover, the proper mode of address,
and was miserable from the conviction that all
would be ruined by her saying "Sir," instead of
"your Grace."   The minister tried to laugh her
out of her fears, and to cheer her by the assurance
that a better-hearted gentleman lived not than the
good Duke of Argyle ; and that she must just speak
to him as she felt.   She departed with her black
trunk slung behind Archy ; and also with extraordinary supplies of cold fowls, mutton, ham, and
cheese—not to speak of letters commendatory to

every manse on the road. What farewells, and
kissings, and waving of handkerchiefs, and drying
of eyes, and gathering of servants and of dogs at
the manse door as the governess rode off on the
white horse, Archy following on the brown! The
proper arrangement of the wooden leg had been a
great mechanical and æsthetic difficulty, but somehow the girls, with a proper disposal of drapery,
had made the whole thing quite *comme il faut*.
Archy too had patched up a saddle of wonderful
structure for the occasion.

Time passed, and in a fortnight, to the joy of
the household, the white mare was seen coming
over the hill, with the brown following; and soon
the governess was once more in the arms of her
friends, and the trunk in those of Archy. Amidst
a buzz of questions, the story was soon told with
much flutter and some weeping—how she had met
the Duke near the castle; how she had presented
her petition, while she could not speak; how his
Grace had expressed his great regard for " his
minister;" and how next day, when she called by
appointment, he had signified his intention of
granting the annuity. " It is like himself," was the

minister's only remark, while his eyes seemed fuller than usual as he congratulated the little governess on her success; and gave an extra bumper, with many a compliment, to old Archy for the manner in which he had guided the horses and their riders. The little governess taught a school for many years, and enjoyed her annuity till near ninety. During her last days, she experienced the personal kindness and tender goodness of the present "Argyle," as she had long before done, of the former "Argyles."

## THE MINISTER AND HIS WORK.

IN Dr Macculloch's "Tour to the Highlands of Scotland," we have the most perfect and eloquent descriptions of scenery; but in Dr Johnson's, the truest yet most complimentary delineation of the character and manners of the people. The physical features of the country are, no doubt, abiding, while its social condition is constantly changing; so that we can now-a-days more easily recognise the truth of the sketches by the former than by the latter tourist. But the minister of whom I write, and the manners of his time, belonged to the era of Johnson, and not to that of Macculloch.

There is something, by the way, peculiarly

touching in that same tour of the old Doctor's, when we remember the tastes and habits of the man, with the state of the country at the time in which he visited it. Unaccustomed to physical exercise, obese in person and short-sighted in vision, he rode along execrable roads, cautiously felt his way across interminable morasses, on a Highland shelty. He had no means of navigating those stormy seas but an open boat, pulled by sturdy rowers, against wetting spray, or tacking from morning till night amidst squalls, rain, and turbulent tideways. He had to put up in wretched pot-houses, sleeping, as he did at Glenelg, "on a bundle of hay, in his riding-coat; while Mr Boswell, being more delicate, laid himself in sheets, with hay over and above him, and lay in linen like a gentleman." In some of the houses, he found but clay floors below and peat-reek around, and nowhere did he find the luxuries of his own favourite London. Yet he never growls or expresses one word of discontent or peevishness. Whether this was owing to his having for the first time escaped the conventionalities of city life; or to the fact of the Highlands being then the last

stronghold of Jacobitism; or to the honour and respect which was everywhere shown towards himself; or, what is more probable, to the genial influence of fresh air and exercise upon his phlegma-
tic constitution, banishing its "bad humours,"—in
whatever way we may account for it, so it was,
that he encountered every difficulty and discomfort with the greatest cheerfulness; partook of the
fare given him and the hospitality afforded to him
with hearty gratitude; and has written about every
class of the people with the generous courtesy of a
well-bred English gentleman.

His opinion of the Highland clergy is not the
least remarkable of his "testimonies," considering
his intense love of Episcopacy, and its forms of
public worship, with his sincere dislike of Presby-
terianism. "I saw," he says, writing of the clergy,
"not one in the Islands whom I had reason to
think either deficient in learning or irregular in
life, but found several with whom I could not converse without wishing, as my respect increased,
that they had not been Presbyterians." Moreover,
in each of the distant islands which the Doctor
visited, he met ministers with whom even he was

able to have genial and scholarly conversation.
"They had attained," he says, "a knowledge as
may be justly admired in men who have no motive
to study but generous curiosity, or, what is still
better, desire of usefulness; with such politeness
as no measure or circle of converse could ever
have supplied, but to minds naturally disposed
to elegance." When in Skye, he remarks of one
of those clergymen, Mr M'Queen, who had been
his guide, that he was "courteous, candid, sensible,
well-informed, very learned;" and at parting, he
said to him, "I shall ever retain a great regard for
you. Do not forget me." In another island, the
small island of Coll, he paid a visit to Mr Maclean,
who was living in a small, straw-thatched, mud-
walled hut, "a fine old man," as the Doctor observed to Boswell, "well dressed, with as much
dignity in his appearance as the Dean of a cathedral!" Mr Maclean had "a valuable library,"
which he was obliged, "from want of accommodation, to keep in large chests;" and this solitary,
shut up "in a green isle amidst the ocean's waves,"
argued with the awful Southern Don about Leib-
nitz, Bayle, etc., and though the Doctor displayed

a little of the bear, owing to the old man's deafness, yet he acknowledged that he "liked his firmness and orthodoxy." In the island of Mull, again, Johnson spent a night under the roof of another clergyman, whom he calls, by mistake, Mr Maclean, but whose name was Macleod,* and of whom he says that he was "a minister whose elegance of conversation, and strength of judgment, would make him conspicuous in places of greater celebrity." It is pleasant to know, on such good authority, that there lived at that time, in these wild and distant parts, ministers of such character, manners, and learning.

The minister of our Highland parish was a man of similar culture and character with those of his brethren, two of whom mentioned by the Doctor were his intimate friends. He had the good fortune, let me mention in passing, to meet the famous traveller at Dunvegan Castle ; and he used to tell, with great glee, how he found him alone in the drawing-room before dinner, poring over some volume on the sofa, and how the Doc-

---

* The grandfather of the present, and the father of the late Rev. Dr Macleod of New York, U.S., both distinguished clergymen.

tor, before rising to greet him kindly, dashed to the ground the book he had been reading, exclaiming, in a loud and angry voice, " The author is an ass ! "

When the minister came to his parish, the people were but emerging from those old patriarchal times of clanship, with its loyal feelings and friendships, yet with its violent prejudices and intense clinging to the past, and to all that was bad as well as good in it. Many of his parishioners had been "out in the '45," and were Prince Charlie men to the core.* These were not characterised by much reli-

---

* The minister himself was a loyal " Hanoverian." This was caused by his very decided Protestantism, and also, no doubt, by his devotion to the Dunvegan family, which, through the influence chiefly of President Forbes, had opposed Prince Charles. The minister, on a memorable occasion, had his Highland and loyal feeling rather severely tried. It happened thus :—When King William IV., like our noble Prince Alfred, was a midshipman in the royal navy, his ship, the *Cæsar*, visited the Western Isles. The minister, along with the other public men in the district, went to pay his respects to his Royal Highness. He was most graciously received, and while conversing with the prince on the quarter-deck, a galley manned with six rowers pulled alongside. The prince asked him to whom it belonged. On being informed that it belonged to a neighbouring proprietor, the additional remark was made, with a kind smile, " He was out, no doubt, in the '45? Of course he was! Ah, doctor, all you Highlanders were rebels, every one of you! Ha—ha—ha!" "Please your Royal Highness," said the minister,

gion—one of the predecessors of our minister had
been commanded by this party not to dare in their
hearing to pray for King George in church, or they
would shoot him dead. He did, nevertheless, pray,
at least in words, but not, we fear, in pure faith.
He took a brace of pistols with him to the pulpit,
and cocking them before his prayer began, he laid
them down before him, and for once at least offered
up his petitions with his eyes open.

There was no law-officer of the crown, not even
a justice of the peace at that time in the whole
parish. The people were therefore obliged to take
the law to some extent into their own hands.
Shortly after our minister came to the parish,
he wrote stating that "no fewer than thirty persons have been expelled for theft, not by sen-
tence of the magistrate, but by the united
efforts of the better sort of the inhabitants. The
good effects of this expulsion have been sen-
sibly felt; but a court of law having been estab-

with a low bow, "I am thankful to say *all* the Highlanders were
not rebels, for had they been so, we might not have had the honour
and happiness of seeing your Royal Highness among us now." The
prince laughed heartily, and complimented the minister on the
felicity of his reply.

lished since then in the neighbourhood, the necessity for such violent means is in a great measure
obviated."

The minister was too far removed from the big
world of church politics, General Assembly de-
bates, controversial meetings and pamphlets, to be
a party man.   It satisfied him to be a *part* of the
great Catholic Church, and of that small section of
it in which he had been born.   The business of his
Presbytery* was chiefly local, and his work was
confined mainly to his parish.

* It may interest some of our southern readers to know that the
government of the Established Church of Scotland is conducted as
follows :—(1.) Over a single parish is the court called the *Kirk-Ses-
sion,* composed of lay members, who are ordained for the office as
Elders and as Deacons, (to attend to the poor,) but always presided over by the minister.   The number of this court varies
according to the size and circumstances of the congregation and
parish. (2.) Over a number of parishes is the *Presbytery,* composed
of all the clergy within a certain district, and a representative
Elder from each Session.   (3.) Over the Presbyteries of a Pro-
vince is the Synod, composed of all the members of the several
Presbyteries ; and, finally, over the whole Church is the General
Assembly, presided over by a nobleman, representing the Sovereign,
and a "moderator" or chairman, elected by the Church, and composed of representatives, lay and clerical, from every presbytery,
and also of laymen from the Royal Burghs and Universities.   These
several courts have many privileges conferred upon them by Act of
Parliament.   Beyond Scotland, they are no more "established"
than the Church of England is beyond England.   Both Churches

After having studied eight years at a university, he entered on his charge with a salary of £40, which was afterwards raised to £80. He ministered to 2000 souls, all of whom—with the exception of perhaps a dozen families of Episcopalians and Roman Catholics—acknowledged him as their pastor. His charge was scattered over 130 square miles, with a sea-board of 100! This is his own description of the ecclesiastical edifices of the parish at the beginning of his ministry :—" There are two churches *so called*, but with respect to decency of accommodation, they might as properly be called sheds or barns. The dimensions of each is no more than forty by sixteen feet, and without seats or bells. It is much to be regretted that since the Reformation little or no attention has been paid to the seating of churches in this country." No such churches can now be found. How the congregation managed to arrange themselves during service in those "sheds," I know not. Did they stand? sit on stones or bunches of heather?

are, by the Act of Union, placed on an equal footing as regards the State in the Colonies. The government of the Church of Scotland is very similar to that of all the Established Protestant Churches on the Continent.

or recline on the earthen floor? Fortunately the minister was an eloquent and earnest preacher, and he may have made them forget their discomfort. But the picture is not pleasing of a congregation dripping wet, huddled together in a shed, without seats, after a long walk across the mountains. Sleeping, at all events, was impossible.

It is worth noticing, as characteristic of the times, that during the first period of his ministry the Scriptures had not been translated into Gaelic. The clergy translated what they read to the people from the English version, with such assistance as could be derived from Bedell's Irish Bible. The Highlanders owed much to Gaelic hymns, composed by some of their own poets, and also to metrical translations of the Psalms,* by Mr Kirke,

* It is just as strange that the eldest son of " the manse " was the first to prepare a metrical translation of the Psalms in Irish, for the use of the Irish Protestant Churches. He also was the chief means of obtaining a new edition of the Gaelic Scriptures for his own countrymen, and of originating and helping on the Education Scheme of the Church of Scotland, which now instructs 20,000 children in the Highlands. In order to supply the hunger for knowledge which these additional means of education would create, he prepared admirable Gaelic school-books, and conducted a monthly magazine in Gaelic for several years, which, it is not too much to say,

minister of Balquhidder, and by the Synod of Argyle. But even if there had been Bibles, many of the people had not the means of education. What could one or two schools avail in so extensive a parish? To meet the wants of the people, a school would require to be in almost every glen.

But preaching on Sunday, even on a stormy winter's day, was the easiest of the minister's duties. There was not a road in the parish. Along the coast indeed for a few miles there was what was charitably called a road, and, as compared with those slender sheep-tracks which wormed their way through the glens, and across some of the wilder passes, it perhaps deserved the name. By this said road country carts, introduced during his days, could toil, pitching, jolting, tossing, in deep ruts, over stones, and through the burns, like waggons in South Africa, and with all the irregular motion of boats in a storm. But for twenty miles inland the hills and glens were as the Danes had left them.

was, in point of talent, interest, usefulness, and genius, the most precious literary boon ever conferred on the Highlands. I hope this allusion to one so recently departed may be kindly interpreted.

The paths which traversed those wilds were journeyed generally on foot, but in some instances
by "the minister's brown horse," one of those sagacious creatures which, with wonderful instinct,
seemed to be able, as Rory used to say, "to smell
out the road" in the dark. The minister used to
boast how the brave animal had, on an emergency,
carried him for seventy-two miles, the greater part
of which was over the roughest bridle paths in the
country. It is hardly possible to convey a just
impression, except to those acquainted with Highland paths and wildernesses, of what the ordinary
labours of such a minister was. Let us select one
day out of many of a Highland pastor's work.

Immediately after service, a Highlander salutes
him, with bonnet off and a low bow, saying,
" John Macdonald in the Black Glen is dying,
and would like to see you, sir." After some inquiry, and telling his wife not to be anxious if he
is late in returning home, he strides off at "a
killing pace" to see his parishioner. The hut is
distant sixteen Highland miles; but what miles!
Not such as are travelled by the Lowland or
Southern parson, with steps solemn and regular

as if prescribed by law. But this journey is over
bogs, along rough paths, across rapid streams
without bridges, and where there is no better
shelter than can be found in a Swiss *châlet*.
After a long and patient pastoral visit to his
dying parishioner, the minister strikes for home
across the hills. But he is soon met by a shepherd, who tells him of a sudden death which has
occurred but a few hours before in a hamlet not
far off; and to visit the afflicted widow will take
him only a few miles out of his course. So be
it, quoth the parson, and he forthwith proceeds
to the other glen, and mingles his prayers with
those of the widow and her children. But the
longest day must have an end, and the last rays
of the sun are gilding the mountain-tops, and
leaving the valleys in darkness. And so our
minister, with less elastic step, ascends towards
the steep *Col*, which rises for 2000 feet, with great
abruptness, from a chain of lakes up past the
"Righi" I have already described. As he nears the
summit, down comes thick, palpable, impenetrable
mist. He is confident that he knows the road *nearly*
as well as the white horse, and so he proceeds with

caution over deep moor-hags until he is lost in
utter bewilderment.    Well, he has before now
spent the night under a rock, and waited until
break of day ; but having eaten only a little
bread and cheese since morning, he longs for
home.    The moon is out, but the light reveals
only driving mist, and the mountain begins to
feel cold, damp, and terribly lonely.    He walks
on, feeling his way with his staff, when suddenly
the mist clears off, and he finds himself on the
slope of a precipice.    Throwing himself on his
back on the ground, and digging his feet into the
soil, he recovers his footing, and with thanksgiving
changes his course.    Down comes the mist again,
thick as before.    He has reached a wood—where
is he ?    Ah! he knows the wood right well, and
has passed through it a hundred times, so he tries
to do so now, and in a few minutes has fallen
down a bank into a pool of water.    But now he
*has* the track, and following it he reaches the spot
in the valley from where he had started two hours
before!    He rouses a shepherd, and they journey
together to a ferry by which he can return home
by a circuitous route.    The boat is there, but the

tide is out, for it ebbs far to seaward at this spot, and so he has to wait patiently for the return of the tide. The tide turns, taking its own time to do so. Half wading, half rowing, they at last cross the strait. It is now daybreak, and the minister journeys homeward, and reaches the manse about five in the morning.

Such land journeys were frequently undertaken, (with adventures more or less trying,) not merely to visit the sick, but for every kind of parochial duty—sometimes to baptize, and sometimes to marry. These services were occasionally performed in most primitive fashion at one of those green spots among the hills. Corrie Borrodale, among the old "shielings," was a sort of half-way-house between the opposite sides of the parish. There, beside a clear well, children have been baptized; and there, among "the bonnie blooming heather," the Highland shepherd has been married to his bonnie blooming bride. There were also in different districts preaching and "catechising," as it was called. The catechising consisted in examining on the Catechism and Scriptures every parishioner who was disposed to attend the meet-

ing, and all did so with few exceptions. It con-
stituted an important part of the minister's regular
work. Every farm and hamlet was thus visited in
rotation; notes were generally kept of the progress
made by each individual in religious knowledge,
and he who was sluggish and careless was put to
shame before his neighbours. Many presbyteries,
at the time we speak of, took yearly account of
the diligence of each member in the discharge of
this branch of his pastoral office : a reckoning and
a superintendence which, we humbly think, might,
with mutual benefit to people and pastor, be re-
vived in the present day. This "exercise" was
generally followed by preaching, both of course
in the open air, when weather permitted. And
no sight could be more beautiful than that of
the venerable minister, seated on the side of a
green and sheltered knoll, surrounded by the
inhabitants of the neighbouring hamlets, each,
as his turn came, answering, or attempting to
answer, the questions propounded with gravity
and simplicity. A simple discourse followed from
the same rural pulpit, to the simple but thoughtful
and intelligent congregation. Most touching was

it then to hear the Psalms rise from among the moorlands, disturbing "the sleep that is among the lonely hills;" the pauses filled by the piping of the plover or some mountain bird, and by the echoes of the streams and water-falls from the rocky precipices. It was a peasant's choir, rude and uncultivated by art, but heard, I doubt not, with sympathy by the mighty angels who sung their own noblest song in the hearing of shepherds on the hills of Bethlehem.

An essential, an important, and a very laborious part of the parish minister's work was the providing for the wants of the poor and the needy. He and his session were intrusted, under powers clearly defined by law, with the administration of the very considerable funds contributed by charity at the church door every Sabbath. The half-yearly, or quarterly apportionment of this fund, however, formed a small portion of the labours implied in providing for the poor. They were carefully visited by minister and elders : their circumstances accurately ascertained ; and in cases of sickness, or of any special trial, where the session allowance was insufficient, there was an ample supply provided by an appeal to the kindness of the more prosperous in the neighbourhood; and whether food, or clothing, or cordials were needed, they were readily granted to an appeal thus made.*

Our minister's work was thus devoted and unwearied for half a century. And there is something peculiarly pleasing and cheering to think

* It is a noteworthy fact, which ought not to be forgotten, that, until the passing of the new Poor-Law Act, twenty years ago, the ministers and elders of the Church of Scotland conducted the whole business connected with the support of the poor, without fee or reward, without a farthing's cost to the public—large towns alone excepted, where there was a legal assessment laid on, as is the case now throughout the country generally. The number of publicly paid officials employed in this management in the present day approaches two thousand, each, as a matter of course, drawing a considerable salary.

And it is still more noteworthy, that, during the gratuitous administration of the sessions, the cost of all the poor in Scotland—including the large towns—went little beyond £150,000 a-year; while under the present system, with rentals largely increased, with wages rising rapidly, the poor cost the country annually upwards of £750,000—that the expense is steadily rising, and that the discontent of the poor is rising as steadily. We do not mean to discuss questions of political economy; but these facts are nevertheless worth recording.

It may be added, also, that in our minister's earlier days there were no law courts established within the parish, and consequently the settling of many of the disputes which will arise among neighbours fell to him and to his elders; but even after such establishment, he and his assessors continued to be the administrators of justice in scores of cases similar to those where the disputants now invariably taste the luxury of law.

of him and of others of the same calling and character in every church, who from year to year pursue their quiet course of holy, self-denying labour, educating the ignorant; bringing life and blessing into the homes of disease and poverty; sharing the burden of sorrow with the afflicted, the widow, and the fatherless; reproving and admonishing, by life and word, the selfish and un-godly; and with a heart ever open to all the fair humanities of our nature ;—a true "divine," yet every inch a man!  Such men, in one sense, have never been alone; for each could say with his Master, "I am not alone, for the Father is with me."  Yet what knew or cared the great, bust-ling, religious world about them ?  Where were their public meetings, with reports, speeches, ad-dresses, "resolutions," or motions about their work? Where their committees and associations of ardent philanthropists, rich supporters, and zealous fol-lowers ?  Where their "religious" papers, so called, to parade them before the world, and to crown them with the laurels of puffs and leading articles? Alone, he, and thousands like him, laboured, the very salt of the earth, the noblest of their race!

## PASSING AWAY.

THE minister, when verging on four-score, became blind. A son of the manse, his youngest, was, to his joy, appointed to be his assistant and successor in the ministry. I cannot forget the last occasion on which "the old man eloquent" appeared in the pulpit. The Holy Communion was about to be dispensed, and, before parting for ever from his flock, he wished to address them once more. When he entered the pulpit, he mistook the side for the front; but old Rory, who watched him with intense interest, was immediately near him, and seizing a trembling hand, placed it on the book-board, thus guiding his master into the right position for addressing

the congregation.   And then stood up that venerable man, a Saul in height among the people, with
his pure white hair falling back from his ample
forehead over his shoulders.   Few, and loving,
and earnest, were the words he spoke, amidst the
profound silence of a passionately-devoted people,
which was broken only by their low sobs, when he
told them that they should see his face no more.
Soon afterwards he died.   The night of his death,
sons and daughters were grouped around his bed,
his wife on one side, old Rory on the other.   His
mind had been wandering during the day.   At
evening he sat up in bed; and one of his daughters,
who supported his head, dropped a tear on his
face.   Rory rebuked her and wiped it off; for it
is a Highland superstition (?), that no tear should
ever drop on the face of a good man dying ;—is it
because it adds to the burden of dying, or is unworthy of the glorious hopes of living ?   Suddenly
the minister stretched forth his hand, as if a child
was before him, and said, "I baptize thee into the
name of the Father, the Son, and the Holy Spirit,"
then falling back, he expired.   It seemed as if it
were his own baptism as a child of glory.

The widow did not long survive her husband. She had, with the quiet strength and wisdom of love, nobly fulfilled her part as wife and mother. And who can know what service a wife and mother is to a family, save those who have had this staff to lean on, this pillow to rest on, this sun to shine on them, this best of friends to accompany them, until their earthly journey is over, or far advanced?

Her last years were spent in peace in the old manse, occupied then and now by her youngest son. But she desired, ere she died, to see her first-born in his Lowland manse far away, and with him and his children to connect the present with the past. She accomplished her wishes, and left an impress on the young of the third generation which they have never lost during the thirty years that have passed since they saw her face and heard her voice. Illness she had hardly ever known. One morning a grandchild gently opened her bed-room door with breakfast. But hearing the low accents of prayer, she quietly closed it again, and retired. When she came again, and tapped and entered, all was still. The good woman seemed asleep in peace; and so she was, but it was the sleep of death.   She was buried in the Highland kirkyard, beside her husband and nine of her children.   There, with sweet young ones, of another generation, who have since then joined them from the same manse, they rest until the resurrection morning, when all will meet "in their several generations."

Old Rory, however, first followed his beloved master.   One evening, after weeks of illness, he said to his wife, "Dress me in my best; get a cart ready; I must go to the manse and bless them all, and then die."   His wife thought at first that his strange and sudden wish was the effect of delirium, and she was unwilling to consent.   But Rory gave the command in a tone which was never heard except when, at sea or on land, he meant to be obeyed. Arrayed in his Sunday's best, the old man, feeble, pale, and breathless, tottered into the parlour of the manse, where the family were soon around him, wondering, as if they had seen a ghost, what had brought him there.   " I bless you all, my dear ones," he said, "before I die."   And, stretching out his hands, he pronounced a patriarchal blessing, and a short prayer for their welfare.   Shaking hands with each, and kissing the hand of his old and dear mistress, he departed. The family group felt awe-struck,—the whole scene was so sudden, strange, and solemn. Next day, Rory was dead.

Old Jenny, the henwife, rapidly followed Rory. Why mention her? Who but the geese or the turkeys could miss her? But there are, I doubt not, many of my readers who can fully appreciate the loss of an old servant who, like Jenny, for half a century has been a respected and valued member of the family, She was associated with the whole household life of the manse. Neither she nor any of those old domestics had ever been mere things, but living persons with hearts and heads, to whom every burden, every joy of the family was known. Not a child but had been received into her embrace on the day of birth; not one passed away but had received her tears on the day of death; and they had all been decked by her in their last as in their first garments. The official position she occupied as henwife had been created for her in order chiefly to relieve her feelings at the thought of her being useless and a burden in her old age. When she died,

it was discovered that the affectionate old creature
had worn next her heart, and in order to be buried
with her, locks of hair cut off in infancy from the
children whom she had nursed.   And here I must
relate a pleasing incident connected with her.
Twenty years after her death, the younger son of
the manse, and its present possessor, was deputed
by his church to visit, along with two of his
brethren, the Presbyterian congregations of North
America.   When on the borders of Lake Simcoe
he was sent for by an old Highland woman, who
could speak her own language only, though she
had left her native hills very many years before.
On his entering her log-hut, the old woman burst
into a flood of tears, and, without uttering a word,
pointed to a silver brooch which clasped the tartan
shawl on her bosom.   She was Jenny's youngest
sister, and the silver brooch she wore, and which
was immediately recognised by the minister, had
been presented to Jenny by the eldest son of the
manse, when at college, as a token of affection for
his old nurse.

Nearly forty years after the old minister had
passed away, and so many of " the old familiar

faces" had followed him, the manse boat, which in shape and rig was literally descended from the famous "Roe," lay becalmed, on a beautiful summer evening, opposite the shore of the glebe. The many gorgeous tints from the setting sun were reflected from the bosom of the calm sea. Vessels, "like painted ships upon a painted ocean," lay scattered along "the Sound," and floated double, ship and shadow. The hills on both sides rose pure and clear into the blue sky, revealing every rock and precipice, with heathery knoll or grassy alp. Fish sometimes broke the smooth unrippled sea, "as of old the Curlews called." The boating party had gone out to enjoy the perfect repose of the evening, and allowed the boat to float with the tide. The conversation happened to turn on the manse and parish.

"I was blamed the other day," remarked the minister, who was one of the party, " for taking so much trouble in improving my glebe, and especially in beautifying it with trees and flowers, because, as my cautious friend remarked, I should remember that I was only a life-renter. But I asked my adviser how many proprietors in the

I

parish—whose families are supposed to have a better security for their lands than the minister has for the glebe—have yet possessed their properties so long as our poor family has possessed the glebe? He was astonished, on consideration, to discover that every property in the parish had changed its owner, and some of them several times, since I had succeeded my father."

"And if we look back to the time since our father became minister," remarked another of the party, "the changes have been still more frequent. The only possessors of their first home, in short, in the whole parish, are the family which had no possessions in it."

"And look," another said, "at those who are in this boat. How many birds are here out of the old nest!" And strange enough there were in the boat the eldest and youngest sons of the old minister, both born on the glebe, and both doctors of divinity; with three sons, ordained clergymen, sitting beside them, in all, five ministers descended from the old minister. The crew was made up of an elderly man, the son of "old Rory" and of a white-haired man, the son of "old Archy,"

both born on the glebe. And these clergymen
represented a few only of the descendants of the
old minister who were enjoying the manifold blessings of life. These facts are mentioned here in
order to connect such mercies with the anxiety expressed sixty years ago by the poor parson himself in the letter to his girls, which I have published.

One event more remains for me to record connected with the old manse, and then the silence of
the hills, in which that lowly home reposes, will
no more be broken by any word of mine about its
inhabitants—except as they are necessarily associated with other "reminiscences." It is narrated
in the Memoir of Professor Wilson, that when the
eldest son of our manse came to Glasgow College, in the heyday of his youth, he was the only
one who could compete, in athletic exercises,
with Christopher North, who was his friend
and fellow-student. The physical strength, acquired in his early days by the manly training
of the sea and hills, sustained his body; while
a spiritual strength, more noble still, sustained his
soul, during a ministry, in three large and difficult

parishes, which lasted, with constant labour, for more than half a century, and until he was just about to enter on his eightieth year—the day of his funeral being the anniversary of his birth. He had married in early life the daughter of one of the most honourable of the earth, who had for upwards of forty years, with punctilious integrity, managed the estates of the Argyle family in the Western Highlands. Her father's house was opposite the old manse, and separated from it by the "Sound." This invested that inland sea which divided the two lovers, with a poetry that made "The Roe" and her perilous voyages a happy vision that accompanied the minister until his last hour. For three or four years he had retired from public life, to rest from his labours, and in God's mercy to cultivate the passive more than the active virtues in the bosom of his own family. But when disposed to sink into the silent pensiveness and the physical depression which often attend old age, one topic, next to the highest of all, never failed to rouse him—even as the dying eagle in its cage, when it sees far off the mountains on which it tried its early flight—and that one was converse about the old parish, about his father, and his youth. And thus it happened that on the very last evening of his life he was peculiarly cheerful, as he told some stories of that long past; and among others a characteristic anecdote of old Rory. How naturally did the prayer of thanksgiving then succeed the memories of those times of peace and early happiness!

That night, his first and last love—the "better half," verily, of his earthly life, was awakened from her anxious slumbers near him, by his complaint of pain. But she had no time to rouse the household ere he, putting his arms round her neck, and breathing the words "My darling" in her ear, fell asleep. He had for more than twenty-five years ministered to an immense congregation of Highlanders in Glasgow; and his public funeral was remarkable, not chiefly for the numbers who attended it, or the crowds which followed it—for these things are common in such ceremonies—but for the sympathy and sorrow manifested by the feeble and tottering Highland men and women, very many of whom were from the old parish, and who, bathed in tears, struggled to keep up with the hearse, in order to be near, until the last possible moment, one for whom they had an enthusiastic attachment. The Highland hills and their people were to him a passion, and for their good he had devoted all the energies of his long life; and not in vain! His name will not, I think, be lost in this generation, wherever, at least, the Celtic language is spoken; and though this notice of him may have no interest to the Southern reader, who may not know, nor care to know, his name, yet every Gael in the most distant colony, who reads these lines, will pardon me for writing them. He belongs to them as they did to him.

## SOME CHARACTERISTICS OF THE HIGHLAND PEASANTRY.

I KNOW little from personal observation about the Highlanders in the far North or in the central districts of Scotland, but I am old enough to have very vivid reminiscences of those in the West; and of their character, manners, and customs as these existed during that transition period which began after "the '45," but has now almost entirely passed away with emigration, the decay of the "kelp" trade, the sale of so many old properties, and the introduction of large sheep farms, deer forests, and extensive shootings.

I have conversed with a soldier—old John Shoemaker, he was called—who bore arms under

Prince Charlie. On the day I met him he had walked several miles, was hale and hearty though upwards of a hundred years old, and had no money save ten shillings, which he always carried in his pocket to pay for his coffin. He conversed quite intelligently about the olden time with all its peculiarities. I have also known very many who were intimately acquainted with the "lairds" and "men" of those days, and who themselves had imbibed all the impressions and views then prevalent as to the world in general, and the Highlands in particular.

The Highlanders whom the tourist meets with now-a-days are very unlike those I used to know, and who are now found only in some of the remote unvisited glens, like the remains of a broken-up Indian nation on the outskirts of the American settlements. The porters who scramble for luggage on the quays of Oban, Inverary, Fort William, or Portree; the gillies who swarm around a shooting-box, or even the more aristocratic keepers—that whole *set*, in short, who live by summer tourists or autumnal sportsmen—are to the real Highlander, in his secluded parish or glen, what a commissionnaire in a hotel at Inn-spruck is to Hofer and his confederates.

The real Highland peasantry are, I hesitate not to affirm, by far the most intelligent in the world. I say this advisedly, after having compared them with those of many countries. Their good-breeding must strike every one who is familiar with them. Let a Highland shepherd from the most remote glen be brought into the dining-room of the laird, as is often done, and he will converse with ladies and gentlemen, partake of any hospitality which may be shown him with ease and grace, and never say or do anything *gauche* or offensive to the strictest propriety. This may arise in some degree from what really seems to be an instinct in the race, but more probably it comes from the familiar intercourse which, springing out of the old family and clan feeling, always subsists between the upper and lower classes. The Highland gentleman never meets the most humble peasant whom he knows without chatting with him as with an acquaintance, even shaking hands with him; and each man in the district, with all his belongings, ancestry and descendants included, is familiarly known to every other. Yet this familiar intercourse never causes the inferior at any time, or for a single moment, to alter the dignified respectful manner which he recognises as due to his superior. They have an immense reverence for those whom they consider "real gentlemen," or those who belong to the "good families," however distantly connected with them. No members of the aristocracy can distinguish more sharply than they do between genuine blood though allied with poverty, and the want of it though allied with wealth. Different ranks are defined with great care in their vocabulary. The chief is always called lord—"the lord of Lochiel," "the lord of Lochbuy." The gentlemen tenants are called "men"—"the man" of such and such a place. The poorest "gentleman" who labours with his own hands is addressed in more respectful language than his better-to-do neighbour who belongs to their own ranks. The one is addressed as "you," the other as "thou;" and should a property be bought by some one who is not connected with the old or good families, he may possess thousands, but he never commands the same reverence as the poor man who has yet "the blood" in him. The "pride and poverty" of the Gael have passed into a proverb, and express a fact.

They consider it essential to good manners and propriety never to betray any weakness or sense of fatigue, hunger, or poverty. They are great admirers in others of physical strength and endurance: those qualities which are most frequently demanded of themselves. When, for example, a number of Highland servants sit down to dinner, it is held as proper etiquette to conceal the slightest eagerness to begin to eat; and the eating, when begun, is continued with *apparent* indifference—the duty of the elder persons being to coax the younger, and especially any strangers that are present, to resume operations after they have professed to have partaken sufficiently of the meal. They always recognise liberal hospitality as essential to a "gentleman," and have the greatest contempt for narrowness or meanness in this department of life. Drunkenness is rarely indulged in as a solitary habit, but too extensively, I must admit, at fairs and other occasions—funerals not excepted—when many meet together from a distance, with time on their hands, and money in their pockets.

The dislike to make their wants known, or to complain of poverty, was also characteristic of them before the poor law was introduced, or famine compelled them to become beggars from the general public. But even when the civilised world poured its treasures, twenty years ago, into the Fund for the Relief of Highland Destitution, the old people suffered deeply ere they accepted any help. I have known families who closed their windows to keep out the light, that their children might sleep on as if it were night, and not rise to find a home without food. I remember being present at the first distribution of meal in a distant part of the Highlands. A few old women had come some miles, from an inland glen, to receive a portion of the bounty. Their clothes were rags, but every rag was washed, and patched together as best might be. They sat apart for a time, but at last approached the circle assembled round the meal depôt. I watched the countenances of the group as they conversed apparently on some momentous question. This I afterwards ascertained to be, which of them should go forward and speak for the others. One woman was at last selected; while the rest stepped back and hung their heads, concealing their eyes with their tattered tartan plaids. The deputy slowly walked towards the rather large official committee, whose attention, when at last directed to her, made her pause. She then stripped her right arm bare, and, holding up the miserable skeleton, burst into tears and sobbed like a child! Yet, during all these sad destitution times, there was not a policeman or soldier in those districts. No food riot ever took place, no robbery was attempted, no sheep was ever stolen from the hills; and all this though hundreds had only shell-fish, or "dulse," gathered on the sea-shore to live upon.

The Highlander is assumed to be a lazy animal, and not over honest in his dealings with strangers. I have no desire to be a special pleader in his behalf, notwithstanding all my national predilections in his favour. But I must nevertheless dissent to some

extent from these sweeping generalisations.   He is
naturally impulsive and fond of excitement, and
certainly is wanting in the steady, persevering effort
which characterises his Southern brother.   But the
circumstances of his country, his small "croft" and
want of capital, the bad land and hard weather,
with the small returns for his uncertain labour,
have tended to depress rather than to stimulate
him.   One thing is certain, that when he is
removed to another clime, and placed in more
favourable circumstances, he exhibits a perseverance and industry which make him rise very
rapidly.

It must be confessed, however, that Highland
honesty is sometimes very lax in its dealings with
the Sassenach.   The Highlander forms no exception, alas, to the tribe of guides, drivers, boatmen,
all over Europe, who imagine that the tourist possesses unlimited means, and travels only to spend
money.   A friend of mine who had been so long
in India that he lost the Highland accent, though
not the language, reached a ferry on his journey
home, and, concealing his knowledge of Gaelic,
asked one of the Highland boatmen what his

charge was. "I'll ask the maister," was his reply. The master being unable to speak English, this faithful mate acted as interpreter. "What will you take from this Englishman?" quoth the interpreter "Ask the fellow ten shillings," was the reply of the honest master, the real fare being five shillings. "He says," explained the interpreter, "that he is sorry he cannot do it under *twenty* shillings, and that's cheap." Without saying anything, the offer was apparently accepted; but while sailing across my friend spoke in Gaelic, on which the interpreter sharply rebuked him in the same language. "I am ashamed of you!" he said; "I am indeed, for I see you are ashamed of your country; och, och, to pretend to me that you were an Englishman! you deserve to pay *forty* shillings—but the ferry, is only five!" Such specimens, however, are found only along the great tourist thoroughfares where they are in every country too common.

I have said that the Highlanders are an intelligent, cultivated people, as contrasted with that dull, stupid, prosaic, incurious condition of mind which characterises so many of the peasantry in other countries. Time never hangs heavily on their hands during even the long winter evenings, when outdoor labour is impossible. When I was young, I was sent to live among the peasantry in "the parish," so as to acquire a knowledge of the language; and living, as I did, very much like themselves, it was my delight to spend the long evenings in their huts, hearing their tales and songs. These huts were of the most primitive description. They were built of loose stones and clay; the walls were thick, the door low, the rooms numbered one only, or in more aristocratic cases two. The floor was clay; the peat-fire was built in the middle of the floor, and the smoke, when amiable and not bullied by a sulky wind, escaped quietly and patiently through a hole in the roof. The window was like a porthole, part of it generally filled with glass and part with peat. One bed, or sometimes two, (with clean home-made sheets, blankets, and counterpane,) a "dresser" with bowls and plates, a large chest, and a corner full of peat, filled up the space beyond the circle about the fire. Upon the rafters above, black as ebony from peat-reek, a row of hens and chickens with a stately cock roosted in a paradise of heat.

Let me describe one of these evenings. Round the fire are seated, some on stools, some on stones, some on the floor, a happy group. Two or three girls, fine, healthy, blue-eyed lassies, with their hair tied up with ribbon snood, are knitting stockings. Hugh, the son of Sandy, is busking hooks; big Archy is pealing willow-wands and fashioning them into baskets; the shepherd Donald, the son of Black John, is playing on the Jews' harp; while beyond the circle are one or two herd boys in kilts, reclining on the floor, all eyes and ears for the stories. The performances of Donald begin the evening, and form interludes to its songs, tales, and recitations. He has two large "Lochaber trumps," for Lochaber trumps were to the Highlands what Cremona violins have been to musical Europe. He secures the end of each with his teeth, and, grasping them with his hands so that the tiny instruments are invisible, he applies the little finger of each hand to their vibrating steel tongues. He modulates their tones with his breath, and brings out of them Highland reels, strathspeys, and jigs,—such wonderfully beautiful, silvery, distinct, and harmonious

K.

sounds as would draw forth cheers and an encore even in St James's Hall.   But Donald, the son of Black John, is done, and he looks to bonny Mary Cameron for a blink of her hazel eye to reward him, while in virtue of his performance he demands a song from her.   Now Mary has dozens of songs, so has Kirsty, so has Flory,—love songs, shearing songs, washing songs, Prince Charlie songs, songs composed by this or that poet in the parish; and therefore Mary asks, What song?   So until she can make up her mind, and have a little playful flirtation with Donald, the son of Black John, she requests Hugh, the son of Sandy, to tell a story. Although Hugh has abundance of this material, he too protests that he has none.   But having betrayed this modesty, he starts off with one of those which are given by Mr Campbell, to whose admirable and truthful volumes I refer the reader.*

* No man knows the Highlanders better than Mr Campbell— very few so well—and I am glad to quote his opinions.   In the introduction to the " Highland Tales," he says :—

" I have wandered among the peasantry of many countries, and this trip but confirmed my old impression.   There are few peasants that I think so highly of, none that I love so well.   Scotch Highlanders have faults in plenty, but they have the bearing of Nature's own gentlemen—the delicate natural tact which discovers, and

When the story is done, improvisation is often tried, and amidst roars of laughter the aptest verses the truest and most authentic specimens of tales, are made, sometimes in clever satire, sometimes with knowing allusions to the weaknesses or pre-dilections of those round the fire. Then follow riddles and puzzles ; then the trumps resume their tunes, and Mary sings her song, and Kirsty and Flory theirs, and all join in chorus, and who cares

the good taste which avoids, all that would hurt or offend a guest. The poorest is ever the readiest to share the best he has with the stranger ; a kind word kindly meant is never thrown away, and whatever may be the faults of this people, I have never found a boor or a churl in a Highland bothy."

" The Highlander sees every year a numerous flood of tourists of all nations pouring through his lochs and glens, but he knows as little of them as they of him. The shoals of herring that enter Loch Fyne know as much of the dun deer on the hill side, as Lon-doners and Highlanders know of each other. The want of a com-mon language here, as elsewhere, keeps Highlands and Lowlands, Celt and Saxon, as clearly separate as oil and water in the same glass." He remarks with equal truth regarding their stories : " I have never heard a story whose point was obscenity publicly told in a Highland cottage ; and I believe that such are rare. I *have* heard them where the rough polish of more modern ways has replaced the polished roughness of 'wild' Highlanders ; and that where even the bagpipes have been almost abolished as profane. I have heard the music of the Cider Cellars in a parlour, even in polished England, where I failed to extract anything else from a group of comfortably dressed villagers."

for the wind outside or the peat-reek inside ! Never was a more innocent or happy group.

This fondness for music from trump, fiddle, or bagpipe, and for song-singing, story-telling, and improvisation, was universal, and imparted a marvellous buoyancy and intelligence to the people.

These peasants were, moreover, singularly inquisitive, and greedy of information. It was a great thing if the schoolmaster or any one else was present who could tell them about other people and other places. I remember an old shepherd who questioned me closely how the hills and rocks were formed, as a gamekeeper had heard some sportsmen talking about this. The questions which were put were no doubt often odd enough. A woman, for example, whose husband was anxious to emigrate to Australia, stoutly opposed the step, until she could get her doubts solved on some geographical point that greatly disturbed her. She consulted the minister, and the tremendous question which chiefly weighed on her mind was, whether it was true that the feet of the people there were opposite to the feet of the people at home ? and if so—what then ?

There is one science the value of which it is very difficult to make a Highlander comprehend, and that is mineralogy. He connects botany with the art of healing; astronomy with guidance from the stars, or navigation; chemistry with dyeing, brewing, &c.; but "chopping bits off the rocks!" as he calls it,—this has always been a mystery. A shepherd, while smoking his cutty at a small Highland inn, was communicating to another in Gaelic his experiences of "mad Englishmen," as he called them. "There was one," said the narrator, "who once gave me his bag to carry to the inn by a short cut across the hills, while he walked by another road. I was wondering myself why it was so dreadfully heavy, and when I got out of his sight I was determined to see what was in it. I opened it, and what do you think it was? But I need not ask you to guess, for you would never find out. It was stones!" "Stones!" exclaimed his companion, opening his eyes. "Stones! Well, well, that beats all I ever knew or heard of them! and did you carry it?" "Carry it! Do you think I was as mad as himself? No! I emptied them all out, but I filled the bag again from the cairn near the house, and gave him good measure for his money!"

The schoolmaster has been abroad in the Highlands during these latter years, and few things are more interesting than the eagerness with which education has been received by the people. When the first deputation from the Church of Scotland visited the Highlands and Islands, in a Government cruiser put at their disposal, to inquire into the state of education and for the establishing of schools in needy districts, most affecting evidence was afforded by the poor people of their appreciation of this great boon. In one island where an additional school was promised, a body of the peasantry accompanied the deputies to the shore, and bade them farewell with expressions of the most tender and touching gratitude; and as long as they were visible from the boat, every man was seen standing with his head uncovered. In another island where it was thought necessary to change the site of the school, a woman strongly protested against the movement. In her fervour she pointed to her girl and said, "She and the like of her cannot walk many miles to the new school, and it was from her dear lips I first heard the words of the blessed gospel read in our house; for God's sake don't take away the school!" Her pleading was successful. Old men in some cases went to school to learn to read and write. One old man, when dictating a letter to a neighbour, got irritated at the manner in which his sentiments had been expressed by his amanuensis. "I'm done of this!" he at length exclaimed. "Why should I have my tongue in another man's mouth when I can learn to think for myself on paper? I'll go to the school and learn to write!" And he did so. A class in another school was attended by elderly people. One of the boys in it, who was weeping bitterly, being asked by the teacher the cause of his sorrow, ejaculated in sobs, "I trapped my grandfather, and he'll no let me up!" The boy was below his grandfather in the class, and having "trapped," or corrected him in his reading, he claimed the right of getting above him, which the old man resisted.

I may notice, for the information of those interested in the education of the Irish or Welsh-speaking populations, that Gaelic is taught in all the

Highland schools, and that the result has been an immediate demand for English. The education of the faculties, and the stimulus given to acquire information, demand a higher aliment than can be afforded by the medium of the Gaelic language alone. But it is not my intention to discourse, in these light sketches, upon grave themes requiring more space and time to do them justice than my space can afford.

Another characteristic feature of the Highland peasantry is the devoted and unselfish attachment which they retain through life to any of their old friends and neighbours. An intimate knowledge of the families in the district is what we might expect. They are acquainted with all their ramifications by blood or by marriage, and from constant personal inquiries, keep up, as far as possible, a knowledge of their history, though they may have been out of the country for years. I marked, last summer, in the Highlands the surprise of a general officer from India, who was revisiting the scenes of his youth, as old men, who came to pay their respects to him, inquired about every member of his family, showing a thorough knowledge of all the marriages which had taken place, and the very names of the children who had been born. "I declare," remarked the general, "that this is the only country where they care to know a man's father or grandfather! What an unselfish interest, after all, do these people take in one, and in all that belongs to him! And how *have* they found all this out about my nephews and nieces, with their children?" Their love of kindred, down to those in whom a drop of their blood can be traced, is remarkable enough, but not so much so as this undying interest in old friends, whether they be rich or poor. Even the bond of a common name—however absurd this appears—has its influence still in the Highlands. I remember when it was so powerful among old people as to create not only strong predilections, but equally strong antipathies towards strangers of whom nothing was known save their name. This is feudalism fossilised. In the Highlands there are other connexions which are considered closely allied to those of blood. The connexion, for instance, between children—it may be of the laird and of

the peasant—who are reared by the same nurse,
is one of these. Many an officer has been
accompanied by his "foster-brother" to "the
wars," and has ever found him his faithful servant and friend unto death. Such a one was
Ewen M'Millan, who followed Col. Cameron, or
Fassifern—as he was called, in Highland fashion,
from his place of residence,—to whom Sir Walter
Scott alludes in the lines

> " Proud Ben Nevis views with awe,
> How, at the bloody Quatre Bras,
> Brave Cameron heard the wild hurrah
> Of conquest as he fell."

The foster-brother was ever beside his dear
master, with all the enthusiastic attachment and
devotion of the old feudal times, throughout
the Peninsular campaign. The 92d Regiment
was commanded by Fassifern, and speaking of
its conduct at the Nive, Napier says:—" How
gloriously did that regiment come forth to the
charge with their colours flying and their national music playing as if going to review!
This was to understand war. The man (Col.
Cameron,) who at that moment, and immediately

after a repulse, thought of such military pomp, was by nature a soldier." Four days after this, though on each of those days the fighting was continued and severe, the 92d was vigorously attacked at St Pierre. Fassifern's horse was shot under him, and he was so entangled by the fall as to be utterly unable to resist a French soldier, who would have transfixed him but for the fact that the foster-brother transfixed the Frenchman. Liberating his master, and accompanying him to his regiment, the foster-brother returned under a heavy fire and amidst a fierce combat to the dead horse. Cutting the girths of the saddle and raising it on his shoulders, he rejoined the 92d with the trophy, exclaiming, " We must leave them the carcase, but they will never get the saddle on which Fassifern sat !" The Gaelic sayings, " Kindred to twenty degrees, fosterage to a hundred," and " Woe to the father of the foster-son who is unfaithful to his trust," were fully verified in M'Millan's case. I may add one word about Colonel Cameron's death as illustrative of the old Highland spirit. He was killed in charging the French at Quatre Bras. The moment he fell, his foster-brother was by his side, carried him out of the field of battle, procured a cart, and sat in it with his master's head resting on his bosom. They reached the village of Waterloo, where M'Millan laid him on the floor of a deserted house by the way-side. The dying man asked how the day went, expressed a hope that his beloved Highlanders had behaved well, and that " his country would believe he had served her faithfully ;" and then commanded a piper, who had by this time joined them, to play a pibroch to him, and thus bring near to him his home among the hills far away. Higher thoughts were not wanting, but these could mingle in the heart of the dying Highlander with " Lochaber no more." He was buried on the 17th by M'Millan and his old brave friend Captain Gordon — who still survives to tell the story — in the *Allée Verte*, on the Ghent road. The following year the faithful foster-brother returned, and took the body back to Lochaber; and there it lies in peace beneath an obelisk which the traveller, as he enters the Caledonian Canal from the south, may see near a cluster of trees which shade the remains of the

Lochiel family, of which Fassifern was a younger branch.*

It must, however, be frankly admitted that there is no man more easily offended, more *thin-skinned*, who cherishes longer the memory of an insult, or keeps up with more freshness a personal, family, or party feud than the genuine Highlander. Woe be to the man who offends his pride or vanity! " I may forgive, but I cannot forget !" is a favourite saying. He will stand by a friend till the last, but let a breach be once made, and it is most difficult ever again to repair it as it once was. The " grudge" is immortal. There is no man who can fight and shake hands like the genuine Englishman.

It is difficult to pass any judgment on the state of religion past or present in the Highlands. From the natural curiosity of the Highlanders, their desire to obtain instruction, the reading of the Bible in the schools, they are on the whole better informed in respect to religion than the poorer peasantry of

* A very interesting memoir of Fassifern, from which these facts are taken, has been written by the Rev. A. Clark, the minister of the parish in which the Colonel is interred. It is published by Murray & Son, Glasgow.

other countries. But when their religious life is
suddenly quickened it is apt to manifest itself for
a time in enthusiasm or fanaticism, for the Highlander " moveth altogether if he move at all."
The people have all a deep religious feeling, but
that again, unless educated, has been often mingled with superstitions which have come down
from heathen and Roman Catholic times. Of
these superstitions, with some of their peculiar
customs, I may have to speak in another
chapter.

The men of " the '45 " were, as a class, half
heathen, with strong sympathies for Romanism or
Episcopacy, as the supposed symbol of loyalty.
I mentioned, in a former sketch, how the parish
minister of that time had prayed with his eyes
open and his pistols cocked. But I have been
since reminded of a fact which I had forgotten,
that one of the lairds who had " followed Prince
Charlie," and who sat in the gallery opposite the
parson, had threatened to shoot him if he dared
to pray for King George, and, on the occasion referred to, had ostentatiously laid a pistol on the
book-board. It was then only that the minister

produced his brace to keep the laird in countenance! This same half-savage laird was, in later years, made more civilised by the successor of the belligerent parson. Our parish minister, on one occasion, when travelling with the laird, was obliged to sleep at night in the same room with him in a Highland inn. After retiring to bed, the laird said, "O minister, I wish you would tell some tale." "I shall do so willingly," replied the minister; and he told the story of Joseph and his brethren. When it was finished, the laird expressed his great delight at the narrative, and begged to know where the minister had picked it up, as it was evidently not Highland. "I got it," quoth the minister, "in a book you have often heard of, and where you may find many other most delightful and most instructive stories, which, unlike our Highland ones, are all true—in the Bible."

I will here recall an anecdote of old Rory, illustrative of Highland superstition in its very mildest form. When "the minister" came to "the parish," it was the custom for certain offenders to stand before the congregation during service, and do penance in a long canvas shirt drawn over their ordinary garments. He discontinued this severe practice, and the canvas shirt was hung up in his barn, where it became an object of awe and fear to the farm servants, as having somehow to do with the wicked one. He resolved to put it to some useful purpose, and what better could it be turned to than to repair the sail of "The Roe," which had been torn by a recent squall? Rory, on whom this task devolved, respectfully protested against patching the sail with the wicked shirt; but the more he did so, the more the minister—who had himself almost a superstitious horror for superstition—resolved to show his contempt for Rory's fears and warnings by commanding the patch to be adjusted without delay, as he had that evening to cross the stormy sound. Rory dared not refuse, and his work was satisfactorily finished, but he gave no response to his master's thanks and praises as the sail was hoisted with a white circle above the boom, marking the new piece in the old garment. As they proceeded on their voyage, the wind suddenly rose, until the boat was staggering gunwale down with as much as she could carry. When passing athwart the mouth of a wide glen, which, like a funnel, always gathered and discharged, in their concentrated force, whatever squalls were puffing and whistling round the hills, the sea to windward gave token of a very heavy blast, which was rapidly approaching " The Roe," with a huge line of foam before it, like the white helmet crests of a line of cavalry waving in the charge. The minister was at the helm, and was struck by the anxiety visible in Rory's face, for they had mastered many worse attacks in the same place without difficulty. " We must take in two reefs, Rory," he exclaimed, " as quickly as possible. Stand by the halyards, boys! quick and handy." But the squall was down upon them too sharp to admit of any preparation. " Reefs will do no good to-day," remarked Rory with a sigh. The water rushed along the gunwale, which was taking in more than was comfortable, while the spray was flying over the weather bow as the brave little craft, guided by the minister's hand, lay close to the wind as a knife. When the squall was at the worst, Rory could restrain himself no longer, but opening his large boat knife, sprang up

L

and made a dash at the sail. Whirling the sharp blade round the white patch, and embracing a good allowance of cloth beyond to make his mark sure, he cut the wicked spot out. As it flew far to leeward like a sea bird, Rory resumed his seat, and, wiping his forehead, said: " Thanks to Providence, that's gone! and just see how the squall is gone with it!" The squall had indeed spent itself, while the boat was eased by the big hole. "I told you how it would be. Oh! never, never, do the like again, minister, for it's a tempting of the devil!" Rory saw he was forgiven, as the minister and his boys burst into a roar of merry laughter at the scene.

## STORIES OF SNOWSTORMS FOR THE FIRESIDE.

### I.—OLD JENNY OF GLEN IMMERN.

WHEN the sheep were sent to the hills, the shielings were no longer of any use, and so they fell into ruins. But for many a year one hut remained far up in Glen Immern, inhabited by "old Jenny." How she came to live there we never heard. Perhaps she had been there when a child with her father and mother, and with others who had passed from her sight, but not from the eye of her heart: and so she would see forms among the hills that others saw not, and hear voices of the old time whispering in her ear, or echoing among the knolls that others heard not.

Thus in the lonely glen Jenny was not alone.
And I think she knew One who was more real
to her than all those dreams of heart—One who
was her Father in heaven, and ever present with
her. It is certain, however, that Jenny was singularly respected. When she came down from the
glen once a year to the "big house," the laird's
wife brought her into the dining-room and chatted
with her, and gave her something from her own
hand to eat and drink as a pledge of friendship.
The minister visited her regularly; and she came
as regularly to see the family, and would remain
for days a welcome guest in the kitchen. Besides
this, she was often sent for to nurse the sick, and
few houses had not received her advice and assistance in time of trouble; for Jenny knew a remarkable collection of "cures,"—that is, medicines
made up from plants and roots,—as remedies for
those accidents and diseases which were common
in the country. These "cures" were at one time
familiar to many in the Highlands, and until educated physicians settled there, they were the only
sources of relief to the sufferer; and very good
service they did. By such means old Jenny be-

came a sort of public character. No one passed her cottage, on the way across the mountains to the thickly-peopled valley on the other side, without calling on her and giving her all the news of the district.

A goat and a few hens were all Jenny's property. But then she got wool from one family, and meal from another, and her peats from a third; so that she lived in such comfort as no forced poor-law ever gave, or can give; for charity did not injure self-respect, and every gift was a sign of kindness. Spring was the trying season, when the winter had almost exhausted all her means of living. The meal was nearly done—potatoes were not then so common among the poor—the pasture was scanty for the goat; and Jenny was sometimes forced to take a journey to visit her kind neighbours down near the sea-coast, driven, like a vessel in a storm, for shelter to a friendly harbour. Well, it so happened that one day a dreadful snowstorm came on just as she was planning an excursion to get some meal, and when her hut was almost empty of food except the little milk she could get from her goat. For a long time that snow-storm was a sort of date in the parish, and people counted so many years before or after "the great storm." Never had they seen such a constant and heavy fall with such deep snowdrifts. When the heavens at last became clear, the whole face of the country seemed changed. It was some time before the thought suddenly occurred to a shepherd—"What has old Jenny been doing all this time?" No sooner was her name mentioned than she at once became the theme of conversation among all the cottages in the Highland hamlet nearest Glen Immern, and throughout the parish. But for many days, such was the state of the weather that no mortal foot could wade through the snow-wreaths, or buffet the successive storms which swept down with blinding fury from the hills. Jenny was given up as lost! When the minister prayed for her there was deep silence in the small church, and manly sighs were heard. At last, three men resolved, on the first day the attempt was possible, to proceed up the long and dreary glen to search for Jenny. They carried food in their plaids, and whatever comforts they thought necessary—nay, they resolved to bring the old

woman home with them, if they found her alive.
So off they went; and many an eye watched those
three black dots among the snow, slowly tracking
their way up Glen Immern.   At last, they reached
a rock at an angle, where the glen takes a turn to
the left, and where the old woman's cottage ought
to have been seen.   But nothing met the eye except a smooth white sheet of glittering snow, sur-
mounted by black rocks; and all below was silent
as the sky above!   No sign of life greeted eye or
ear.   The men spoke not, but muttered some ex-
clamations of sorrow.   "She is alive!" suddenly
cried one of the shepherds; "for I see smoke."
They pushed bravely on.   When they reached the
hut, nothing was visible except the two chimneys;
and even those were lower than the snow-wreath.
There was no immediate entrance but by one of
the chimneys.   A shepherd first called to Jenny
down the chimney, and asked if she was alive; but
before receiving a reply, a large fox sprang out of
the chimney, and darted off to the rocks.

"Alive!" replied Jenny; "but thank God you
have come to see me!   I cannot say come in by
the door; but come down—come down."

In a few minutes her three friends easily descended by the chimney, and were shaking Jenny's hand warmly.   Hurried questions were put and answered.

"Oh, woman! how have you lived all this time?"

"Sit down and I will tell you," said old Jenny, whose feelings now gave way to a fit of hysterical weeping.   After composing herself, she continued, " How did I live?" you ask, Sandy.   "I may say, just as I have always lived—by the power and goodness of God, who feeds the wild beasts."

"The wild beasts indeed," replied Sandy, drying his eyes; "did you know that a wild beast was in your own house?   Did you see the fox that jumped out of your chimney as we entered?"

"My blessings on the dear beast!" said Jenny, with fervour.   "May no huntsman ever kill it! and may it never want food either summer or winter!"

The shepherds looked at one another by the dim light of Jenny's fire, evidently thinking that she had become slightly insane.

"Stop, lads," she continued, "till I tell you the

story. I had in the house, when the storm began, the goat and hens. Fortunately, I had fodder gathered for the goat, which kept it alive, although, poor thing, it has had but scanty meals. But it lost its milk. I had also peats for my fire, but very little meal; yet I never lived better; and I have been able besides to preserve my bonnie hens for summer. I every day dined on flesh meat too, a thing I have not done for years before; and thus I have lived like a lady."

Again the shepherds were amazed, and asked in a low voice, as if in pity for her state, "Where did you get meat, Jenny?"

"From the old fox, Sandy!"

"The fox!" they all exclaimed.

"Ay, the fox," said Jenny; "just the dear, old fox, the best friend I ever had. I'll tell you how it was. The day of the storm he looked into the chimney, and came slowly down, and set himself on the rafter beside the hens, yet never once touched them. Honest fellow! he is sorely miscalled; for he every day provided for himself, and for me, too, like a kind neighbour, as he was. He hunted regularly like a gentleman, and brought in game in abundance for his own dinner—a hare almost every day—and what he left I got, and washed, and cooked, and eat, and so I have never wanted! Now that he has gone, you have come to relieve me."

"God's ways are past finding out!" said the men, bowing down their heads with reverence.

"Praise Him," said Jenny, "who giveth food to the hungry!"

## II.—THE WIDOW AND HER SON.

A WIDOW, who, I have heard, was much loved for her "meek and quiet spirit," left her home in "the parish," early one morning, in order to reach, before evening, the residence of a kinsman who had promised to assist her to pay her rent. She carried on her back her only child. The mountain-track she pursued passes along the shore of a beautiful salt-water loch; then through a green valley, watered by a peaceful stream which flows from a neighbouring lake. It afterwards winds along the margin of this solitary lake, until, near its farther end, it suddenly turns

into an extensive copse-wood of oak and birch.
From this it emerges half-way up a rugged mountain side; and, entering a dark glen, through which
a torrent rushes amidst great masses of granite, it
conducts the traveller at last, by a zigzag ascent,
up to a narrow gorge, which is hemmed in upon
every side by giant precipices, with a strip of
blue sky overhead, all below being dark and
gloomy.

From this mountain-pass the widow's dwelling
was ten miles distant.   She had undertaken a long
journey, but her rent was some weeks overdue, and
the sub-factor had threatened to dispossess her.

The morning on which she left her home gave
promise of a peaceful day.   Before noon, however,
a sudden change took place in the weather.   To
the northward, the sky became black and lowering.   Masses of clouds fell down upon the hills.
Sudden gusts of wind began to whistle among
the rocks, and with black squalls to ruffle the
surface of the lake.   The wind was succeeded
by rain, and the rain by sleet, and the sleet by
a heavy fall of snow.   It was the month of
May, and that storm is yet remembered as the

"great May storm." The wildest day of winter never saw snowflakes falling faster, or whirling with more fury through the mountain-pass, filling every hollow and whitening every rock!

Little anxiety about the widow was felt by the villagers, as many ways were pointed out by which she might have escaped the fury of the storm. She could have halted at the steading of this farmer, or the shieling of that shepherd, before it had become dangerous to cross the hill. But early in the morning of the succeeding day they were alarmed to hear from a person who had come from the place to which the widow was travelling, that she had not made her appearance there.

In a short time about a dozen men mustered to search for the missing woman. At each house on the track they heard with increasing fear that she had been seen pursuing her journey the day before. The shepherd on the mountain could give no information regarding her. Beyond his hut there was no shelter; nothing but deep snow; and between the range of rocks, at the summit of the pass, the drift lay thickest. There the storm must have blown with a fierce and bitter blast. It was by no means an easy task to examine the deep wreaths which filled up every hollow. At last a cry from one of the searchers attracted the rest, and there, crouched beneath a huge granite boulder, they discovered the dead body of the widow.

She was entombed by the snow. A portion of a tartan cloak which appeared above its surface led to her discovery. But what had become of the child? Nay, what had become of the widow's clothes? for all were gone except the miserable tattered garment which hardly covered her nakedness? That she had been murdered and stripped, was the first conjecture suggested by the strange discovery. But being in a country in which one murder only had occurred within the memory of man, the notion was soon dismissed from their thoughts. She had evidently died where she sat, bent almost double; but as yet all was mystery as to her boy and her clothing. Very soon, however, the mystery was cleared up. A shepherd found the child alive in a sheltered nook in the rock, very near the spot where his mother sat cold and stiff in death. He lay in a bed of heather and fern, and round him were swathed all the clothes which his mother had stripped off herself to save her child! The story of her self-sacrificing love was easily read.

The incident has lived fresh in the memory of many in the parish; and the old people who were present in the empty hut of the widow, when her body was laid in it, never forgot the minister's address and prayers, as he stood beside the dead. He was hardly able to speak for tears, as he endeavoured to express his sense of that woman's worth and love, and to pray for her poor orphan boy.

More than fifty years had passed away, when the eldest son of " the manse," then old and gray-headed, went to preach to his Highland congregation in Glasgow, on the Sunday previous to that on which the Lord's Supper was to be dispensed. He found a comparatively small congregation assembled, for snow was falling heavily, and threatened to continue all day. Suddenly he recalled the story of the widow and her son, and this again recalled to his memory the text:—" He shall be as the shadow of a great rock in a weary land."

He resolved to address his people from these words, although he had carefully prepared a sermon on another subject.

In the course of his remarks he narrated the circumstances of the death of the Highland widow, whom he had himself known in his boyhood. And having done so, he asked, "If that child is now alive, what would you think of his heart, if he did not cherish an affection for his mother's memory? and what would you think of him if the sight of her clothes, which she had wrapt round him, in order to save his life at the cost of her own, did not touch his heart, and even fill him with gratitude and love too deep for words? Yet what hearts have you, my hearers, if, over the memorials of your Saviour's sacrifice of Himself, which you are to witness next Sunday, you do not feel them glow with deepest love, and with adoring gratitude?"

Some time after this, a messenger was sent by a dying man with a request to see the minister. This was speedily complied with. The sick man seized him by the hand, as he seated himself beside his bed, and, gazing intently in his face, said, "You do not, you cannot recognise me. But I know you, and knew your father before you. I have been a wanderer in many lands. I have visited every quarter of the globe, and have fought and bled for my king and country. But while I served my king, I forgot my God. Though I have been some years in this city, I never entered a church. But the other Sunday, as I was walking along the street, I happened to pass your church door when a heavy shower of snow came on, and I entered the lobby for shelter, but, I am ashamed to say, not with the intention of worshipping God, or of hearing a sermon. But as I heard the singing of psalms, I went into a seat near the door; then you preached, and I heard you tell the story of the widow and her son." Here the voice of the old soldier faltered, his emotion almost choked his utterance; but, recovering himself for a moment, he cried, " I am that son!" and burst into a flood of tears. "Yes," he continued, " I am that son! Never, never, did I forget my mother's love. Well might you ask, what a heart should mine have been if she had been forgotten by me! Though I never saw her, dear to me is her memory, and my only desire now is, to lay my bones beside hers in the old churchyard among the hills. But, sir, what breaks my heart, and covers me with shame, is this —that until now I never saw the love of Christ in giving Himself for me,—a poor, lost, hell-deserving sinner. I confess it! I confess it!" he cried, looking up to heaven, his eyes streaming with tears. Then pressing the minister's hand close to his breast, he added, " It was God made you tell that story. Praise be to His holy name, that my dear mother did not die in vain, and that the prayers which I was told she used to offer for me have been at last answered; for the love of my mother has been blessed by the Holy Spirit, for making me see, as I never saw before, the love of the Saviour. I see it, I believe it; I have found deliverance now where I found it in my childhood,— in the cleft of the rock—the Rock of Ages!" and, clasping his hands, he repeated, with intense fervour, " Can a mother forget her sucking child, that she should not have compassion on the son of her womb? She may forget; yet will I not forget thee!"

He died in peace.

M

## TACKSMEN AND TENANTS.

THE "upper" and "lower" classes in the Highlands were not separated from each other by a wide gap. The thought was never suggested of a great proprietor above, like a leg of mutton on the top of a pole, and the people far below, looking up to him with envy. On reviewing the state of Highland society, one was rather reminded of a pyramid whose broad base was connected with the summit by a series of regular steps. The dukes or lords, indeed, were generally far removed from the inhabitants of the land, living as they did for the greater part of the year in London; but the minor chiefs, such as " Lochnell," " Lochiel," " Coll," " Macleod," " Raasay," &c.,

resided on their respective estates, and formed centres of local and personal influence. They had good family mansions; and in some instances the old keep was enlarged into a fine baronial castle, where all the hospitality of the far north was combined with the more refined domestic arrangements of the south. They had also their handsome "barge," or well-built, well-rigged "smack" or "wherry;" and their stately piper, who played pibrochs with very storms of sound after dinner, or, from the bow of the boat, with the tartan ribands fluttering from the grand war-pipe, spread the news of the chief's arrival for miles across the water. They were looked up to and respected by the people. Their names were mingled with all the traditions of the country: they were as old as its history, indeed, practically as old as the hills themselves. They mingled freely with the peasantry, spoke their language, shared their feelings, treated them with sympathy, kindness, and, except in outward circumstances, were in all respects one of themselves. The poorest man on their estate could converse with them at any time in the frankest manner, as with friends whom they could trust. There was between them an old and firm attachment.

This feeling of clanship, this interest of the clan in their chief, has even lived down to my own recollection. It is not many years ago—for I heard the incident described by some of the clan who took part in the *émeute*—that a new family burial-ground was made on an old property by a laird who knew little of the manners or prejudices of the country, having lived most of his time abroad. The first person he wished to bury in this new private tomb near " the big house " was his predecessor, whose lands and name he inherited, and who had been a true representative of the old stock. But when the clan heard of what they looked upon as an insult to their late chief, they formed a conspiracy, seized the body by force, and after guarding it for a day or two, buried it with all honour in the ancient family tomb on

" The Isle of Saints, where stands the old gray cross."

The Tacksmen at that time formed the most important and influential class of a society which has now wholly disappeared in most districts. In

no country in the world was such a contrast presented as in the Highlands between the structure
of the houses and the culture of their occupants.
The houses were of the most primitive description;
they consisted of one story—had only what the
Scotch call a *but and a ben;* that is, a room at each
end, with a passage between, two garret rooms
above, and in some cases a kitchen, built out at
right angles behind. Most of them were thatched
with straw or heather. Such was the architecture
of the house in which Dr Johnson lived with the
elegant and accomplished Sir Allan Maclean, on
the island of Inchkenneth. The old house of
Glendessary, again, in "the parish," was constructed, like a few more, of wicker work; the
outside being protected with turf, and the interior
lined with wood. "The house and the furniture,"
writes Dr Johnson, "were ever always nicely
suited. We were driven once, by missing our
passage, to the hut of a gentleman, when, after a
very liberal supper, I was conducted to my chamber, and found an elegant bed of Indian cotton,
spread with fine sheets. The accommodation was
flattering; I undressed myself, and found my feet

in the mire.   The bed stood on the cold earth, which a long course of rain had softened to a puddle."   But in these houses were gentlemen, nevertheless, and ladies of education and high-breeding. Writing of Sir Allan Maclean and his daughters, Johnson says :—" Romance does not often exhibit a scene that strikes the imagination more than this little desert in these depths and western obscurity, occupied, not by a gross herdsman or amphibious fisherman, but by a gentleman and two ladies of high rank, polished manners, and elegant conversation, who, in a habitation raised not very far above the ground, but furnished with unexpected neatness and convenience, practised all the kindness of hospitality and the refinement of courtesy."   It was thus, too, with the old wicker-house of Glendessary, of which not a trace now remains.   The interior was provided with all the comfort and taste of a modern mansion.   The ladies were accomplished musicians, the harp and piano sounded in those " halls of Selma," and their descendants are now among England's aristocracy.

These gentlemen-tacksmen were generally men of education.   They had all small but well-selected

libraries, and had not only acquired some knowledge of the classics, but were fond of keeping up
their acquaintance with them. It was not an uncommon pastime with them when they met together to try who could repeat the greatest number
of lines from Virgil or Horace, or who among them,
when one line was repeated, could *cap* it with
another line commencing with the same letter as
that which ended the former. All this may seem
to many to have been profitless amusement; but it
was not such amusement as rude and uncultivated
boors would have indulged in, nor was it such as
is likely to be imitated by the rich farmers who
now pasture their flocks where hardly a stone
marks the site of those old houses.

I only know one surviving gentleman-tacksman
belonging to the period of which I write, and he is
ninety years of age, though in the full enjoyment
of his bodily health and mental faculties. About
forty years ago, when inspecting his cattle, he was
accosted by a pedestrian with a knapsack on his
back, who addressed him in a language which was
intended for Gaelic. The tacksman, judging him
to be a foreigner, replied in French, which met no

response but a shake of the head, the tacksman's French being probably as bad as the tourist's Gaelic. The Highlander then tried Latin, which kindled a smile of surprise, and drew forth an immediate reply. This was interrupted by the remark that English would probably be more convenient for both parties. The tourist, who turned out to be an Oxford student, laughing heartily at the interview, gladly accepted the invitation of the tacksman to accompany him to his thatched house, and share his hospitality. He was surprised, on entering " the room," to see a small library in the humble apartment. " Books here!" he exclaimed, as he looked over the shelves. " Addison, Johnson, Goldsmith, Shakespeare—what! Homer, too?" The farmer, with some pride, begged him to look at the Homer. It had been given as a prize to himself when he was a student at the university. My old friend will smile as he reads these lines, and will wonder how I heard the story.*

It was men like these who supplied the High-

---

* Since the above was written, he has passed away in perfect peace, and with an eye undimmed, though he was in his ninety-fifth year.

lands with clergymen, physicians, lawyers, and the army and navy with many of their officers. It is not a little remarkable that the one island of Skye, for example, should have sent forth from her wild shores since the beginning of the last wars of the French Revolution, 21 lieutenant-generals and major-generals; 48 lieutenant-colonels; 600 commissioned officers; 10,000 soldiers; 4 governors of colonies; 1 governor-general; 1 adjutant-general; 1 chief baron of England; and 1 judge of the Supreme Court of Scotland. I remember the names of 61 officers being enumerated, who, during "the war," had joined the army or navy from farms which were visible from one hill-top in "the parish." These times have now passed away. The Highlands furnish few soldiers or officers. Even the educated clergy are becoming few.

One characteristic of these tacksmen which more than any other forms a delightful reminiscence of them, was their remarkable kindness to the poor. There was hardly a family which had not some man or woman who had seen better days, for their guest, during weeks, months, perhaps years. These forlorn ones might have been very

distant relations, claiming that protection which a
drop of kindred blood never claimed in vain; or former neighbours, or the children of those who were
neighbours long ago ; or, as it often happened, they
might have had no claim whatever upon the hospitable family beyond the fact that they were
utterly destitute, yet could not be treated as
paupers, and had in God's providence been cast on
the kindness of others, like waves of the wild sea
breaking at their feet.  Nor was there anything
" very interesting" about such objects of charity.
One old gentleman-beggar I remember, who used
to live with friends of mine for months, was singularly stupid, and often bad-tempered.  A decayed
old gentlewoman, again, who was an inmate for
years in one house, was subject to fits of great depression, and was by no means pleasant company.
Another needy visitor used to be accompanied by
a female servant.  When they departed after a
sojourn of a few weeks, the servant was generally
laden with wool, clothing, and a large allowance of
tea and sugar, contributed by the hostess for the
use of " the mistress," who thus obtained supplies
from different families during summer, which kept

herself and her red-haired domestic comfortable in their small hut during the winter. " Weel, weel," said the worthy host, as on one occasion he saw the pair depart, " it's a puir situation being a beggar's servant, like yon woman carrying the poke." Now this hospitality was never dispensed with a grudge, but with all tenderness and the nicest delicacy. These "genteel beggars" were received into the family, had comfortable quarters assigned to them in the house, partook of all the family meals ; and the utmost care was taken by old and young that not one word should be uttered, nor anything done, which could for a moment suggest to them the idea that they were a trouble, a bore, an intrusion, or anything save the most welcome and honoured guests. This attention, according to the minutest details, was almost a religion with the old Highland "gentleman" and his family.

The poor of the parish, strictly so called, were, with few exceptions, wholly provided for by the tacksmen. Each farm, according to its size, had its old men, widows, and orphans depending on it for their support. The widow had her free house,

which the farmers and the "cottiers" around him
kept in repair. They drove home her peats for
fuel from "the Moss;" her cow had pasturage on
the green hills. She had land sufficient to raise
potatoes, and a small garden for vegetables. She
had hens and ducks too, with the natural results of
eggs, chickens, and ducklings. She had sheaves of
corn supplied her, and these, along with her own
gleanings, were threshed at the mill with the tacksman's crop. In short, she was tolerably comfortable, and very thankful, enjoying the feeling of
being the object of true charity, which was returned by such labour as she could give, and by
her hearty gratitude.

But all this was changed when those tacksmen
were swept away to make room for the large
sheep farms, and when the remnants of the people
flocked from their empty glens to occupy houses
in wretched villages near the sea-shore, by way of
becoming fishers—often where no fish could be
caught. The result has been that "the parish,"
for example, which once had a population of 2200
souls, and received only £11 per annum from
public (church) funds for the support of the poor,

expends now under the Poor-law upwards of £600 annually, with a population diminished by one-half, but with poverty increased in a greater ratio. This, by the way, is the result generally, when money awarded by law, and distributed by officials, is substituted for the true charity prompted by the heart, and dispensed systematically to known and well-ascertained cases, which draw it forth by the law of sympathy and Christian duty. I am quite aware how very chimerical this doctrine is held to be by some political economists, but in these days of heresy in regard to older and more certain truths, it may be treated charitably.*

The effect of the poor-law, I fear, has been to destroy in a great measure the old feelings of self-respect which looked upon it as a degradation to

---

* In no case can a poor-law meet the wants of the deserving poor. In every case it must be supplemented by systematic benevolence. If it attempts, *by means of a few officials*, to deal kindly and liberally with every case of poverty, it will soon pauperise and demoralise the country. If, on the other hand, it applies such stringent tests as starvation and extreme distress alone can submit to, a vast mass of unrelieved suffering must be the result. Christian charity has yet to fill up, as it has never done, the gap between legal paupers and the deserving poor.

receive any support from public charity when living, or to be buried by it when dead. It has loosened also, those kind bonds of neighbourhood, family relationship, and natural love which linked the needy to those who had the ability to supply their wants, and whose duty it was to do so, and which was blessed both to the giver and receiver. Those who ought on principle to support the poor are tempted to cast them on the rates, and thus to lose all the good derived from the exercise of Christian almsgiving. The poor themselves have become more needy and more greedy, and scramble for the miserable pittance which is given and received with equal heartlessness.

The temptation to create large sheep-farms has no doubt been great. Rents are increased, and more easily collected. Outlays are fewer and less expensive than upon houses, steadings, &c: But should more rent be the highest, the noblest object of a proprietor? Are human beings to be treated like so many things used in manufactures? Are no sacrifices to be demanded for their good and happiness? Granting, for the sake of argument, that profit, in the sense of obtaining more money, will be found in the long run to measure what is best for the people as well as for the landlord, yet may not the converse of this be equally true—that the good and happiness of the people will in the long run be found the most profitable? Proprietors, we are glad to hear, are beginning to think that if a middle-class tenantry, with small arable farms of a rental of from £20 to £100 per annum, were again introduced into the Highlands, the result would be increased rents. Better still, the huge glens, along whose rich straths no sound but the bleat of sheep or the bark of dogs is now heard for twenty or thirty miles, would be tenanted, as of yore, with a comfortable and happy peasantry.

In the meantime, emigration has been to a large extent a blessing to the Highlands, and to a larger extent still a blessing to the colonies. It is the only relief for a poor and redundant population. The hopelessness of improving their condition, which rendered many in the Highlands listless and lazy, has in the colonies given place to the hope of securing a competency by prudence and industry. These virtues have accordingly

sprung up, and the results have been comfort and
independence.    A wise political economy, with
sympathy for human feelings and attachments,
will, I trust, be able more and more to adjust
the balance between the demands of the old and
new country, for the benefit both of proprietors
and people.    But I must return to the old tenants.

Below the gentlemen-tacksmen were those who
paid a much lower rent, and who lived very comfortably, and shared hospitably with others the
gifts God had given them.    I remember a group
of men, tenants in a large glen, which now "has
not a smoke in it," as the Highlanders say,
throughout its length of twenty miles.    They had
the custom of entertaining in rotation every traveller who cast himself upon their hospitality.    The
host on the occasion was bound to summon his
neighbours to the homely feast.    It was my good
fortune to be a guest when they received the present minister of " the parish," while *en route* to visit
some of his flock.    We had a most sumptuous
feast—oat-cake, crisp and fresh from the fir :;
cream, rich and thick, and more beautiful than
nectar, whatever that may be ; blue Highland

cheese, finer than Stilton ; fat hens, slowly cooked
on the fire in a pot of potatoes, without their skins,
and with fresh butter—"stoved hens," as the
superb dish was called ; and, though last, not
least, tender kid, roasted as nicely as Charles
Lamb's cracklin' pig. All was served up with the
utmost propriety, on a table covered with a pure
white cloth, and with all the requisites for a comfortable dinner, including the champagne of elastic,
buoyant and exciting mountain air. The manners
and conversation of those men would have pleased
the best-bred gentleman. Everything was so
simple, modest, unassuming, unaffected, yet so
frank and cordial. The conversation was such as
might have been heard at the table of any intelligent man. Alas ! there is not a vestige remaining
of their homes. I know not whither they are gone,
but they have left no representatives behind. The
land in the glen is divided between sheep, shepherds, and the shadows of the clouds.

There were annual festivals of the Highland
tenantry, which deeply moved every glen. These
were the Dumbarton and Falkirk "Trysts," or
fairs for cattle and sheep. What preparations

N

were made for these gatherings, on which the rent and income of the year depended! What a collecting of cattle, of drovers, and of dogs,—the latter being the most interested and excited of all the members of the caravan. What speculations as to how the " market " would turn out. What a shaking of hands in boats, wayside inns, and on decks of steamers by the men in homespun cloth, gay tartans, or in the more correct new garbs of Glasgow or Edinburgh tailors! What a pouring in from all the glens, increasing at every ferry and village, and flowing on, a river of tenants and proprietors, small and great, to the market! What that market was I know not from personal observation, nor desire to know.

> " Let Yarrow be unseen, unknown,
>     If now we're sure to rue it ;
> We have a vision of our own,
>     Ah, why should we undo it ? "

The impression left in early years is too sublime to be tampered with. I have a vision of miles of tents, of flocks, and herds, surpassed only by those in the wilderness of Sinai ; of armies of Highland sellers trying to get high prices out of the English-

men, and Englishmen trying to put off the High-
landmen with low prices—but all in the way of
" fair dealing."

When any person returned who had been himself at the market, who could recount its ups and
downs, its sales and purchases, with all the skir-
mishes, stern encounters, and great victories, it was
an eventful day in the tacksman's dwelling ! A
stranger not initiated into the mysteries of a great
fair might have supposed it possible for any one to
give all information about it in a brief business
form. But there was such an enjoyment in details, such a luxury in going over all the prices, and
all that was asked by the seller and refused by the
buyer, and asked again by the seller, and again
refused by the buyer, with such nice financial
fencing of "splitting the difference," or giving back
a "luck-penny," as baffles all description. It was
not enough to give the prices of three-year-olds
and four-year-olds, yell cows, crock ewes, stirks,
stots, lambs, tups, wethers, shots, bulls, &c., but
the stock of each well-known proprietor or breeder
had to be discussed. Colonsay's bulls, Corrie's
sheep, Drumdriesaig's heifers, or Achadashenaig's

wethers, had all to be passed under careful review. Then followed discussions about distinguished "beasts," which had "fetched high prices;" their horns, their hair, their houghs, and general "fashion," with their parentage. It did not suffice to tell that this or that great purchaser from the south had given so much for this or that "lot," but his first offer, his remarks, his doubts, his advance of price, with the sparring between him and the Highland dealer, must all be particularly recorded, until the final shaking of hands closed the bargain. And after all was gone over, it was a pleasure to begin the same tune again with variations. But who that has ever heard an after-dinner talk in England about a good day's hunting, or a good race, will be surprised at this endless talk about a market?

I will close this chapter with a story told of a great sheep-farmer (not one of the old "gentleman tenants" verily!) who, though he could neither read nor write, had nevertheless made a large fortune by sheep-farming, and was open to any degree of flattery as to his abilities in this department of labour. A buyer, knowing his weakness, and anxious to ingratiate himself into his good graces, ventured one evening over their whisky-toddy to remark, "I am of opinion, sir, that you are a greater man than even the Duke of Wellington!" "Hoot toot!" replied the sheep-farmer, modestly hanging his head with a pleasing smile, and taking a large pinch of snuff. "That's too much—too much by far—by far." But his guest, after expatiating for a while upon the great powers of his host in collecting and concentrating upon a Southern market a flock of sheep, suggested the question, "Could the Duke of Wellington have done *that?*" The sheep-farmer thought a little, snuffed, took a glass of toddy, and slowly replied, "The Duke of Wellington was, nae doot, a clever man; very, very clever, I believe. They tell me he was a good sojer; but then, d'ye see, he had reasonable men to deal with—captains, and majors, and generals that could understand him,—every one of them, both officers and men; but I'm no so sure after all if he could manage say twenty thousand sheep, besides black cattle, that couldna understand one word he said, Gaelic or English, and bring every hoof o' them to Fa'kirk Tryst! I doot it—I doot it! But *I* have often done that." The inference was evident.

## MARY CAMPBELL'S MARRIAGE.

MARY CAMPBELL was a servant in the old manse, about sixty years ago, and was an honest and bonnie lassie. She had blue eyes and flaxen hair, with a form as "beautiful as the fleet roe on the mountain," a very Malvina to charm one of the heroes of old Ossian. Her sweetheart was not, however, an "Oscar of the spear," a "Cuchullin of the car," or a Fingal who "sounded his shield in the halls of Selma," but a fine-looking shepherd lad named Donald Maclean, who "wandered slowly as a cloud" over the hills at morn after his sheep, and sang his songs, played his trump, and lighted up Mary's face with his looks at even. For two years they served together;

and, as in all such cases, these years seemed to
them like a single day. Yet no vows were exchanged, no engagement made between them.
Smiles and looks, improvised songs full of lovers'
*chaffing*, dances together as partners in the kitchen
to Archy M'Intyre's fiddle, an inclination to work
at the same hay-rick, to reap beside each other
on the same harvest rigs, and to walk home together from the kirk ;—these were the only signi-
ficant signs of what was understood by all, that
handsome Donald and bonnie Mary were sweet-
hearts.

It happened to them as to all lovers since the
world began ; the old story of want of smoothness
in the river of affection was repeated in their case.
It had the usual eddies and turns which are found
in all such streams, and it had its little falls, with
tiny bubbles, that soon broke and disappeared in
rainbow hues, until the agitated water rested once
more in a calm pool, dappled with sunlight, and
overhung with wild flowers.

But a terrible break and thundering fall at last
appeared in the approach of rich Duncan Stewart
from Lochaber ! Duncan was a well-to-do small

tenant, with a number of beeves and sheep. He
was a thrifty money-making bachelor, who never
gave or accepted bills for man or for beast, but
was contented with small profits and ready cash,
secured at once and hoarded in safety with Car-
rick, Brown, & Company's Ship Bank, Glasgow,
there to grow at interest while he was sleeping—
though he was generally "wide-awake." He was
a cousin of Mary's "thrice removed," but close
enough to entitle him to a hearing when he came
to court her; and on this very errand he arrived
one day at the manse, where—alas! for poor
Donald Maclean—he was, as a matter of course,
hospitably received.

Duncan had seen Mary but once, but having
made up his mind as to her fair appearance, which
it was not difficult for him to do, and having
ascertained from others that she was in every respect a properly-conducted girl, and a most accomplished servant, who could work in the field or
dairy, in the kitchen or laundry,—and that beside
the fire at night her hands were the most active
in knitting, sewing, carding wool, or spinning—he
concluded that she was the very wife for Duncan

Stewart of Blairdhu.  But would Mary take him?
A doubt never crossed his mind upon that point.
His confidence did not arise from his own good
looks, for they, to speak charitably, were doubtful,
even to himself.  He had high cheek-bones, small
teeth, not innocent of tobacco, and a large mouth.
To these features there was added a sufficient
number of gray hairs sprinkled on the head and
among the bushy whiskers, to testify to many
more years than those which numbered the age of
Mary.  But Duncan had money—a large amount
of goods laid up for many years—full barns and
crowded sheep-folds.  He had a place assigned to
him at Fort-William market such as a well-known
capitalist has on the Exchange.  He was thus the
sign of a power which tells in every class of society.
Are no fair merchant's daughters, we would respectfully ask, affected in their choice of husbands
by the state of their funds?  Has a coronet no influence over the feelings?  Do the men of substance make their advances to beauties who have
no wealth, without some sense of the weight of
argumemt which is measured by the weight of
gold in their proffered hand?  Do worth and

character, and honest love, and *sufficient* means, always get fair play from the fair, when opposed by rivals having less character and less love, but with more than *sufficient* means? According to the reader's replies to these questions will be his opinion as to the probability of Duncan winning Mary, and of Mary forsaking poor Donald and accepting his "highly respectable" and wealthy rival.

It must be mentioned that another power came into play at this juncture of affairs, and that was an elder sister of Mary's, who lived in the neighbourhood of the farmer, and who was supposed, by the observing dames of the district, to have "set her cap" at Duncan. But it was more the honour of the connexion than love which had prompted those gentle demonstrations on the part of Peggy. She wished to give him the hint, as it were, that he need not want a respectable wife for the asking; although, of course, she was quite happy and contented to remain in her mother's house, and help to manage the small croft, with its cow, pigs, poultry, and potatoes. Duncan, without ever pledging himself, sometimes seemed

to acknowledge that it might be well to keep
Peggy on his list as a reserve corps, in case he
might fail in his first battle. The fact must be
confessed, that such marriages of "convenience"
were as common in the Highlands as elsewhere.
Love, no doubt, in many cases, carried the day
there, as it does in Greenland, London, or Tim-
buctoo. Nevertheless the dog-team, the blubber,
the fishing-tackle, of the North will, at times, tell
very powerfully on the side of their possessor,
who is yet wanting in the softer emotions; and
so will the cowries and cattle of Africa, and the
West-end mansion and carriage of London. The
female heart will everywhere, in its own way,
acknowledge that "love is all very well, when
one is young, but "—— And with that prudential
"but," depend upon it the blubber, cowries, and
carriage are sure to carry the day, and leave poor
Love to make off with clipped wings!

Duncan of Blairdhu so believed, when he proposed to Mary through the minister's wife, who
had never heard the kitchen gossip about the
shepherd, and who was delighted to think that
her Mary had the prospect of being so comfort-

ably married. All the *pros* and *cons* having been set before her, Mary smiled, hung her head, pulled her fingers until every joint cracked, and, after a number of "could not really says," and "really did not knows," and "wondered why he had asked her," and "what was she to do," &c., followed by a few hearty tears, she left her mistress, and left the impression that she would in due time be Mrs Duncan Stewart. Her sister Peggy appeared on the scene, and, strange to say, urged the suit with extraordinary vehemence. She spoke not of love, but of honour, rank, position, comfort, influence, as all shining around on the Braes of Lochaber. Peggy never heard of the shepherd; but had she done so, the knowledge would have only moved her indignation. Duncan's cousinship made his courtship a sort of family claim—a social right. It was not possible that her sister would be so foolish, stupid, selfish, as not to marry a rich man like Mr Stewart. Was she to bring disgrace on herself and people by refusing him? So Mary was too gentle for Peggy, and she bent like a willow beneath the breeze of her appeals. She would have given worlds to have been able to say that she was engaged to Donald; but that was not the case. Would Donald ask her? She loved him too well to betray her feelings so as to prompt the delicate question, yet she wondered why he did not come to her relief at such a crisis. Did he know it? Did he suspect it?

Donald, poor lad, was kept in ignorance of all these diplomatic negotiations; and when at last a fellow-servant expressed his suspicions, he fell at once into despair, gave up the game as lost, lingered among the hills as long as possible, hardly spoke when he returned home at night, seemed to keep aloof from Mary, and one evening talked to her so crossly in his utter misery, that next morning, when Duncan Stewart arrived at the manse, Peggy had so arranged matters that Mary before the evening was understood to have accepted the hand of the rich farmer.

The news was kept secret. Peggy would not speak; Mary could not. Duncan was discreetly silent, and took his departure to arrange the marriage, the day for which was fixed before he left. The minister's wife and the minister congratulated Mary. Mary gave no response, but pulled her fingers more energetically and nervously than ever. This was all taken as a sign of modesty. The shepherd whistled louder than before for his dogs, and corrected them with singular vehemence; he played his trumps with greater perseverance, and sang his best songs at night; but there was no more dancing, and he did not walk with Mary from the kirk. The other servants winked and laughed, and knew there was "something atween them," then guessed what it was, then knew all about it; yet none presumed to tease Donald or Mary. There was a something which kept back all intrusion, but no one seemed to know what that something was.

The marriage dress was easily got up by the manse girls, and each of them added some bonnie gift to make Mary look still more bonnie. She was a special favourite, and the little governess with the work of her own hands contributed a good deal to Mary's wardrobe.

All at once the girls came to the conclusion that Mary did not love Duncan. She had no interest in her dress; she submitted to every attention as if it were a stern duty; her smile was not joyous.  Their suspicions were confirmed when the cook, commonly called Kate Kitchen, confided to them the secret of Mary's love for the shepherd—all, of course, in strict confidence; but every fair and gentle attempt was made in vain to get her to confess.  She was either silent, or said there was nothing between them, or that she would do all that was right, and so on, or would dry her eyes with her apron as she left the room. These interviews were not satisfactory, and so they were soon ended; a gloom gathered over the wedding; there was a want of enthusiasm about it; every one felt drifting slowly to it without any reason strong enough for pulling in an opposite direction.  Why won't Donald propose?  His proud heart is breaking, but he thinks it too late, and will give no sign.  Why does not Mary refuse Duncan—scorn him, if you will, and cling to the shepherd?  Her little proud heart is also break-ing, for the shepherd has become cold to her. She thinks he ought to have asked her before now, or even yet proposed a runaway marriage, carried her off, and she would have flown with him, like a dove gently held in an eagle's talons, over hill and dale, to a nest of their own, where love alone would have devoured her. But both said, "'Tis too late!" Fate, like a magic power, seemed to have doomed that she must marry Duncan Stewart.

The marriage was to come off at the house of a tacksman, an uncle of the bride's, about two miles from the manse; for the honour of having a niece married to Blairdhu demanded that special attention should be shown on the occasion. A large party was invited. There were about a score of the tenantry of the district, with the minister's family, and a few of the gentry, such as the sheriff and his wife, and the doctor; some friends who accompanied Duncan from Lochaber; big Sandy Cameron from Lochiel; Archy, son of Donald, from Glen Nevis; and Lachlan, the son of young Lachlan, from Corpach. How they all managed to dispose of themselves in the *but and ben*, including the centre closet, of Malcolm Morrison's house, has never yet been explained. Those who have known the capacity of Highland houses, —the capacity of being full, and yet able to accommodate more, have thought that the walls possessed some expansive power, the secret of which has not come down to posterity. On that marriage-day a large party was assembled. On the green outside the house, were many Highland carts, which had conveyed the guests; while the horses, with ungainly hops, their fore-legs being tied together at the fetlock, cropped the green herbage at freedom, until their services were required within the next twelve hours. Droves of dogs were busy making one another's acquaintance; collie dogs and terriers—every tail erect or curled, and each, with bark and growl, asserting its own independence. Groups of guests, in home-spun clothes, laughed and chatted round the door waiting for the hour of marriage. Some of "the ladies" were gravely seated within, decked out in new caps and ribands; while servant-women, with loud voices and louder steps, were rushing to and fro, as if in desperation, arranging the dinner. This same dinner was a very ample one of stoved hens and potatoes, legs of mutton, roast ducks, corned beef, piles of cheese, tureens of curds and cream, and oat-cakes piled in layers. Duncan

Stewart walked out and in, dressed in a full suit of blooming Stuart tartan, with frills to his shirt, which added greatly to his turkey-cock appearance.

But where was the bride? She had been expected at four o'clock, and it was now past five. It was understood that she was to have left the manse escorted by Hugh, the son of big John M'Allister. The company became anxious. A message of inquiry was at last despatched, but the only information received was that the bride had left the manse at two o'clock, immediately after the manse party. A herd-boy was again despatched to obtain more accurate tidings, and the governess whispered in his ear to ask particularly about the whereabouts of Donald, the shepherd. But the boy could tell nothing, except that Hugh and the bride had started on horseback three hours before; and as for Donald, he was unwell in bed, for he had seen him there rolled up in blankets, with his face to the wall. The excitement became intense. Duncan Stewart snuffed prodigiously; Malcolm, Mary's uncle, uttered sundry expressions by no means becoming; Peggy, full of alarming surmises, wrung her hands, and threw herself on a bed in the middle closet. The ladies became perplexed; the sheriff consulted the company as to what should be done. The doctor suggested the suicide of the bride. The minister suspected more than he liked to express. But two men mounted the best horses, and taking a gun with them—why, no one could conjecture—started off in great haste to the manse. The timid bird had flown, no one knew whither. The secret had been kept from every human being. But if she was to leave the parish it could only be by a certain glen, across a certain river, and along one path, which led to the regions beyond. They conjectured that she was *en route* for her mother's home, in order to find there a temporary asylum. To this glen, and along this path, the riders hurried. The marriage party, in the meantime, "took a refreshment," and made M'Pherson, the bagpiper, play reels and strathspeys, to which the young folks danced, while the older people brewed whisky punch, and assured Duncan Stewart that the mystery would soon be satisfactorily cleared up. Duncan seemed to enjoy his tumbler, and pretended to laugh at the odd joke—for a joke he said it was. Peggy alone refused to be comforted. Hour after hour passed, but no news of the bride. The ladies began to yawn, and the gentlemen to think how they should spend the night; until at last all who could not be accommodated within the elastic walls by any amount of squeezing, dispersed, after house and barn were filled, to seek quarters at the manse or among the neighbouring farms.

The two troopers who rode in pursuit of Mary came at last, after a hard ride of twenty miles, to a small inn, which was the frontier house of the parish, and whose white walls marked, as on a peninsula, the ending of one long uninhabited glen, and the commencement of another. As they reached this solitary and wayside place, they determined to put up for the night. The morning had been wet, and clouds full of rain had gathered after sunset on the hills. On entering the kitchen of the "change house," they saw some clothes drying on a chair opposite the fire, with a "braw cap" and ribands suspended near them, and dripping with moisture. On making inquiry, they were informed that these belonged to a young woman who had arrived there shortly before, behind Hugh, the son of big John M'Allister of the manse, who had returned with the horse by another road over the hill. The woman was on her way to Lochaber, but her name was not known. Poor Mary was caught! Her pursuers need not have verified their conjectures by entering her room and upbraiding her in most unfeeling terms, telling her, before locking the door in order to secure her, that she must accompany them back in the morning and be married to Duncan Stewart, as sure as there was justice in the land. Mary spoke not a word, but gazed at them as in a dream.

At early dawn she was mounted behind one of these moss-troopers, and conducted in safety to the manse, as she had requested to see the family before she went through the ceremony of marriage. That return to the manse was an epoch in its history. The shepherd in the meantime had disappeared, and so had Hugh M'Allister. When Mary was ushered into the presence of the minister, and the door was closed, she fell on her knees before him, and, bending her forehead until she rested it on his outstretched hand, she burst forth into hysterical weeping. The minister soothed her, and bid her tell him frankly what all this was about. Did she not like Stewart? Was she unwilling to marry him? "Unwilling to marry him!" cried Mary, rising up, with such flashing eyes and dramatic manner as the minister had never seen in her before, or thought it possible for one so retiring and shy to exhibit; "I tell you, sir, I would sooner be chained to a rock at low water, and rest there until the tide came and choked my breath, than marry that man!" And Mary, as if her whole nature was suddenly changed, spoke out with the vehemence of long-restrained freedom breaking loose at last in its own inherent dignity. "Then, Mary, dear," said the minister, patting her head, "you shall never be married to mortal man against your will, by me or any one else." "Bless you, dear, dear sir," said Mary, kissing his hand.

Duncan heard the news. "What on earth, then," he asked, "is to be done with the dinner?"

for the cooking had been stopped.  To his Lochaber friends he whispered certain old sayings borrowed from sea and land—as, for example, that
" there are as good fish in the sea as ever came out
of it "—that

> " She who winna when she may,
>   May live to rue 't another day,"—

and so on.  Blairdhu spoke and acted like one
who pitied, as a friend, the woman whom he
thought once so wise as to have been willing to
marry him.  Yet his question was a serious one,
and was still unanswered :—" What was to become
of the dinner ? "  Mary's uncle suggested the
answer.  He took Duncan aside, and talked con-
fidentially and earnestly to him.  His communications were received with a smile, a grunt, and a
nod of the head, each outward sign of the inward
current of feeling being frequently repeated in the
same order.  The interview was ended by a request from Duncan to see Peggy.  Peggy gave
him her hand, and squeezed his with a fervour
made up of hysterics and hope.  She wept, however, real tears, pouring forth her sympathies
for the bridegroom in ejaculatory gasps, like

jerks for breath, when mentioning a man of his "res—pect—a—bil—i—ty." Before night, a match was made up between Duncan and Peggy: she declaring that it was done to save the credit of her family, though it was not yesterday that she had learned to esteem Mr Stewart; he declaring that he saw clearly the hand of Providence in the whole transaction—that Mary was too young and too inexperienced for him, and that the more he knew her, the less he liked her. The hand of Providence was not less visible when it conveyed a dowry of £50 from Peggy's uncle with his niece. The parties were "proclaimed" in church on the following Sunday and married on Monday—and so both the credit of the family and the dinner were saved.

But what of Mary? She was married to the shepherd, after explanations and a "scene" which, as I am not writing fiction but truth, I cannot describe, the details not having come to me among the traditions of "the parish."

Donald enlisted as a soldier in some Highland regiment, and his faithful Mary accompanied him to the Peninsula. How, as a married man, he

managed to enlist at all, and she to follow him as
his wife, I know not. But I presume that in those
days, when soldiers were recruited by officers who
had personally known them and their people, and
to whom the soldier was previously attached, many
things were permitted and favours obtained which
would be impossible now. Nor can I tell why
Mary was obliged to return home. But the rules
or necessities of the service during war demanded
this step. So Mary once more appeared at the
manse, in the possession of about £60, which she
had earned and saved by working for the regiment, and which Donald had intrusted, along with
an only daughter, to his wife's care. The money
was invested by the minister. Mary, as a matter
of course, occupied her old place in the family,
and found every other fellow-servant, but Donald,
where she had left them years before. No one
received her with more joy than Hugh M'Allister,
who had been her confidant and best man. But
what stories and adventures Mary had to tell!
And what a high position she occupied at the old
kitchen fireside! Everything there was as happy
as in the days of " auld lang syne," and nothing

wanting save Donald's blithe face and merry trumps.

Neither Mary nor Donald could write, nor could they speak any language except Gaelic. Their stock of English was barely sufficient to enable them to transact the most ordinary business. Was it this want, and the constant toil and uncertain marches of a soldier during war, which had prevented Donald from writing home to his wife? For, alas! two long years passed without her having once heard from him.

After months of anxious hope had gone by, Mary began to look old and careworn. The minister scanned the weekly newspaper with intense anxiety, especially after a battle had been fought, to catch Donald's name among the list of the dead or wounded. He had written several times for information, but with little effect. All he could hear was that Donald was alive and well. At last the news came that he was married to another woman. A soldier journeying homewards from the same regiment, and passing through the parish, had said so to several persons in the village, after he had had "his glass." But the soldier was gone long before he could be cross-questioned. Mary heard the news, and though scorning the lie, as she said it was, she never alluded to the fearful story. Still the secret wound was evidently injuring her health; her cheek became paler, her "natural force abated" while at her work, and Kate Kitchen had on more than one occasion discovered tears dropping on the little girl's face, as her mother combed her hair, or laid her down to sleep.

There was not a person in the house who did not carry poor Mary's burden, and treat her with the utmost delicacy. Many an expression, calculated to strengthen her faith in God, and to comfort her, was uttered at family prayers, which she always attended. Yet she never complained, never asked any sympathy; she was quiet, meek, and most unselfish, like one who tried to bear alone her own sorrow, without troubling others. She worked diligently, but never joined in the chorus song which often cheered the hours of labour. She clung much to Hugh M'Allister, who, like a shield, cast aside from her the cruel darts which were shot in the parish by insinuations of Donald's unfaithfulness, or the repetition of the story told by the soldier.

The fifth year of desolation had reached mid-summer, and it was clear that Mary was falling into permanent bad health. One day, having toiled until the afternoon at the making of a hay-stack, she sat down to rest upon some hay near it. Above, lads and lasses were busy tramping, under the superintendence of Hugh M'Allister. Hugh suddenly paused in the midst of his work. and, gazing steadfastly for a minute or two at a distant person approaching the manse from the gate, said, with a suppressed voice, and a "hush" which commanded silence, "If Donald Maclean is in life, that's him!" Every eye was directed to the traveller, who, with a knapsack on his back, was slowly approaching. "It's a beggar," said Kate Kitchen. "It's like Donald, after all," said another, as the sounds of the traveller's feet were heard on the narrow gravel walk. "It is him, and none but him!" cried Hugh, as he slid down to the ground, having seen Donald's face as he took off his cap and waved it. Flying to Mary, who had been half asleep from fatigue, he seized her

by the hand, raised her up, and putting his
brawny arm round her neck, kissed her; then
brushing away a tear from his eye with the back
of his rough hand, he said, "God bless you! this
is better than a thousand pounds, any day!"
Mary, in perplexity and agitation, asked what he
meant, as he dragged her forward, giving her a
gentle push as they both came round the haystack
which concealed Donald from their view. With
a scream she flew to him, and, as they embraced
in silence, a loud cheer rose from the stack, which
was speedily hushed in silent sobs even from the
strong men.

What an evening that was at the manse! If
ever Donald heard the falsehood about his second
marriage, there was no allusion to it that night.
He had returned to his wife and child with honourable wounds, a Waterloo medal, and a pension for
life. He and Mary settled down again at the
manse for many months, and the trump was again
heard, as in the days of yore. On the last night
of the year Donald insisted on dancing once more
with Mary, in spite of his lame leg and the
laughter of his girl.

I will not follow their adventures further, beyond stating that they removed to Glasgow; that Donald died, and was buried thirty years ago in the old churchyard of " the parish;" that the daughter was married, but not happily; that Mary fought a noble, self-denying battle to support herself by her industry, and her army savings, the capital of which she has preserved until now.

When nearly eighty years of age, she went on a pilgrimage to visit Donald's grave. " Do you repent marrying him, and refusing Duncan Stewart?" I asked her on her return. " Repent!" she exclaimed, as her fine old face was lighted up with sunshine; " I would do it all again for the noble fellow!"

Mary lived in Glasgow, respected by all who knew her, and died two or three years ago.

## CHURCHYARDS AND FUNERALS.

THE Highland churchyard is a spot which seldom betrays any other traces of human art or care than those simple headstones which mark its green graves. In very few instances is it enclosed ; its graves generally mingle with the mountain pasture and blooming heather, and afford shelter to the sheep and lamb from the blast of winter and the heat of summer. But although not consecrated by holy prayer and religious ceremony, these are, nevertheless, holy spots in the hearts and memories of the peasantry, who never pass them without a subdued look, which betokens a feeling of respect for the silent sleepers. To deck a father's or mother's grave, would be, in the estimation of the Highlander, to turn it into a flower-garden. He thinks it utter vanity to attempt to express his grief or respect for the departed by any ornament beyond the tombstone, whose inscription is seldom more than a statistical table of birth and death.

Many of those Highland churchyards, so solitary and so far removed from the busy haunts of men, are, nevertheless, singularly touching and beautiful. Some are on green islands whose silence is disturbed only by the solemn thunder of the great ocean wave, or the ripple of the inland sea; some are in great wide glens, among bracken and blooming heather, round the ruins of a chapel, where prayers were once offered by early missionaries, who with noble aim and holy ambition penetrated these wild and savage haunts; while others break the green swards about the parish church on ground where God has been worshipped since the days of St Columba.

One of the most beautiful I ever visited is on a small green island in Loch Shiel in Argyleshire. The loch for nearly twenty miles is as yet innocent of roads on either shore, so that the tourist who visits the place has to navigate the lake in a rude country boat; and if he attempts to sail, he must probably do so with blankets attached to the oar, and then trust to a fair wind. Yet what can be more delicious than thus to glide along the shore with a crew that won't speak till they are spoken to, and in silence gaze upon the ever-varying scene —to skim past the bights and bays with their reedy margins—the headlands tufted with waving birch —the gulfy torrents pouring down their foaming waterfalls and " blowing their trumpets from the steeps"—with the copse of oak and hazel, that covers the sides of the mountain from the deep dark water up to the green pasture, and beyond, the bare rocks that pierce the blue.

Not unlikely the crew, when they take to their oars, will sing " Ho Morag," in honour of Prince Charlie, " the lad wi' the philabeg," who on the green alluvial plain at the head of the loch—where his monument now stands — first unfurled his banner, to regain the British crown; and if you don't know this romantic episode in history, the boatmen will point out with pride the glens where the Camerons, Macdonalds, Stewarts, and Macleans poured down their kilted clans, the last "old guard" of the feudal times, to do battle for "the yellow-haired laddie;" and unless you cordially believe (at least until you leave Loch Shiel) that you would have joined them on that day, with the probability even of losing your head and your common sense, you are not in a fit state of spirit to enjoy the scene.

Half way up this lake, and at its narrowest portion, there is a beautiful green island, which stretches itself so far across as to leave but a narrow passage for even the country boat. Above it, and looking down on it, rises Ben Reshobal for 2000 feet or more, with its hanging woods, gray rocks, dashing streams, and utter solitude. On the island is an old chapel, with the bell,—now we believe preserved by the Laird,—which long ago so often broke the silence of these wilds on holy days of worship or of burial. There lie chiefs and vassals, fierce cateran robbers of sheep and cattle, murderers of opposing clans, with women and children, Catholic and Protestant, Prince Charlie men, and men who served in army and navy under George the Third. How silent is the grave-yard!

You sit down among the ruins and hear only the bleat of sheep, the whish-whish of the distant waterfalls, the lapping of the waves, or the wind creeping through the archways and mouldering windows.    The feuds and combats of the clans are all gone ; the stillness and desolation of their graves alone remain.

But "the parish" churchyard is not much less picturesque.    It is situated on a green plateau of table-land which forms a ledge between the low sea-shore and hilly background.    A beautiful tall stone cross from Iona adorns it ; a single Gothic arch of an old church remains as a witness for the once consecrated ground, and links the old " cell" to the modern building, which in architecture—shame to modern Lairds—is to the old one what a barn is to a church.    The view, however, from that churchyard, of all God's glorious architecture above and below, makes one forget those paltry attempts of man to be a fellow-worker with Him in the rearing and adorning of the fitting and the beautiful.    There is hardly in the Highlands a finer expanse of inland seas, of castled promontories, of hills beyond hills, until cloudland and highland mingle; of precipice and waterfall, with all the varied lights and shadows which heathy hill sides, endless hill tops, dark corries, ample bays and rocky shores, can create at morn, noonday, or evening, from sun and cloud,—a glorious panorama extending from the far west beyond the giant point of Ardnamurchan, " the height of the great ocean," to the far east, where Ben Cruachan and "the Shepherds of Etive Glen" stand sentinels in the sky. No sea king could select a more appropriate resting-place than this, from whence to catch a glimpse, as his spirit walked abroad beneath the moonlight, of galleys coming from the Northland of his early home; nor could an old saint find a better, if he desired that after death the mariners, struggling with stormy winds and waves, might see his cross from afar, and thence, *in extremis*, snatch comfort from this symbol of faith and hope; nor could any man, who in the frailty of his human nature shrunk from burial in lonely vault, and who wished rather to lie where birds might sing, and summer's sun shine, and winter's storms lift their voices to God, and the beautiful world be ever above and around him, find a spot more congenial to his human feelings than the kirkyard of "the parish."

The Celt has a strong desire, almost amounting to a decided superstition, to lie beside his kindred. He is intensely social in his love of family and tribe. It is long ere he takes to a stranger as bone of his bone and flesh of his flesh. When sick in the distant hospital, he will, though years have separated him from home and trained him to be a citizen of the world, yet dream in his delirium of the old burial-ground. To him there is in this idea a sort of homely feeling, a sense of friendship, a desire for a congenial neighbourhood, that, without growing into a belief of which he would be ashamed, unmistakably circulates as an instinct in his blood, and cannot easily be dispelled. It is thus that the poorest Highlanders always endeavour to bury their dead with kindred dust. The pauper will save his last penny to secure this boon.

A woman, for example, from "the main land," somewhere in Kintail, was married to a highly respectable man in one of the Hebrides which need not be specified. When she died, twelve of her relations, strong men, armed with oak sticks, journeyed sixty miles to be present at her funeral. They quietly expressed their hope to her husband, that his wife should be buried in her own country and beside her own people. But on ascertaining from him that such was not his purpose, they declared their intention to carry off the body by force. An unseemly struggle was avoided only through the husband being unable to find any one to back him in his refusal of what was deemed by his neighbours to be a reasonable request. He therefore consented, and accompanied the body to the churchyard of her family.

This feeling is carried to a length which, in one instance I have heard of, was too ludicrous to be dignified even by the name of superstition. A Highland porter, who carried our bag but the other day, and who has resided for thirty years in the low country, sent his amputated finger to be buried in the graveyard of the parish beside the remains of his kindred! It is said that a bottle of whisky was sent along with the finger that it might be entombed with all honour!—but I don't vouch for the truth of the latter part of the story. I never heard who dug the grave of the finger—whether it was "I, says the owl"—nor who attended the funeral, nor what monument was erected over the respected member. But there, nevertheless, it lies, and I doubt not that the porter will one day lie beside it.

This desire of being interred with kindred dust or with "the faithful ones," as they express it, is so strong, that I have known a poor man selling all his potatoes, and reducing himself to great suffering, in order to pay the expense of burying his wife in a distant churchyard among her people; and that, too, when the minister of his parish offered to bury her at his own expense in the churchyard of the parish in which the widower resided. Only a year or two ago a pauper in the parish of K———, begged another poor neighbour to see her buried beside her family. When she died, twelve men assembled, carried her ten miles off, dug her grave, and paid all the expenses of her funeral, which, had she been buried elsewhere, would have been paid by the parish.

It is still a very common belief among the peasantry that shadowy funeral processions pre-

cede the real ones, and that "warnings" are given
of a coming death by the crowing of cocks, the
ticking of the death watch, the howling of dogs,
voices heard by night, the sudden appearance of
undefined forms of human beings passing to and
fro, &c.

It has also been the custom of the poorest persons to have all their dead clothes prepared for
years before their death, so as to insure a decent
orderly interment.  To make these clothes was a
task often imposed upon the ladies, or females in
a parish who were good at their needle.  The
pattern of the shroud was a fixed one, and special
instructions were given regarding it by the initiated.
Such things are common even now among Highland
families who have emigrated to Glasgow.  A short
time ago a highly respectable lady in that city,
when she found that her illness was dangerous, gave
a confidential servant the key of a box, where, in
the event of death, all would be found that was
required to dress her body for the grave.

The old wrapping of the body was woollen
cloth, and the Gaelic term used to express it, (olla-
nach,) which may be translated "woollening," is

still used to describe the dressing of the body before burial.* The old stone coffin is dug up in the Highlands as elsewhere, but the coffins hol-

* I have somewhere read that in some English Parliament, if I remember rightly, in the reign of Henry VII., it was enacted, in the interest no doubt of the wool trade, that corpses should be dressed in woollen grave-clothes.

Since the above was written two correspondents have kindly favoured me with communications as to the laws enacted in England and Scotland, on the wrapping of dead bodies in woollen for burial. An English correspondent writes—

"The Act to which you refer for the encouragement of the woollen trade, was passed 30 Charles II., stat. 1, c. 3, 1678. The Act was unpopular and fell into disuse, and was finally repealed 54 Geo. III., c. 108, 1814.

"The Rev. G. F. Townsend (now of Burleigh Street Church, Strand) refers to this in his 'History of Leominster,' published October 1862, of which place he was vicar, and gives some curious extracts from the parish register on this subject. He also gave me one of the original certificates—and I now present it to you, as it may be of some little service to you.

"Pope, you may remember, refers to the custom :—

"'Odious ! in woollen : 'twould a saint provoke !'
Were the last words the fair Narcissa spoke :
'No! let a charming chintz and Brussels lace
Wrap my cold hands and shade my lifeless face !'"

The following is the quaint certificate referred to :—

"Mrs Eliz. Watcham, of the Borough of Leominster, in the County of Hereford, maketh Oath, That Mr Solomon Long, of the Borough aforesaid, of the County aforesaid, lately deceased, was not put in, wrapt, or wound up, or Buried in any Shirt, Shift, Sheet or Shroud, made or mingled with Flax, Hemp, Silk, Hair, Gold or Silver, or other than what is made of Sheeps-Wooll only : Nor in any Coffin lined or faced with any Cloth, Stuff, or any other

lowed out of the solid log—one of which was discovered a few years ago in Lochaber—seem, as far as I know, to have been peculiar to the Highlands.

Thing whatsoever, made or mingled with Flax, Hemp, Silk, Hair, Gold, or Silver, or any other Material, contrary to the late Act of Parliament for Burying in Woollen, but Sheeps-Wooll only. Dated the Third Day of October, in the Third Year of the Reign of our Sovereign Lord George the Second, by the Grace of GOD, King of Great-Britain, France and Ireland, Defender of the Faith, Annoq ; Dom' 1729.

"Sealed and Subscribed by us who
were present, and Witnesses
to the Swearing of the abovesaid Affidavit.

"PENELOPE POWELL.
ELIZ. × JONES.

"I, Caleb Powell, do hereby Certify, that the Day and Year abovesaid, the said Eliz. Watcham came before me, and made such Affidavit as is above specified, according to the late Act of Parliament, Intituled, an 'Act for Burying in Woollen.' Witness my Hand, the Day and Year first above-written.

"CALEB POWELL."

A Scotch correspondent writes us on the same subject :—

"There are various old Scottish statutes regulating the cloth to be used at burials. One is the statute of James VII. 1686, cap. 16, enacting that no 'corps' should be buried in any cloth but 'plain linen, or cloth of hards, made and spun within the kingdom,' and specially *prohibiting* the use of 'Holland ; or other linen-cloth made in other kingdoms, and all silk, hair, or *woolen*, gold or silver, or any other stuff whatsoever, than what is made of flax or hards, spun and wrought within the kingdom.' And two responsible parties in the parish had to certify in the case of every burial that the statute had been complied with ; and had to bring a certificate to that effect to the minister of the parish who was then to

The Gaelic term still in use for a coffin (caisil chrò,) the "wattle enclosure," points to what we doubt not was equally peculiar to the Highlands, that of surrounding the dead body with slender branches of trees, and bending them firmly together with *withs* or twisted rods of hazel or willow, and thus interring it.

From the time of death till that of interment, the body is watched day and night. A plate of salt is always placed upon the breast. Candles are also frequently lighted around it. These are the remains of Roman Catholic customs. When the body, on the day of funeral, is carried a considerable distance, a *cairn* of stones is always raised on the

record the same. The statute was re-enacted, with some sumptuary clauses in 1695, but both were repealed in the *last* Scottish parliament (1707, c. 14) before the union.—That Act *forbade* the use of linen at burials ; and ordered that ' hereafter no corps of any person of what condition or quality soever shall be buried in linen of whatever kind; and that *where linen has been made use of about dead bodies formerly, plain woolen cloath or stuff shall only be made use of in all time coming.'*

" The preambles of the first two statutes declare the object to be the encouragement of linen manufacture in the kingdom, and the prevention of the exportation of money for foreign goods ; and the preamble of Queen Anne's Act (1707), declares its object to be the encouragement of ' the manufacture of wool ' within the kingdom."

spots where the coffin has rested, and this cairn is from time to time renewed by friends and relatives. Hence the Gaelic saying or prayer with reference to the departed, " Peace to thy soul, and a stone to thy cairn !"—thus expressing the wish, that the remembrance of the dead may be cherished by the living.

The bagpipe is sometimes still played at funerals. Five or six years ago a medical man, greatly beloved and respected for his skill and kindness to the poor, died at Fort William from fever, caught in the discharge of his duties. The funeral was attended by about 1400 people. Strong men wept, and women threw themselves on the ground in the agony of their impassioned sorrow. Three pipers headed the procession, playing the wild and sad lament of " I 'll never, I 'll never, I 'll never return." —The whole scene has been described to me by those present as having been most deeply affecting. Many tourists who have ascended Ben Nevis, will remember that green and beautiful churchyard where he lies, near Fort William, and which looks up to the overhanging mountain, and down upon the sea and Inverlochy Castle, with the dark peat-moss of the Lochy beyond, and farther still, the hills of Lochiel.

But after these digressions I must return to the churchyard of " the parish."

There are two graves which lie side by side across the ruins of the old archway I have spoken of. The one is an old stone coffin, the other a grassy hillock—and I shall tell what I have heard, and what I know about their inhabitants.

## THE OLD STONE COFFIN;

### OR, THE TOMB OF THE SPANISH PRINCESS.

IN the year 1588, the good ship "Florida," one
of the Spanish Armada, was driven into the
harbour of Tobermory, in Mull, by the great storm
which scattered that proud fleet. The ship was
visited by the chief of the Macleans of Duart, the
remains of whose castle are still among the most
picturesque objects on the shores of the Sound of
Mull. The clan Maclean had a feud at the time
with the clan Macian, of Ardnamurchan, immediately opposite Tobermory harbour, and for some
"consideration" or other, Maclean of Duart, their
chief, induced a party of Spanish soldiers to aid
him in attacking his rival. Having revenged him-

self by the powerful and unexpected aid of the Spaniards, he failed to implement his bargain with them, and shortly afterwards, whether through treachery or not is uncertain, the "Florida" was blown up. The body of a female was washed on shore and buried in a stone coffin in the consecrated ground of "the parish." She has ever since been dignified by the name of "the Spanish Princess."

Oliver Cromwell sent a vessel to the Highlands, commanded by a Captain Pottinger, to coerce some of the rebellious Highland Popish chiefs. This vessel was wrecked upon a rock opposite Duart, and only a few years ago the spot was examined, in which, according to tradition, Pottinger's body was buried, when human remains were discovered. Some of the guns of the vessel have also, I believe, been seen.

So much for true history:* now for the High-

* In the year 1740, Spaldin, the diver, was sent by the British Government to regain some of the treasure which was supposed to have been sunk in the "Florida." He succeeded only in obtaining ten of the guns, which are now at Inverary Castle. I myself have a portion of one of the black oak planks which was raised at the time.

Mr Gregory, in his learned and accurate History of the Highlands,

land myth founded on these facts.  It is literally translated from the *ipsissima verba* of an old woman.

"In the time that is gone, the daughter of the King of Spain, in her sleep of the night, beheld in a dream a hero so splendid in form and mien, as to fill her whole heart with love.  She knew that he was not of the people of Spain, but she knew not what his race, his language, or his country was.  She had no rest by day or by night, seeking for the beautiful youth who had filled her heart, but seeking him in vain.  At last she resolved to visit other lands, and got a ship built—a great ship with three masts, and with sails as white as the young snow one night old.  She went to many countries and to many lands, and whenever she reached land she invited all the nobles of the neighbourhood to come on board her great ship.  She entertained them

confirms the tradition of Maclean of Duart having been instrumental in destroying the " Florida."  He states that Spain, being at that time at peace with Scotland, though at war with England, demanded reparation for the savage and inhospitable conduct of Maclean of Duart, and that the records of council in Edinburgh show that the Highland chief had to confess his guilt and sue for pardon, as one who had justly forfeited his life.

royally. There were feasting, and wine and music, dice and dancing. All were glad to be her guests, and very many gave her the love of their hearts ; but among them all she found not her love, the hero of her bright night-dream, (her whisper.) She went from one harbour to another—from one kingdom to another. She went to France, and to England. She went to Ireland and to Lochlinn. She went to the 'Green Isle of the Ocean at the end of the land of the world,' (Scandinavia.) She made feasting and music wherever she went. Around her all was gaiety and gladness—the song and the harp—the wine, and the voice of laughter—hilarity and heartiness, but within her breast all was dark, and cold, and empty.

"At length, passing by the land under the wave, (the flat island of Tyree,) she came near the kingdom of *Sorcha*, (Ardnamurchan,) and after this to 'Mull of the great mountains,' to the harbour of all harbours, curved like a bent bow, sheltered from every wind and every wave. Here the great ship of the three masts and of the white sails cast her anchor, and here, as in all other ports, the daughter of the King of Spain sent invitations to

Q

all the nobles of the neighbouring country to visit her on board her ship. Here many a bold steersman of the *Birlinns* who quailed not before ocean's wrath, many a brave swordsman who rejoiced in the field of slaughter, and many a daring rider who could quell the wildest steed, with the owner of many a hospitable house whose door was never shut, and many a leader of numerous hosts who never turned their face from the foe, came on board the great ship. But all were strangers unto her, until at length the Lord of Duart, the chief of the numerous, the warlike, the renowned Macleans, shone upon her sight. Then did her heart leap with joy, and soon turn to rest in gladness; for he was her vision of the night, and the desire of her heart, in quest of whom she had travelled to so many lands.

"It was then that there was the magnificent and royal entertainment. There was red wine in '*cup, iorn*, and *cuach*,' (cup, goblet, and bicker.) There was music of sweetest sound. Sorrow was laid down, and joy was lifted on high. The daughter of the King of Spain had a sunbeam in the heart, and brightness in the countenance.

The Lord of Duart was so blinded by her beauty and her nobleness that he saw not the black gulf before him. He surrendered himself entirely to her loveliness, and great was the happiness of their converse. He forgot that in the strong black castle of frowning Duart, he had left a youthful bride. On board of the great ship days passed like moments in the midst of enjoyment; but not faster flew the days than rumour flew to Duart, proclaiming to the forsaken lady of the castle the unfaithfulness of her lord. The colour left her cheeks, sleep departed from her eyes, gnawing jealousy entered her heart, and fierce revenge filled her mind. Often as she turned on her pillow, as often turned she a new plan in her head for the destruction of her who had robbed her of her love; but none of these did satisfy her. At long and at last, (at length and at worst,) she contrived a plan which succeeded in drawing the Lord of Duart, and him alone, to the land; and, one of her most attached followers * being on board the

---

* "Most attached follower," *Cōta-eneais*—"coat of the waist," and *Leinê chrios*—"skirt of the girdle," are the terms used in Gaelic to denote a thoroughly devoted follower. It was customary of old, when a lady married beyond her father's clan, as was generally the

ship, set fire to the store of powder, which, with sound louder than the thunder of the skies, rent the great ship of the three masts and the snow-white sails into ten thousand pieces, bringing death and utter destruction on all who were on board, and, saddest woe! on the beautiful and loving daughter of the King of Spain.

"The Lady of Duart rejoiced. Her lord wished not to show his grief, nor to keep in remembrance the wandering love he had given to a stranger. Thus, though he sent followers to gather the remains of the fair daughter of the King of Spain, and to bury her in holy ground, and though they laid her bones in the (*Cil*) churchyard of the holy Columba (Callum Cille) in Morven, she was committed to the dust without priest or prayer—without voice of supplication or psalm of repose—silently and secretly in the blackness of midnight.

case, that she took with her two or more of her family followers, who always formed a sort of body-guard to her, considering themselves entirely at her disposal, and at her command were ready to stab husband or son. Many strange interminglings of names and races have thus arisen. In the very centre of Lochaber there are several Burkes and Boyles. On inquiry I found that these had come from Ireland ages ago as the followers of an Irish lady, who had married MacDonald of Keppoch. There the descendants still are.

"It chanced, shortly after this, that two young men in Morven, bound in ties of closest friendship, and freely revealing to one another all that was in their hearts, began to speak with wonder of the many great secrets of the world beyond the grave. They spoke, and they spoke of what was doing in the habitation of the spirits beyond the thick veil that hides the departed from the friends who sorrow so sorely after them. They could not see a ray of light — they could discover nothing. At length they mutually promised and vowed, that whichever of them was first called away, would, while engaged in the dread task of *Fair'e Chlaidh,* or, 'Watching of the churchyard,'* tell to the

---

* This is a curious idea. In many parts of the Highlands it is believed to this day, that the last person buried has to perform the duty of sentinel over the churchyard, and that to him the guardianship of the spirits of those buried before is in some degree committed. This post he must occupy until a new tenant of the tomb releases him. It is not esteemed as an enviable position, but one to be escaped if possible ; consequently, if two neighbours die on the same day, the surviving relatives make great efforts to be first in closing the grave over their friend. I remember an old nurse, who was mourning the death of a sweet girl whom she had reared, exclaiming with joy when she heard, on the day after her funeral, of the death of a parishioner, "Thank God ! my dear darling will have to watch the graves no longer ! "

A ludicrous but striking illustration of this strange notion oc-

survivor all that he could reveal regarding the abode of the departed ; and here the matter was left.

"Not long after it fell out that one of them, full as his bone was of marrow, yielded to the sway of death. His body, after being carried *Deas iŭl*\* (according to the course of the sun) around the

curred three years ago in the parish of A——. An old man and an old woman, dwelling in the same township, but not on terms of friendship—for the lady, *Kate Ruadh*, (or red-headed Kate,) was more noted for antipathies than attachments—were both at the point of death. The good man's friends began to clip his nails —an office always performed just as a person is dying. He knowing that his amiable neighbour was, like himself, on the verge of the grave, roused himself to a last effort, and exclaimed, "Stop, stop ; you know not what use I may have for all my nails, in compelling Kate Ruadh to keep *Fair'e Chlaidh*, (to watch the churchyard,) in place of doing it myself !"

\* *Deas iŭl*—"a turn the right or the south way ;" *i.e.*, following the course of the sun. This is said to be a Druidical practice, followed in many places to this day. Very recently it was customary in the churchyard of "the parish" to carry the bier around the stone cross which stands there, and to rest it for a few minutes at its base before committing the body to the grave. It is still customary with people, if any food or drink goes wrong in the throat, to exclaim *Deas iŭl*, apparently as a charm ; and sending the bottle round the table in the course of the sun, is as common in the south as in the north. The *south* seems to have been held in high estimation by the Celts. Thus the *right* hand is termed the *south* hand : *Deas*. The same word is used to signify "the being prepared or ready," "the being expert," and "being handsome in person."

stone cross in the churchyard of Callum Cille, (Columba,) in Morven, and allowed to rest for a time
at the foot of that cross, was laid amid the dust of
his kindred.  His surviving comrade, Evan of the
Glen, mourned sore for the loss of his friend; and
much awe and fear came upon him as he remembered the engagement made between them; for
now the autumn evening was bending, (or waning,)
and like a stone rolling down a hill is the faint
evening of autumn.  The hour of meeting drew
nigh, and regard to the sacredness of a promise
made to him who was now in the world of ghosts,
as well as regard for his own courage, decided him
to keep the tryst, (meeting.)  With cautious, but
firm step he approached the *Cill*, and looked for
his departed friend, to hear the secrets of the land
of ghosts.  Quickly as his heart beat at the
thought of meeting the spirit of his friend, he
soon saw what made it quiver like the leaf of the
aspen tree.  He saw the gray shade of him who
had, at one time, been his friend and his faithful
comrade; but he saw all the ' sheeted spectres'
of the populous churchyard moving in mournful
procession around the boundary of their dark

abodes, while his friend seemed to lead the dread and shadowy host. But his eye was soon drawn by the aspect of utter woe presented by one white form which kept apart from the rest, and moved with pain which cannot be told. Forgetful of what had brought him to the *Cill*, he drew near this sight of woe, and heard a low and most plaintive song, in which the singer implored the aid of him whose 'ship was on the ocean,' bewailed her miserable condition, in a land of strangers, far from father and from friends, laid in the grave without due or holy rites, and thus she moaned—

'Worm and beetle, they are whistling
Through my brain—through my brain;
Imps of darkness, they are shrieking
Through my frame—through my frame.'

"Evan, whose heart was ever soft and warm towards the unhappy, asked her the cause of her grief, and whether he could lighten it. She blessed him that he, in the land of the living, had spoken to her in the land of the dead; for now she said she might be freed from evil, and her spirit might rest in peace.

"She told him that she was Clara Viola, daughter of the King of Spain. She told him of the bright

vision of her youthful dream, and how, after drawing her over many an ocean, and bringing her to
many lands, it had, like the *Dreag*,* the shooting-
star of night, suddenly vanished in darkness, or,
like the flame of the *sky-fire*, (lightning,) quickly
ended in thunder and in ruin. She pointed out
the grave into which she had been cast without
holy rites. She implored of him to raise her
bones—to wash them in the holy well of Saint
*Molŭag* in Lismore ; thereafter to carry them to
the kingdom of Spain ; and she described a place
where he would get a chest full of gold, and a
chest full of silver.

"With many fears, but with the courage of a
hero, he accomplished what the princess asked of
him. He washed her bones in the Sainted Well
of Molŭag, in Lismore, and her name is now attached (bound) to the spring, *Tobar Clàr Mheolain*
(pronounced *Clāūr Ve-ŏ-len*), the Well of Clara
Viola.† Thereafter he set off for the kingdom of

---

* *Dreag* signifies the death of a Druid, and is the common name
still for a bright meteor or shooting-star, implying the belief that
the spirits of the *Druids* departed in fiery chariots.

† A well in the churchyard of St Moluag, in Lismore, does
actually bear this name, "*Tobar Claur-Ve-o-len*"—but I cannot in
the least certify that it is derived from that of the Spanish princess.

Spain, and though it was a long way off, he was not long in reaching it. He soon made his way to the palace of the King of Spain, and that was the palace of many windows, of many towers, and of many doors, doors which were never closed— the great house of feasts and of royal hospitality. He was received with honour. He got the chest full of gold, and the chest full of silver, and many a reward besides. But when the King of Spain heard how his beautiful daughter had been treated in Albin, (Scotland,) his heart swelled with wrath and his face flamed with fury. He ordered his three strongest and most destructive ships of war to be immediately fitted out, his three best and bravest captains to command them, to sail as fast as possible to the three best harbours in Scotland, —one in the Kyles of Bute, one in the 'Horseshoe' of Kerrera, and one in the Bay of Tobermory, Mull, and there to load them all with the limbs of Scottish men and of Scottish women.

" One ship did come to Tobermory Bay, and fearful she looked, as with masts bending, and great guns roaring, she leaped and bellowed along the Sound of Mull. She was commanded by Captain

Pottinger. He was skilful in sailing, firmer in fighting, and besides had great knowledge of magic, (Druidism.) He spoke the direst threats against the people of Mull, and said that he would sweep the island with a besom—that he would leave it bare.

" The people of Mull were seized with great fear, and the Lord of Duart, though dreading no ordinary foe, had many things to move him. He found no rest in his house or out of it. He sorrowed for the past, and he dreaded what was to come. Not thinking any human power of avail against the great and deadly war-ship of Spain, commanded by a man deep in magic, he and his men sought evil from magic also, (Druidism,) and with effectual spells and charms, gathered all the witches of Mull, the *Doideagan muileach*, to one meeting-place. He told them of the dire threat of Captain Pottinger, and begged them to raise a wind which would sink his ship, even in the harbour that was better than any other harbour. The *Doideag* asked him if Captain Pottinger, when uttering his threat of devastation, had said 'With

God's help?' 'He did not.' 'Good is that!' said she.

"She and her companions began their work. What *übag, obag,* and *gisreag* (charm, incantation, and canting) they used I know not, ('Christ's cross between us and them all!' here exclaims the narrator ;) but I know that she tied a straw-rope to a *Braa,* (a *quern*-stone,) passed the rope over one of the rafters of the house, and raised the quern-stone as far as she could. As the quern-stone rose the wind rose; but all the strength of the *Doideag* could not raise it high, for Captain Pottinger could put weight on the stone and keep it down. She summoned her sisters from various quarters: one *Laovag Thirisdeach* from Tiree, *Maol-Odhar* from Kintyre, and *Cas a' Mhogain riabhaich* from Cowal.* They came to

---

* The names of the witches may be thought of very little consequence ; but it is interesting to observe that these are names all implying some personal deformity or peculiarity, and show that the witches were more objects of dislike than respect. *Doideag* means little frizzle, applied to anything dry and withered, but more especially to frizzled hair ; *Laovag* signifies hoofie, clootie, or spindle-shanked ; *Cas a' Mhogain riabhaich,* the foot of the russet, or brindled old stocking—*Osan* is the ordinary term for stocking ; *Mogan,* Scottice *Hoggan,* a ragged stocking without a sole ; *Moal-*

her aid and pulled at the rope. They could not raise it higher. Some of them flew through the air to the ship, and in the shape of cats ascended the rigging. They numbered nine. Captain Pottinger said he was stronger than these—that he feared them not. They increased to fifteen, reached the very top of the mast, and scrambled along all the yard-arms, and up and down the shrouds. Captain Pottinger was stronger than these yet, and defied them all.

"At last the *Doideag* seeing her work like to fail, called on a very strong man, *Domhnull Dubh Làidir* (black Donald the strong) to hold the rope and keep the quern-stone from falling lower. He seized the rope with the grasp of death, and with his muscles stretched and strained he held fast the quern-stone.

"The *Doideag* quickly flew to Lochaber to beg

---

*odhar*, bald and dun; *Gormal mhor*, the great blue-eye, is the only one who has a respectable name.

One of my story-tellers gave a different list of the witches engaged in this work. *Luideag, Agus Doideag, Agus Corrag Nighinn Iag Bhàin, Cas a' mhogain Riabhaich á Gleancomham, Agus Gorm-shuil mhor bhàr na Maighe, Raggie* and *Frizzle*, and the finger of White John's Daughter, — that is, "*Hogganfoot* from Glenco, and Great Blue-Eye from Moy," (in Lochaber.)

for the assistance of *Great Gormal* of Moy, whose powers were more than that of all the others put together. *Gormal* yielded to the request, and no sooner did she spread her wings on the air than the tempest raged and roared, blowing the sea to *spin-drift*, tearing the trees from the ground, and splintering the adamant rock. Captain Pottinger feeling that evil was approaching, resolved to leave the bad neighbourhood, and ordered his cable to be cut with speed. His sailors began to do so with gladness; but when the hatchet was raised aloft to strike the blow, the wind blew the iron head off the handle before it could reach the cable. Not an axe-head would remain on the haft. *Gormal* soon reached the harbour. In the likeness of a cat, larger than ever was seen before, she climbed to the top of the mast and sang—

> ' Aha, Captain Pottinger, thou didst boast
> Last year to desolate Mull's coast,
> But now, Hoo-hoo! thy ship is lost! '

And with this, Captain Pottinger and his men, and the great deadly war-ship of Spain, sank down into the depths."

And so ends the Highland myth!

## THE GRASSY HILLOCK;

### OR, THE GRAVE OF FLORY CAMERON.

WE might expect to find peculiar types of character among a people who possess, as the Highlanders do, a vivid fancy, strong passions, and keen affections; who dwell among scenery of vast extent and great sublimity, shut up in their secluded valleys, separated even from their own little world by mountains and moorlands or stormy arms of the sea; whose memories are full of the dark superstitions and wild traditions of the olden time; who are easily impressed by the mysterious sights and sounds created by mists and clouds and eerie blasts, among the awful solitudes of nature; and who cling with passionate fondness to home and family, as to the very life and soul of the otherwise desert waste around them. But I never met, even in the Highlands, with a more remarkable example of the influence of race and circumstances than Flora, or rather Flory Cameron.

The first time I saw her was when going to the school of "the parish," early on an autumnal morning. The school was attached to the church, and the churchyard was consequently near it. The churchyard, indeed, with its headstones and flat stones, its walled tombs, and old ruined church, was fully appreciated by us, as an ideal place for our joyous games, especially for "hide and seek," and "I spy." Even now, in spite of all the sadder memories of later years, I can hardly think of the spot without calling up the blithe face of some boy peering cautiously over the effigy of an old chief, or catching the glimpse of a kilt disappearing behind a headstone, or hearing a concealed titter beside a memorial of sorrow.

As I passed the churchyard for the first time in the sober dawning of that harvest day, I was arrested by seeing the figure of a woman wrapt

in a Highland plaid, sitting on a grave, her head
bent and her hands covering her face, while her
body slowly rocked to and fro. Beside her was a
Highland terrier that seemed asleep on the grave.
Her back was towards me, and I slipped away
without disturbing her, yet much impressed by
this exhibition of grief.

On telling the boys what I had seen, for the
grave and its mourner were concealed at that
moment from our view by the old ruin, they,
speaking in whispers, and with an evident feeling
of awe or of fear, informed me that it was "Flory
the witch," and that she and her dog had been
there every morning since her son had died months
before; and that the dog had been a favourite of
her son's, and followed the witch wherever she
went. I soon shared the superstitious fear for
Flory which possessed the boys; for, though they
could not affirm, in answer to my inquiries, that
she ever travelled through the air on a broom-
stick, or became a hare at her pleasure, or had
ever been seen dancing with demons by moonlight in the old church, yet one thing was certain, that the man or woman whom she blessed

R

was blessed indeed, and that those whom she cursed were cursed indeed. " Is that really true?" I eagerly asked. " It is true as death!" replied the boy Archy Macdonald, shocked by my doubt; "for," said he, " did not black Hugh Maclean strike her boy once at the fair, and did she not curse him when he went off to the herring fishery? and wasn't he and all in the boat drowned? True! ay, it's true." " And did she not curse," added little Peter M'Phie, with vehemence, " the ground officer for turning old Widow M'Pherson out of her house? Was he not found dead under the rock? Some said he had been drunk; but my aunt, who knew all about it, said it was because of Flory's curse, nothing else, and that the cruel rascal deserved it too." And then followed many other terrible proofs of her power, clinched with the assurance from another boy that he had once heard " the maister himself say, that he would any day far rather have her blessing than her curse!"

This conversation prepared me to obey with fear and trembling a summons which I soon afterwards unexpectedly received. Flory had one day, unseen by me, crossed the playground, when we were too busy to notice anything except the ball for which we were eagerly contending at our game of "shinty." She heard that I was at the school, and seeing me, sent a boy to request my presence. As I came near her, the other boys stood at a respectful distance, watching the interview. I put out my hand frankly, though tremblingly, to greet her. She seized it, held it fast, gazed at my face, and I at hers. What she saw in mine I know not, but hers is still vividly before me in every line and expression. It was in some respects very strange and painfully impressive, yet full of affection, which appeared to struggle with an agonised look of sorrow that ever and anon brought tears down her withered cheeks. Her eyes seemed at one time to retire into her head, leaving a mere line between the eyelashes, like what one sees in a cat when in the light; they then would open slowly, and gradually increase until two large black orbs beamed on me, and I felt as if they drew me unto them by a mysterious power. Pressing my hand with one of hers, she stroked my head fondly, muttering to herself all the time, as if in prayer. She then said, with deep feeling, "Oh, thou calf of my heart! my love, my darling, son and grandson of friends, the blessed! let the blessing of the poor, the blessing of the widow, the blessing of the heart be on thee, and abide with thee, my love, my love!" And then, to my great relief, she passed on. In a little while she turned and looked at me, and, waving a farewell, went tottering on her way, followed by the dog. The boys congratulated me on my interview, and seemed to think I was secure against any bodily harm. I think the two parties in our game that day, competed for my powerful aid.

I often saw Flory afterwards, and instead of avoiding her, felt satisfaction rather in having my hand kissed by her, and in receiving the blessing, which in some kind form or other she often gave. Never, during the autumn and winter months when I attended that Highland school, did she omit visiting the grave on which I first saw her. The plashing rain fell around her, and the winds blew their bitter blast, but there she sat at early morning, for a time to weep and pray. And even when snow fell, the black form of the widow, bent in sorrow, was only more clearly revealed. Nor was she ever absent from her seat below the pulpit on Sunday. Her furrowed countenance with the strange and tearful eye, the white *mutch* with the black ribbon bound tightly round the head, the slow rocking motion, with the old, thin, and withered body,—all are before me, though forty years have passed since then.

In after years, the present minister of the parish, and son of "the manse," told me more about Flory than I then knew. The account given to me by the boys at school was to some extent true. She was looked upon as a person possessing an insight into the character of people and their future, for her evil predictions had in many cases been fulfilled. She had remarkable powers of discernment, and often discovered elements of disaster in the recklessness or wickedness of those whom she denounced; and when these disasters occurred in any form, her words were remembered, and her predictions attributed to some supernatural communications with the evil one. Although the violence of her passion was so terrible when roused by any act of cruelty

or injustice, that she did not hesitate to pour i
forth on the objects of her hate, in solemn impre-
cations expressed in highly-wrought and poetic
language; yet Flory herself was never known to
claim the possession of magic powers.* She
spoke, she said, but the truth, and cursed those

* In many Highland parishes—ay, and in Scotch and English
ones too—there were persons who secretly gave charms to cure
diseases and prevent injuries to man or beast. These charms have
come down from Popish times. A woman still lives, I believe, in the
"parish" who possessed a charm which the minister was resolved to
obtain from her, along with the solemn promise that she would never
again use it. We understand that if any charm is once repeated to
and thus possessed by another, it cannot, according to the law which
regulates those supposed powers of darkness, be used again by its
original owner. It was with some difficulty that the minister at
last prevailed on "the witch" to repeat her charm. She did so,
in a wild glen in which they accidentally met. She gave the charm
with loud voice, outstretched arm, and leaning against the stem of
an old pine-tree, while the minister quietly copied it into his note-
book, as he sat on horseback. "Here it is, minister," she said,
"and to you or your father's son alone would I give it, and once
you have it, it will pass my lips no more :—

    "The charm of God the Great
      The free gift of Mary :
      The free gift of God :
      The free gift of every Priest and Churchman :
      The free gift of Michael the Strong :
      That would put strength in the sun."

Yet all this echo of old ecclesiastical thunder was but "a charm
for sore eyes!" Whether it could have been used for greater, if
not more useful purposes, I know not.

only who deserved it, and had her curses not all come true? Her violent passion or hysteria was her only demoniacal possession.

Flory was not by any means an object of dislike. She was as ardent and vehement in her attachments as in her hates, and the former were far more numerous than the latter. Her sick and afflicted neighbours always found in her a sympathising and comforting friend. With that strange inconsistency by which so much light and darkness, good and evil, meet in the same character, Flory, to the minister's knowledge, had been the means of doing much good in more than one instance by her exhortations and her prayers, to those who had been leading wicked lives; while her own life as a wife and a mother had been strictly moral and exemplary. She had been early left a widow, but her children were trained up by her to be gentle, obedient, and industrious, and she gave them the best education in her power.

But it was God's will to subdue the wild and impassioned nature of Flory by a series of severe chastisements. When a widow, her eldest son, in the full strength of manhood, was drowned at sea; and her only daughter and only companion died. One son alone, the pride of her heart, and the stay of her old age, remained, and to him she clung with her whole heart and strength. He deserved, and returned her love. By his industry he had raised a sufficient sum of money to purchase a boat, for the purpose of fishing herring in some of the Highland lochs—an investment of capital which in good seasons is highly advantageous. All the means possessed by Donald Cameron were laid out on this boat and both he and his mother felt proud and happy as he launched it free of debt and was able to call it his own. He told his mother that he expected to make a little fortune by it, that he would then build a house, and get a piece of land, and that her old age would be passed under his roof in peace and plenty. With many a blessing from Flory the boat sailed away. But Donald's partner in the fishing speculation turned out a cowardly and inefficient seaman. The boat was soon wrecked in a storm. Donald, by great exertion, escaped with his life. He returned to his mother a beggar, and so severely injured that he survived the wreck of his boat and fortune but a few weeks.

There was not a family in the parish which did not share the sorrow of poor Flory.

I received the following account of his funeral now before me, from the minister, who was so much struck by all he saw and heard on that occasion that he noted down the circumstances at the time. I shall give it in his own words :—

"When I arrived at the scene of woe, I observed the customary preparations had been judiciously executed, all under the immediate superintendence of poor Flory. On entering the apartment to which I was conducted, she received me with perfect composure and with all that courteous decorum of manner so common in her country. Her dress she had studiously endeavoured to render as suitable to the occasion as circumstances would admit. She wore a black woollen gown of a peculiar, though not unbecoming form, and a very broad black riband was tightly fastened round her head, evidently less with regard to ornament than to the aching pain implanted there by accumulated suffering. According to the custom of the country she drank to the health of each individual present, prefacing each health with a few kind words. In addressing the schoolmaster, who had been assiduous in his attentions towards her, she styled him the 'counsellor of the dying sufferer, the comforter of the wounded mourner.' Another individual present she addressed as 'the son of her whose hand was bountiful, and whose heart was kind,' and in like manner, in addressing me, she alluded very aptly and very feelingly to the particular relation in which I then stood towards her. She then retired with a view of attending to the necessary preparations amongst the people assembled without the house. After a short interval, however, she returned, announcing that all was in readiness for completing the melancholy work for which we had convened. Here she seemed much agitated. Her lips, and even her whole frame seemed to quiver with emotion. At length, however, she recovered her former calmness, and stood motionless and pensive until the coffin was ready to be carried to the grave. She was then requested to take her station at the head of the coffin, and the black cord attached to it was extended to her. She seized it for a moment, and then all self-possession vanished. Casting it from her, she rushed impetuously forward, and clasping her extended arms around the coffin, gave vent to all her accumulated feelings in the accents of wildest despair. As the procession slowly moved onwards, she narrated in a sort of measured rhythm her own sufferings, eulogised the character of her son, and then, alas! uttered her wrath against the man to whose want of seamanship she attributed his death. I would it were in my power to convey her sentiments as they were originally expressed. But though it is impossible to convey them in their pathos and energy, I shall endeavour to give a part of her sad and bitter lamentation by a literal translation of her words.

" ' Alas! alas! woe's me, what shall I do?
Without husband, without brother,
Without substance, without store :
A son in the deep, a daughter in her grave,
The son of my love on his bier—
Alas! alas! woe's me, what shall I do?

" ' Son of my love, plant of beauty,
Thou art cut low in thy loveliness ;
Who'll now head the party at their games on the plains
    of Artornish?

The swiftest of foot is laid low.
Had I thousands of gold on the sea-cover'd rock,
I would leave it all and save the son of my love.
But the son of my love is laid low—
Alas! alas! woe's me, what shall I do?

"'Land of curses is this!—where I lost my family and my
    friends,
My kindred and my store,
Thou art a land of curses for ever to me—
Alas! alas! what shall I do?

"'And, Duncan, thou grandson of Malcolm,
Thou wert a meteor of death to me;
Thine hand could not guide the helm as the hand of my
    love.
But, alas the stem of beauty is cut down,
I am left alone in the world,
Friendless and childless, houseless and forlorn—
Alas! alas! woe's me what shall I do?'

"Whilst she chanted forth these and similar lamentations, the funeral procession arrived at the place of interment, which was only about a mile removed from her cottage. The grave was already dug. It extended across an old Gothic arch. Under it Flory sat for some moments in pensive silence. The coffin was placed in the grave, and when it had been adjusted with all due care, the attendants were about to proceed to cover it. Here, however, they were interrupted. Flory arose, and

motioning to the obsequious crowd to retire, she
slowly descended into the hollow grave, placed
herself in an attitude of devotion, and continued
for some time engaged in prayer to the Almighty.

"The crowd of attendants had retired to a little
distance, but being in some degree privileged, or
at least considering myself so, I remained leaning
upon a neighbouring grave-stone as near to her as
I could without rudely intruding upon such great
sorrow. I was however too far removed to hear
distinctly the words which she uttered, especially
as they were articulated in a low and murmuring
tone of voice. The concluding part of her address
was indeed more audibly given, and I heard her
bear testimony with much solemnity to the fact
that her departed son had never provoked her to
wrath, and had ever obeyed her commands. She
then paused for a few moments, seemingly anxious
to tear herself away, but unable to do so. At
length she mustered resolution, and after impress-
ing three several kisses on the coffin, she was
about to arise. But she found herself again interrupted. The clouds which had hitherto been
lowering were now dispelled, and just as she was

slowly ascending from the grave, the sun burst forth in full splendour from behind the dark mist that had hitherto obscured its rays. She again prostrated herself, this time under the influence of a superstitious belief still general in the Highlands, that bright sunshine upon such occasions augurs well for the future happiness of the departed. She thanked God 'that the sky was clear and serene when the child of her love was laid in the dust.' She then at length arose, and resumed her former position under the old archway, which soon re-echoed the ponderous sound of the falling earth upon the hollow coffin.

"It was indeed a trying moment to her. With despair painted on her countenance, she shrieked aloud in bitter anguish, and wrung her withered hands with convulsive violence. I tried to comfort her, but she would not be comforted. In the full paroxysm of her grief, however, one of the persons in attendance approached her. 'Tears,' said her friend, 'cannot bring back the dead. It is the will of Heaven—you must submit.' 'Alas!' replied Flory, 'the words of the lips—the words of the lips are easily given, but they heal not the broken heart!' The offered consolation, however, was effectual thus far, that it recalled the mourner to herself, and led her to subdue for the time every violent emotion. She again became alive to everything around, and gave the necessary directions to those who were engaged in covering up the grave. Her directions were given with unfaltering voice, and were obeyed by the humane neighbours with unhesitating submission. On one occasion indeed, and towards the close of the obsequies, she assumed a tone of high authority. It was found that the turf which had been prepared for covering the grave was insufficient for the purpose, and one of the attendants not quite so fastidious as his countrymen, who in such cases suffer not the smallest inequality to appear, proposed that the turf should be lengthened by adding to it. The observation did not escape her notice. Flory fixed her piercing eye upon him that uttered it, and after gazing at him for some moments with bitter scorn, she indignantly exclaimed, 'Who talks of patching up the grave of my son? Get you gone! cut a green sod worthy of my beloved.' This imperative order was instantly obeyed. A suitable turf was procured, and the grave was at length covered up to the entire satisfaction of all parties. She now arose, and returned to her desolate abode, supported by two aged females, almost equally infirm with herself, and followed by her dog.

"But Flory Cameron did not long remain inactive under suffering. With the aid of her good friend, the parish schoolmaster, she settled with scrupulous fidelity, all her son's mercantile transactions; and with a part of the very small reversion of money accruing to herself she purchased a neat freestone slab, which she has since erected as the 'Tribute of a widowed mother to the memory of a dutiful son.' Nor has her attention been limited to the grave of her son. Her wakeful thoughts seem to have been the subject of her midnight dreams. In one of the visions of the night, as she herself expressed it, her daughter appeared to her, saying, that she had honoured a son and passed over a daughter. The hint was taken. Her little debts were collected; another slab was provided on which to record the name and merits of a beloved daughter; and, to his honour I mention it, a poor mason employed in the neighbourhood entered so warmly into the feeling by which Flory was actuated that he gave his labour gratuitously in erecting this monument of parental affection. But though the violence of her emotion subsided, Flory Cameron's grief long remained. In church, where she was a regular attendant, every allusion to family bereavement subdued her, and often, when that simple melody arose in which her departed son was wont very audibly to join, she used to sob bitterly, uttering with a low tone of voice, 'Sweet was the voice of my love in the house of God.' Frequently I have met her returning from the burying-ground at early dawn and at evening twilight, accompanied by her little dog, once the constant attendant of her son; and whilst I stood conversing with her I have seen the daisy which she had picked from the grave of her beloved, carefully laid up in her bosom. But her grief is now assuaged. Affliction at length tamed the wildness of her nature, and subdued her into a devotional frame. She ceased to look for earthly comfort, but found it in Christ. She often acknowledged to me with devout sub-

S

mission that the Lord, as He gave, had a right to take away, and that she blessed His name; and that as every tie that bound her to earth had been severed, her thoughts rose more habitually to the home above, where God her Father would at last free her from sin and sorrow and unite her to her dear ones."

Flory continued to visit the grave of her children as long as her feeble steps could carry her thither. But her strength soon failed, and she was confined to her poor hut. One morning, the neighbours, attracted by the howling of her dog, and seeing no smoke from her chimney, entered unbidden, and found Flory dead and lying as if in calm sleep in her poor bed. Her body was laid with her children beneath the old arch and beside the stone coffin of the Spanish Princess.

## THE SCHOOLMASTER.

THE parish schoolmaster of the past belonged to a class of men and to an institution peculiar to Scotland. Between him and the parish clergyman there was a close alliance formed by many links. The homes and incomes of both, though of very unequal value, were secured by Act of Parliament, and provided by the heritors of the parish. Both held their appointments for life, and could be deprived of them only for heresy or immorality, and that by the same kind of formal "libel," and trial before the same ecclesiastical court. Both were members of the same church, and had to subscribe the same confession of faith; both might have attended the same university, nay, passed through the same curriculum of eight years of preparatory study for the ministry.

The schoolmaster was thus a sort of prebendary or minor canon in the parish cathedral—a teaching presbyter and coadjutor to his preaching brother. In many cases "the master" was possessed of very considerable scholarship and culture, and was invariably required to be able to prepare young men for the Scotch universities, by instructing them in the elements of Greek, Latin, and Mathematics. He was by education more fitted than any of his own rank in the parish to associate with the minister. Besides, he was generally an elder of the kirk, and the clerk of the kirk session; and, in addition to all these ties, the school was usually in close proximity to the church and manse. The master thus became the minister's right hand and confidential adviser, and the worthies often met. If the minister was a bachelor—a melancholy spectacle too often seen! —the schoolmaster more than any other neighbour cheered him in his loneliness. He knew all the peculiarities of his diocesan, and especially when he might "step up to the manse for a chat" without being thought intrusive. If, for example, it was Monday—the minister's Sunday of rest—and if the day was wet, the roads muddy, the trees dripping, the hens miserable, and seeking shelter under carts in the farmyard, he knew well that ere evening came, the minister would be glad to hear his rap breaking the stillness of the manse. Seated together in the small study before a cheerful fire, they would then discuss many delicate questions affecting the manners or morals of the flock, and talk about the ongoings of the parish, its births, marriages, and deaths; about its poor, sick, or dying sufferers; about the state of the crops, and the expectation of good or bad "Fiars prices," and the consequent prospects of good or bad stipends, which these regulated. The chances of repairs or additions being obtained for manse, church, or school, would also be considered; preachers and preachings criticised; Church and State politics discussed—both being out-and-out Tories; knotty theological points argued connected with Calvinism or Arminianism; with all the minor and

more evanescent controversies of the hour.  Or, if
the evening was fine, they would perhaps walk in
the garden to examine the flowers and the vegetables, and *dander* over the glebe to inspect the
latest improvements, when the master was sure to
hear bitter complaints of the laziness of "the
minister's man" John, who had been threatened to
be turned off for years, but who took the threats
with about as much ease of mind as he did his
work.  Before parting, they probably partook of a
humble supper of eggs and toasted cheese, soft as
thick cream, washed down by one glass of Edinburgh ale, or, to be perfectly honest, one tumbler
of whisky toddy, when old Jenny was told to be
sure that the water was boiling.

A schoolmaster who had received licence to
preach, and who consequently might be presented
to a parish, if he could get one, belonged to the
aristocracy of his profession.  Not that he lived
in a better house than his unlicensed brother, or
received higher emoluments, or wore garments less
japanned from polished old age.  But the man in
the pulpit was greater than the man in the school,
addressed larger pupils, and had larger prospects.

Among those schoolmasters who were also preachers, it would have been possible, I daresay, to have found a specimen occasionally of the Dominie Sampson type, with peculiarities and eccentricities which easily accounted for his failure as a preacher, and his equally remarkable want of success as a teacher. There were also a few, perhaps, who had soured tempers, and were often crabbed and cross within school and out of it. But let us not be too severe on the poor Dominie! He had missed a church from want of a patron, and, it must be acknowledged, from want of the gift of preaching, which he bitterly termed "the gift of the gab." In college he had taken the first rank in his classes: and no wonder, then, if he was a little mortified in seeing an old acquaintance who had been a notorious dunce obtain a good living through some of those subtle and influential local or political agencies, or the "pow'r o' speech i' the poopit," neither of which he could command, and who, when preferred, became oleaginous on the tiends, and slowly jogged along the smooth road of life on a punchy, sleek horse, troubled chiefly about the great number of his children and the small number of his "chalders."  It is no wonder, I say, that the disappointed Dominie was mortified at this, compelled as he was, poor fellow, to whip his way, tawse in hand, through the mud of A B C, and syntax, Shorter Catechism, and long division, on a pittance of some sixty pounds a year.  Nay, as it often happened, the master had a sore at his heart which few knew about.  When he was a tutor long ago in the family of a small laird, he had, we shall suppose, fallen in love with the laird's daughter Mary, whose mind he had first wakened into thought, and first led into the land of poetry.  She was to have married him, but not until he should get a parish, for the laird would not permit his fair star to move in any orbit beneath that of the manse circle.  And long and often had the parish been expected, and just when the presentation seemed to be within his nervous grasp, it had vanished through some unexpected mishap, and with its departure hope became more deferred, and the heart more sick, until at last Mary married, and so changed all things to her old lover.  She had not the pluck to stand by the master when the Laird of Blackmoss was pressing for her hand. And then the black curly hairs of the master turned to gray as the dream of his life vanished, and he awoke to the reality of a heart that can never love another, and to a school with its A B C and syntax. But somehow the dream comes strangely back in all its tenderness as he strokes the hair of some fair girl in the class and looks into her eyes; or it comes darkly back in all its bitterness, and a fire begins to burn at his heart, which very possibly passes off like a shock of electricity along his right arm, and down the black tawse, finally discharging itself with a flash and a roar into some lazy mass of agricultural flesh who happens to have a vulgar look like the Laird of Blackmoss, and an unprepared lesson.

It often happened that those who were uncommonly bad preachers, were, nevertheless, admirable teachers, especially if they had found suitable wives, and were softened by the amenities of domestic life; above all when they had boys of their own to "drill." The parish school then became one of no mean order. The glory of the old Scotch teacher of this stamp, was to *ground*

his pupils thoroughly in " the elements." He hated
all shams, and placed little value on what was
acquired without labour. To master details, to
stamp grammar rules and prosody rules, thoroughly understood, upon the minds of his pupils
as with a pen of iron; to move slowly, but accurately through a classic, this was his delight; not
his work only, but his recreation, the outlet of his
tastes and energies. He had no long-spun theories
about education, nor ever tried his hand at adjusting the fine mechanism of boys' motives. " Do your
duty and learn thoroughly, or be well licked;"
"Obedience, work, and no humbug," were the sort
of Spartan axioms which expressed his views.
When he found the boys honest at their work, he
rejoiced in his own. But if he found one who
seemed bitten with the love of Virgil or Homer; if
he discovered in his voice or look, by question or
answer, that he "promised to be a good classic,"
the dominie had a tendency to make that boy a
pet. On the annual examination by the presbytery, with what a pleased smile did he contemplate
his favourite in the hands of some competent and
sympathising examiner! And once a year on

such a day the dominie might so far forget his stern and iron rule as to chuck the boy under the chin, clap him fondly on the back, and give him sixpence.

I like to call those old teaching preachers to remembrance. Take them all in all they were a singular body of men; their humble homes, poor salaries, and hard work, presenting a remarkable contrast to their manners, abilities, and literary culture. Scotland owes to them a debt of gratitude that can never be repaid; and many a successful minister, lawyer, and physician, is able to recall some one of those old teachers as his earliest and best friend, who first kindled in him the love of learning, and helped him in the pursuit of knowledge.

In cities the schoolmaster may be nobody, lost in the great crowd of professional and commercial life, unless that august personage the Government Inspector appears in the school, and links its master and pupil teachers to the august and mysterious Privy Council located in the official limbo of Downing Street. But in a country parish, most of all in a Highland parish, to which we must now return, the schoolmaster or "master" occupied a most important position.

The schoolmaster of "the parish" half a century ago was a strong-built man, with such a face, crowned by such a head, that taking face and head together, one felt that he was an out-and-out *man*. A Celt he evidently was, full of emotion, that could be roused to vehemence, but mild, modest, subdued, and firm. He had been three years at Glasgow University, attending the Greek, Latin, and logic classes. How he, the son of a *very* small farmer, could support himself is partly explained by the account we have given of student life at that time in Glasgow college. He had brought, no doubt, a supply of potatoes, salt herrings, sausages, and dried cod or ling from Barra, with a mutton ham or two from home. And thus he managed, with a weekly sum which an unskilled labourer would consider wretched wages, to educate himself for three years at the University. He eventually became the schoolmaster, elder, session-clerk, precentor, post-master, and catechist of "the parish," —offices sufficient perhaps to stamp him as incompetent by the Privy Council Committee acting under a "minute," but nevertheless capable of being all duly discharged by "the master."

The school of course was his first duty, and there he diligently taught some fifty or sixty scholars in male and female petticoats for five days in the week, imparting knowledge of the "usual branches," and also instructing two or three pupils, including his own sons, in Greek, Latin, and mathematics. I am obliged to confess that neither the teacher nor the children had the slightest knowledge of physiology, chemistry, or even household economy. It is difficult to know, in these days of light, how they got on without it: for the houses were all constructed on principles opposed in every respect to the laws of health as we at present understand them, and the cooking was confined chiefly to potatoes and porridge. But whether it was the Highland air which they breathed, or the rain which daily washed them, or the absence of doctors, the children who ought to have died by rule did not, but were singularly robust and remarkably happy. In spite of bare feet and uncovered heads they seldom had colds, or, if they had, as Charles Lamb says, " they took them kindly."

His most important work next to the school was catechising. By this is meant, teaching the " Shorter Catechism" of the Church to the adult parishioners. The custom was, that at certain seasons of the year, when the people were not busy at farm-work, they were assembled in different hamlets throughout the parish : if the weather was wet, in a barn ; if fine, on the green hill-side, and there, by question and answer, with explanatory remarks, to indoctrinate them into the great truths of religion. Many of the people in the more distant valleys, where even the small " side schools" could not penetrate, were unable to read, but they had ears to hear, and hearts to feel, and through these channels they were instructed. These meetings were generally on Saturdays when the school was closed. The sick also had the benefit of the catechist's teaching and prayers.

The schoolmaster, I have said, was also postmaster. But then the mail was but weekly, and by no means a heavy one. It contained only a few letters for the sheriff or the minister, and half-a-dozen to be delivered as opportunity offered to outlying districts in the parish, and these, with three or four newspapers a week old, did not occupy much of his time. The post, moreover, was never in a hurry. "Post haste" was unknown in those parts: the "poste restante" being much more common. The "runner" was a sedate walker, and never lost sight of his feelings as a man in his ambition as a post. Nor was the master's situation as "precentor" a position like that of organist in Westminster or St Paul's. His music was select, and confined to three or four tunes. These he modulated to suit his voice and taste, which were peculiar and difficult to describe. But the people understood both, and followed him on Sundays as far as their own peculiar voices and tastes would permit: and thus his musical calling did not at all interfere with his week-day profession.

It is impossible to describe the many wants which he supplied and the blessings which he con-ferred. There were few marriages of any paro-chial importance at which he was not an honoured guest. In times of sickness, sorrow, or death, he was sure to be present with his subdued manner, tender sympathy, and Christian counsel. If any one wanted advice on a matter which did not seem of sufficient gravity to consult about at the manse, " the master" was called in. If a dying man wanted a trustee, who would deal kindly and honestly with his widow and children, the master was sure to be nominated. He knew every one in the parish, and all their belongings, as minutely as a man on the turf knows the horses and their pedigree.

I need not add that he was a true friend of the inmates of the manse, and the minister trusted him as he did no other man. And so it happened that when the "minister" was dying the school-master watched him by night, and tended him as an old disciple would have done one of the prophets, and left him not until with prayer he closed his eyes.

His emoluments for all this labour were not extravagant. Let us calculate. He had £15 as schoolmaster; £5 in school fees; £7 as postmaster; £1 as session clerk; £1 as leader of church psalmody ; £5 as catechist ; £34 in all, with house and garden. He had indeed a bit of ground with two or three cows, a few sheep, and a few acres for potatoes, and oats or barley, but for all this he paid rent. So his emoluments were not large. The house was a thatched cottage with what the Scotch call a "butt and ben ;" the "butt" being half kitchen, half bedroom, with a peat-fire on the floor, the "ben" having also a bed, but being dignified by a grate. Between them was a small bed-closet separated from the passage by a wicker partition. All the floors were clay. Above was a garret or loft reached by a ladder, and containing amidst a dim light a series of beds and shakes-down like a barrack. In this home father, mother, and a family of four sons and three daughters were accommodated. The girls learned at home,—in addition to " the three r's" learned at school,—to sew and spin, card wool, and sing songs ; while the boys, after preparing their Virgil or arithmetic sums for next day, went in the evening to fish, to work in the garden, or on the farm, to drive the cattle home, to cut peats for fuel or stack them, to reap ferns and house them for

T

bedding the cattle in winter, or make "composts" for the fields, and procure for them moss and other unmentionable etceteras. When darkness came they gathered round the fire, while some wove baskets, repaired the horses' harness or their own shoes, made fishing lines and "busked" hooks; others would discourse sweet music from the trump, and all in their turn tell stories to pass the time pleasantly. The grinding of meal for porridge or *fuarag* was a common occupation. This *fuarag* was a mixture made up of meal freshly ground from corn that had been well toasted and dried before the fire, and then whipped up with thick cream,—a dainty dish to set before a king! The difficulty in making it good was the getting of corn freshly toasted and meal freshly ground. It was prepared by means of a quern, which at that time was in almost every house. The quern consisted of two round flat stones, of about a foot in diameter, and an inch or so thick, corresponding to the grinding stones in a mill. The lower stone was fixed, and the upper being fitted into it by a circular groove, was made to revolve rapidly upon it, while the corn was poured through a hole in the upper stone to be ground between the two. It was worked thus. A clean white sheet was spread over the bed in the kitchen. The mill was placed in the centre. One end of a stick was then inserted into a hole in the upper stone to turn it round, while the other end of the stick, to give it a purchase and keep it steady, was fixed in the twist of a rope, stretched diagonally from one bedpost to another. The miller sat in the bed, with a leg on each side of the quern, and seizing the stick, rapidly turned the stone, while the parched corn was poured in. When ground it was taken away and cleaned of all husks. The dry new meal being whipped up with rich cream the fuarag was ready, and then— lucky the boy who got it! I cannot forget the mill or its product, having had the privilege of often sharing in the labours of the one, and enjoying the luxury of the other.

Our schoolmaster could not indeed give entertainments worthy of a great educational institute, nor did he live in the indulgence of any delicacies greater than the one I have dwelt upon, if, indeed, there was any greater then in existence. There was for breakfast the never-failing porridge and milk—and such milk!—with oat-cakes and bar-ley scones for those who preferred them, or liked them as a top-dressing. On Sundays there were tea and eggs. The dinner never wanted noble potatoes, with their white powdery waistcoats, re-vealing themselves under the brown jackets. At that time they had not fallen into the " sere and yellow leaf," but retained all their pristine youth and loveliness as when they rejoiced the heart of some Peruvian Inca in the land of their nativity. With such dainties, whether served up " each like a star that dwelt apart," or mashed with milk or a little fresh butter into a homogeneous mass, what signified the accompaniments ? Who will inquire anxiously about them ? There may have been sometimes salt herring, sometimes other kinds of sea-fish—lythe, rock-cod, mackerel, or saithe, but oftener the unapproachable milk alone ! At times a fat hen, and bit of pork, or blackfaced mutton, would mar the simplicity of the dinner. When these came, in Providence, they were appreciated. But whatever the food, all who partook of it ate it heartily, digested it with amazing rapidity, and never were the worse, but always the better for it. No one had headaches, or ever heard of medicine except in sermons ; and all this is more than can be said of most feasts, from those of the excellent Lord Mayor of London downwards, in all of which the potatoes and milk are shamefully ignored, while salt herring and potatoes—the most savoury of dishes—and even fuarag, are utterly forgotten.

Handless people, who buy everything they require, can have no idea how the schoolmaster and his family managed to get clothes ; yet they always were clothed, and comfortably too. There was wool afforded by their own few sheep, or cheaply obtained from their neighbours, and the mother and daughters employed themselves during the long winter nights in carding and spinning it. Then Callum the weaver took in hand to weave it into tartans, of any known Celtic pattern : and Peter the tailor undertook to shape it into comely garments for father or son ; while the female tailors at home had no difficulty in arranging suitable garments out of their own portion of the wool. As for shoes, a hide or two of leather was purchased, and John the shoemaker, like Peter the tailor, would come to the house and live there, and tell his stories, and pour out the country news, and rejoice in the potatoes, and look balmy over the fuarag.  Peter the tailor, when he went, left beautiful suits of clothes behind him ; John the shoemaker completed the adornment by most substantial shoes—wanting polish, probably, and graceful shapes, but nevertheless strong and victorious in every battle with mud and water, and possessing powerful thongs and shining tackets. And thus the family were clothed—if we except the kilts of the younger boys, which necessarily left Nature, with becoming confidence in her powers, to a large portion of the work about the limbs.  The master's suit of black was also an exception.  When that suit was purchased was a point not easily determined.  It was generally understood to have been obtained when the schoolmaster went on his first and last journey to see George IV. in Edinburgh.  The suit was folded in his large green chest behind the door, and was only visible once a year at the communion, or when some great occasion, such as a marriage or a funeral, called it forth into sunlight.  The tartan coat and home-made woollen trousers were at such times exchanged for black broadcloth, and the black silk neckcloth for a white cravat; and then the schoolmaster, with his grave countenance and gray whiskers, and bald head, might pass for a professor of theology or the bishop of a diocese.

The worthy schoolmaster is long since dead. He died, as he had lived, in peace with God and man. The official residence has been changed to another part of the parish; and when I last saw the once happy and contented home of the good man, with whom I had spent many happy days, the garden was obliterated, the footpaths covered with grass, and the desolation of many years was over it. Verily, the place that once knew him knows him no more.

## THE "FOOLS."

NO one attempting to describe from personal knowledge the characteristics of Highland life, can omit some mention of the fools. It must indeed be admitted that the term "fool" is ambiguous, and embraces individuals in all trades, professions, and ranks of society. But those I have in my mind were not so injurious to society, nor so stupid and disagreeable, as the large class commonly called "fools." Nor is the true type of "fool," a witless idiot like the Cretin, nor a raving madman, fit only for Bedlam;—but "a pleasant fellow i' faith, with his brains somewhat in disorder."

I do not know whether "fools" are held in such

high estimation in the Highlands as they used to be in that time which we call "our day." It may be that the poor laws have banished them to the calm and soothing retreat of the workhouse; or that the moral and intellectual education of the people by government pupils and Queen's scholars have rendered them incapable of being amused by any abnormal conditions of the intellect; but I am obliged to confess that I have always had a foolish weakness for "fools"—a decided sympathy with them—which accounts for their occupying a very fresh and pleasing portion of my reminiscences of the " parish."

. The Highland "fool" was the special property of the district in which he lived. He was not considered a burthen upon the community, it was felt to be a privilege to assist him. He wandered at his own sweet will wherever he pleased, " ower the muir amang the heather;" along highways and byways, with no let or hindrance from parish beadles, rural police, or poor-law authorities.

Every one knew the "fool," and liked him as a sort of *protégé* of the public. Every house was open to him, though he had his favourite places of call. But he was too wise to call as a fashionable formal visitor, merely to leave his card and depart if his friend was "not at home." The temporary absence of landlord or landlady made little difference to him. He came to pay a visit, to enjoy the society of his friends, and to remain with them for days, perhaps for weeks, possibly even for months. He was sure to be welcomed, and never treated uncivilly or sent away until he chose to depart. Nay, he was often coaxed to prolong the agreeable visit which was intended as a compliment to the family, and which the family professed to accept as such. It was, therefore, quite an event when some rare fool arrived, illustrious for his wit. His appearance was hailed by all in the establishment, from the shepherds, herds, workmen, and domestic servants, up to the heads of the family, with their happy boys and girls. The news spread rapidly from kitchen to drawing-room—"'Calum,' 'Archy,' or 'Duncan' fool is come!" and all would gather round him to draw forth his peculiarities.

It must be remembered that the Highland kitchen, which was the "fool's" stage, court, reception and levee room, and which was cheered at night by his brilliant conversation, was like no other similar culinary establishment, except, perhaps, that in an old Irish house. The prim model of civilised propriety, with its pure well-washed floors and whitewashed walls, its glittering pans, burnished covers, clean tidy fireside with roasting-jack, oven and hot-plate—a sort of cooking drawing-room, an artistic studio for roasts and boils—was utterly unknown in the genuine Highland mansion of a former generation. The Highland kitchen had, no doubt, its cooking apparatus, its enormous pot that hung from its iron chain amidst the reek in the great chimney; its pans embosomed in glowing peats, and whatever other instrumentality (possibly an additional peat fire on the floor) was required to prepare savoury joints, with such barn-door dainties as ducks and hens, turkeys and geese—all supplied from the farm in such quantities as would terrify the modern cook and landlady if required to provide them daily from the market. The cooking of the Highland kitchen was also a continued process, like that on a passenger steamer on a long voyage. Different classes had to be served at different periods of the day, from early dawn till night. There were, therefore, huge pots of superb potatoes "laughing in their skins," and pots as huge of porridge poured into immense wooden dishes, with the occasional dinner luxury of Braxy—a species of mutton which need not be too minutely inquired into. These supplies were disposed of by the frequenters of the kitchen, dairymaids and all sorts of maids, with shepherds, farm-servants male and female, and herd lads full of fun and grimace, and by a constant supply of strangers, with a beggar and probably a "fool" also at the side-table. The kitchen was thus a sort of caravanserai, in which crowds of men and women, accompanied by sheep-dogs and terriers, came and went; and into whose precincts ducks, hens, and turkeys strayed as often as they could to pick up *débris*. The world in the drawing-room was totally separated from this world in the kitchen, except when invited to it by the young lady of the family, who in her turn acted as housekeeper. The "gentry" in "the room" were supposed to look down upon it as on things belonging to another sphere, governed by its own laws and customs, with which they had no wish to interfere. And thus it was that "waifs" and "fools" came to the kitchen and fed there, as a matter of course, having a bed in the barn at night. All passers-by got their "bite and sup" in it readily and cheerfully. Servants' wages were nominal, and food was abundant from moor and loch, sea and land. To do justice to the establishment I ought to mention that connected with the kitchen there was generally a room called "the Servants' Hall," where the more distinguished strangers — such as the post or packman, with perhaps the tailor or shoemaker when these were necessarily resident for some weeks in the house— took their meals along with the housekeeper and more "genteel" servants.

I have, perhaps, given the impression that these illustrious visitants, the "fools," belonged to that parish merely in which the houses that they frequented were situated. This was not the case. The fool was quite a cosmopolitan. He wandered like a wild bird over a large tract of country, though he had favourite nests and places of refuge. His selection of these was judiciously made according to the comparative merits of the treatment which he received from his many friends. I have known some cases in which the attachment became so great between the fool and the household that a hut was built and furnished for his permanent use. From this he could wander abroad when he wished a change of air or society. Many families had their fool—their Wamba or jester—who made himself not only amusing but useful, by running messages and doing out-of-the-way jobs requiring little wit but often strength and time.

As far as my knowledge goes, or my memory serves me, the treatment of these parish "characters" was most considerate. Any teasing or annoyance which they received detracted slightly, if at all, from the sum of their happiness, and was but the friction which elicited their sparks and crackling fun. The herd boys round the fireside at night could not resist applying it, nor their elders from enjoying it; while the peculiar claims of the fool to be considered lord or king, admiral or general, an eight-day clock or brittle glass, were cheerfully acquiesced in. Few men with all their wits about them could lead a more

free or congenial life than the Highland fool with
his wit alone.

One of the most distinguished fools of my acquaintance was " Allan-nan-Con," or Allan of the
Dogs.   He had been drafted as a soldier, but
owing to some breach of millitary etiquette on
his part, when under inspection by Sir Ralph
Abercromby, he was condemned as a fool, and
immediately sent home.   I must admit that
Allan's subsequent career fully confirmed the cor-
rectness of Sir Ralph's judgment.   His peculiarity
was his love of dogs.   He wore a long loose great-
coat bound round his waist by a rope.   The great-
coat bagged over the rope, and within its loose
and warm recesses a number of pups nestled while
on his journey, so that his waist always seemed to
be in motion.   The parent dogs, four or five in
number, followed on foot, and always in a certain
order of march, and any straggler or undisciplined
cur not keeping his own place received sharp admonition from Allan's long pike-staff.   His head-
dress was a large Highland bonnet, beneath which
appeared a small sharp face, with bright eyes and
thin-lipped mouth full of sarcasm and humour.

Allan spent his nights often among the hills. "My house," he used to say, "is where the sun sets." He managed, on retiring to rest, to arrange his dogs round his body so as to receive the greatest benefit from their warmth. Their training was the great object of his life; and his pupils would have astonished any government inspector by their prompt obedience to their master's commands and their wonderful knowledge of the Gaelic language.

I remember on one occasion when Allan was about to leave "the manse," he put his dogs, for my amusement, through some of their *drill*, as he called it. They were all sleeping round the kitchen fire, the pups freed from the girdle, and wandering at liberty, when Allan said, "Go out, one of you my children, and let me know if the day is fair or wet." A dog instantly rose, while the others kept their places, and with erect tail went out. Returning, it placed itself by Allan's side, so that he might by passing his hand along its back discover whether it was wet or dry! "Go," he again said, "and tell that foolish child"—one of the pups—"who is frolicking outside of

the house, to come in." Another dog rose, departed, and returned wagging his tail and looking
up to Allan's face. "Oh, he won't come, won't
he? Then go and bring him in, and if necessary
by force!" The dog again departed, but this
time carried the yelping pup in his mouth, and
laid it at Allan's feet. "Now, my dear children,
let us be going," said Allan, rising, as if to proceed on his journey. But at this moment two
terriers began to fight,—though it seemed a mimic
battle,—while an old sagacious-looking collie never
moved from his comfortable place beside the fire.
To understand this scene you must know that
Allan had taken offence at the excellent sheriff
of the district because of his having refused him
some responsible situation on his property, and to
revenge himself he had trained his dogs to act
the drama which was now in progress. Addressing the apparently sleeping dog, whom he called
"the Sheriff," he said, "There you lie, you lazy
dog, enjoying yourself when the laws are breaking by unseemly disputes and fights! But what
care you if you get your meat and drink! Shame
upon you, Sheriff. It seems that I even must

U

teach you your duty. Get up this moment, sir, or I shall bring my staff down on your head, and make these wicked dogs keep the peace!" In an instant "the Sheriff" rose and separated the combatants.

It was thus that, when any one offended Allan past all possibility of forgiveness, he immediately trained one of the dogs to illustrate his character, and taught it lessons, by which in every house he could turn his supposed enemy into ridicule. A farmer, irritated by this kind of *dogmatic* intolerance, ordered Allan to leave his farm. "Leave it, forsooth!" replied Allan with a sarcastic sneer. "Could I possibly, sir, take it with me, be assured I would do so rather than leave it to you!"

When Allan was dying he called his dogs beside him, and told them to lie close and keep him warm, as the chill of death was coming over him. He then bade them farewell, as his "children and best friends," and hoped they would find a master who would take care of them and teach them as he had done. The old woman, in whose hut the poor fool lay, comforted him by telling him how, according to the humane belief of her country, all

whom God had deprived of reason were sure to
go to heaven, and that he would soon be there. "I
don't know very well," said Allan, with his last
breath, "where I am going, as I never travelled
far; but if it is possible, I will come back for my
dogs; and, mind you," he added, with emphasis,
"to punish the Sheriff for refusing me that situation!"

Another most entertaining fool was Donald
Cameron. Donald was never more brilliant than
when narrating his submarine voyages, and his
adventures, as he walked along the bottom of the
sea passing from island to island. He had an
endless variety of stories about the wrecks which
he visited in the caverns of the deep, and above all
of his interviews with the fish, small and great,
whom he met during his strange voyages, or
journeys, rather. I remember his once telling me
the following with grave earnestness, as we sat
together fishing from a rock:—"I was sadly put
about on one occasion, my boy, when coming from
the island of Tyree. Ha! ha! ha! It makes me
laugh to think of it now, though at the time it was
very vexing. It was very stormy weather, and the

walking was difficult, and the road long. I became very hungry at last, and looked out for some
hospitable house where I could find rest and refreshment. I was fortunate enough to meet a
turbot, an old acquaintance, who invited me, most
kindly, to a marriage party, which was that day to
be in his family. The marriage was between a
daughter of his own, and a well-to-do flounder.
So I went with the decent fellow, and entered a
fine house of shells and tangle, most beautiful to
look upon. The dinner came, and it was all one
could wish. There was plenty, I assure you,
to eat and drink, for the turbot had a large
fishing bank almost to himself to ply his trade
on, and he was too experienced to be cheated
by the hook of any fisherman. He had also been
very industrious, as indeed were all his family.
So he had good means. But as we sat down
to our feast, my mouth watering, and just as I
had the bountiful board under my nose, who
should come suddenly upon us with a rush, but a
tremendous cod, that was angry because the turbot's daughter had accepted a poor, thin, flat
flounder, instead of his own eldest son, a fine red-

rock cod? The savage, rude brute gave such a fillip with his tail against the table, that it upset, and what happened, my dear, but that the turbot, with all the guests, flounders, skate, haddock, and whiting, thinking, I suppose, that it was a sow of the ocean, (a whale,) rushed away in a fright; and I can tell you, calf of my heart, that when I myself saw the cod's big head and mouth and staring eyes, with his red gills going like a pair of fanners, and when I got a touch of his tail, I was glad to be off with the rest; so I took to my heels and escaped among the long tangle. Pfui! what a race of hide-and-seek that was! Fortunately for me I was near the Point of Ardnamurchan, where I landed in safety, and got to Donald M'Lachlan's house wet and weary. Wasn't that an adventure? And now," concluded my friend, " I'll put on, with your leave, a very large bait of cockles on my hook, and perhaps I may catch some of that rascally cod's descendants!"

" Barefooted Lachlan," another parish worthy, was famous as a swimmer. He lived for hours in the water, and alarmed more than one boat's crew, who perceived a mysterious object—it might be the sea-serpent—a mile or two from the shore, now appearing like a large seal, and again causing the water to foam with gambols like those of a much larger animal. As they drew near, they saw with wonder what seemed to be the body of a human being floating on the surface of the water. With the greatest caution an oar was slowly moved towards it; but just as the supposed dead body was touched, the eyes, hitherto shut, in order to keep up the intended deception, would suddenly open, and with a loud shout and laugh, Lachlan would attempt to seize the oar, to the terror and astonishment of those who were ignorant of his fancies. The belief in his swimming powers—which in truth were wonderful—became so exaggerated that his friends, even when out of sight of land, would not have been surprised to have been hailed and boarded by him. If any unusual appearance was seen on the surface of the water along the coast of the parish, and rowers paused to consider whether it was a play of fish or a pursuing whale, it was not unlikely that one of them would at last say, as affording the most probable solution of the mystery, " I believe myself it is Barefooted Lachlan !"

Poor Lachlan had become so accustomed to this kind of fishy existence that he attached no more value to clothes than a merman does. He looked upon them as a great practical grievance. To wear them on his aquatic excursions was at once unnecessary and inconvenient, and to be obliged, despite of tides and winds, to return from a distant swimming excursion to the spot on the shore, where they had been left, was to him an intolerable bore. A tattered shirt and kilt were not worth all this trouble. In adjusting his wardrobe to meet the demands of the sea, it must be confessed that Lachlan forgot the fair demands of the land. Society at last rebelled against his judgment, and the poor-law authorities having been appealed to, were compelled to try the expensive but necessary experiment of boarding Lachlan in a pauper asylum in the Lowlands, rather than permit him to wander about unadorned as a fish out of water. When he landed at the Broomielaw of Glasgow, and saw all its brilliant gas lights, and beheld for the first time in his life a great street with houses which seemed palaces, he whispered with a smile to his keepers, " Surely this is heaven ! am I right ?" But when he passed onward to his asylum, through the railway tunnel with its smoke and noise, he trembled with horror, declaring that now, alas ! he was in the lower regions and lost for ever. The swimmer did not prosper when deprived of his long freedom among the winds and waves of ocean, but died in a few days after entering the well-regulated home provided for his comfort by law. Had it not been for his primitive taste in clothes, and his want of appreciation of any better or more complete covering than his tanned skin afforded, I would have protested against his being confined in a workhouse as a cruel and needless incarceration, and pleaded for him as Wordsworth did for his Cumberland beggar :—

> " As in the eye of Nature he has lived,
> So in the eye of Nature let him die ! "

While engaged in the unusual task of writing the biographies of fools, I cannot forget one who, though not belonging to " the parish," was

better known perhaps than any other in the
North. The man I speak of was "Gillespic
Aotrom," or "light-headed Archy," of the Isle of
Skye. Archy was perhaps the most famous
character of his day in that island. When I first
made his acquaintance a quarter of a century ago,
he was eighty years of age, and had been a notorious and much-admired fool during all that
period — from the time, at least, when he had
first babbled folly at his mother's knee. Archy,
though a public beggar, possessed excellent manners. He was welcomed in every house in Skye ;
and if the landlord had any appreciation of wit, or
if he was afraid of being made the subject of some
sarcastic song or witty epigram, he was sure to ask
Archy into the dining-room after dinner, to enjoy
his racy conversation. The fool never on such
occasions betrayed the slightest sense of being
patronised, but made his bow, sat down, accepted
with respect, ease, and grace his glass of wine or
whisky punch, and was ready to engage in any
war of joke or repartee, and to sing some inimit-
able songs, which hit off with rare cleverness the
infirmities and frailties of the leading people of

the island—especially the clergy. Some of the
clergy and gentry happened to be so sensitive to
the power and influence of this fool's wit, which
was sure to be repeated at "kirk and market,"
that it was alleged they paid him black-mail in
meat and money to keep him quiet, or obtain
his favour. Archy's practical jokes were as remarkable as his sayings. One of these jokes was
the following. An old acquaintance of mine, a
minister in Skye, who possessed the kindest dis-
position and an irreproachable moral character,
was somehow more afraid of Archy's sharp tongue
and witty rhymes than most of his brethren.
Archy seemed to have detected intuitively his
weak point, and though extremely fond of the
parson, yet he often played upon his good-nature
with an odd mixture of fun and selfishness. On
the occasion I refer to, Archy in his travels arrived
on a cold night at the manse when all its inmates
were snug in bed, and the parson himself was
snoring loudly beside his helpmate. A thundering knock at the door awakened him, and thrust-
ing his head, enveloped in a thick white night-
cap, out of the window, he at once recognised the

tall, well-known form of Archy. " Is that you, Archy ? Oich, oich ! what do you want, my good friend, at this hour of the night ?" blandly asked the old minister. " What could a man want at such an hour, most reverend friend," replied the rogue, with a polite bow, " but his supper and his bed !" " You shall have both, good Archy," said the parson, at the same time wishing Archy on the other side of the Coolins. Dressing himself in his home-made flannel unmentionables, and throwing a shepherd's plaid over his shoulders, he descended and admitted the fool. He then provided a sufficient supper for him in the form of a large supply of bread and cheese, with a jug of milk. During the repast Archy told his most recent gossip and merriest stories, concluding by a request for a bed. "You shall have the best in the parish, good Archy, take my word for it !" quoth the old dumpy and most amiable minister. The bed alluded to was the hay-loft over the stable, which could be approached by a ladder only. The minister adjusted the ladder and begged Archy to ascend. Archy protested against the rudeness. " You call that, do you, one of the best beds in Skye ? You, a minister, say so ?

On such a cold night as this, too? You dare to say this to *me?*" The old man, all alone, became afraid of the gaunt fool as he lifted his huge stick with energy. But had any one been able to see clearly Archy's face, they would have easily discovered a malicious twinkle in his eye betraying some plot which he had been concocting probably all day. "I do declare, Archy," said the parson, earnestly, "that a softer, cleaner, snugger bed exists not in Skye!" "I am delighted," said Archy, "to hear it, minister, and must believe it since *you* say so. But you know it is the custom in our country for a landlord to show his guest into his sleeping apartment, isn't it? and so I expect you to go up before me to my room, and just see if all is right and comfortable. Please ascend!" Partly from fear and partly from a wish to get back to his own bed as soon as possible, and out of the cold of a sharp north wind, the simple-hearted old man complied with Archy's wish. With difficulty, waddling up the ladder, he entered the hay-loft. When his white rotund body again appeared as he formally announced to his distinguished guest how perfectly comfortable the resting-place provided for him was, the ladder, alas! had been removed, while Archy calmly remarked, "I am rejoiced to hear what you say! I don't doubt a word of it. But if it is so very comfortable a bed - room, you will have no objection, I am sure, to spend the night in it. Good night, then, my much-respected friend, and may you have as good a sleep and as pleasant dreams as you wished me to enjoy." So saying he made a profound bow and departed with the ladder over his shoulder. But after turning the corner and listening with fits of suppressed laughter to the minister's loud expostulations and earnest entreaties—for never had he preached a more energetic sermon, or one more from his heart—and when the joke afforded the full enjoyment which was anticipated, Archy returned with the ladder, and advising the parson never to tell *fibs* about his fine bed-rooms again, but to give what he had without imposing upon strangers, he let him descend to the ground, while he himself ascended to the place of rest in the loft.

Archy's description of the whole scene was ever afterwards one of his best stories, to the minister's great annoyance.

In some way or other he had been grievously offended by another of the clergy, on whom he revenged himself by robbing his hen-roost of a large cock, with splendid yellow feathers and a noble comb. Archy having carefully cut open and disembowelled the cock, without injuring its magnificent plumage, formed it into a helmet. Concealing it under his great-coat, and occupying a prominent seat in church, immediately opposite the pulpit, he patiently waited, with becoming gravity, until the minister had reached the climax of his discourse, and was eloquently addressing the congregation, when, stooping down, he adjusted his helmet, tying the legs of the cock under his chin, its tail feathers drooping behind, and the head, with its glowing comb and appendages, stuck up before; then assuming his former position, with folded arms, he gazed on the minister, who, it may be well believed, returned the gaze with awful gravity. While the congregation joined him in the gaze, their gravity was considerably less.

A friend of mine met Archy on the highway, and, wishing to draw him out, asked his opinion of several travellers as they passed. The first was a very tall man. Archy remarked that he had never seen any man before so near heaven! Of another he said that he had "the sportsman's eye and the soldier's step," which was singularly true in its description.

A Skye laird who was fond of trying a pass of arms with Archy, met him one day gnawing a bone. "Shame on you, Archy," said the laird, "why do *you* gnaw a bone in that way?" "And to what use, sir," asked Archy in reply, "would you have me put it?" "I advise you," said the laird, "to throw it in charity to the first dog you meet." "Is that your advice? then I throw it to yourself!" said Archy, shying the bone at the laird's feet.

While correcting these sheets, an old woman from Skye, now in Glasgow, and who knew Archy well, has repeated to me the words which he never failed to use with reverence as his grace before meat. They seem to contain some allusion to the sin of the evil eye, so much feared and hated by the old Highlanders. I translate them literally:—

> " May my heart always bless my eyes ;
> And my eyes bless all they see ;
> And may I always bless my neighbour,
> Though my neighbours should never bless me.　Amen."

By this time I fear that my sedate and wise readers will conclude that a sympathy with fools comes very naturally to me. I must bow my head to the implied rebuke. It is, I know, a poor defence to make for my having indulged, however briefly, in such biographies, that the literary world has produced many longer ones of greater fools less innocent of crime, less agreeable, and less beneficial to society, than those which I have so imperfectly recorded among my reminiscences of the old Highlands.*

But lest any one should imagine for a moment that I treat lightly the sufferings of those deprived

---

* Since writing the above, I have heard of a distinguished general officer who left the Highlands in his youth, but returned a short time ago to visit his early home, who, with great seriousness and *naïveté*, said to my informant, " Will you believe me when I tell you that among the many things so long associated with my remembrances, and which I miss much—are —are—pray don't laugh at me when I confess it—are my old friends the fools!" I heartily sympathise with the general !

of God's highest gift of reason, let me say that *my* fools were generally strong and healthy in body, and in many cases, as I have already hinted, took a share in farm-work, boating, fishing, &c., and the treatment which they received was, on the whole, humane and benevolent. At the same time I do not forget another very different class, far lower in the scale of humanity, which, owing to many circumstances that need not be detailed here, was a very large one in the Highlands—I mean, creatures weak in body and idiotic in mind, who, in spite of the tenderest affection on the part of their poor parents, were yet miserable objects for which no adequate relief existed. Such cases indeed occur everywhere throughout the kingdom to a greater extent, I think, than most people are aware of. Those idiots are sometimes apparently little re-moved above the beasts that perish, yet they nevertheless possess a Divine nature never wholly extinguished, which is capable of being developed to a degree far beyond what the most sanguine could anticipate who have not seen what wise, patient, benevolent, and systematic education is capable of accomplishing. The coin with the

X

King's image on it, though lying in the dust with the royal stamp almost obliterated, may be again marveilously cleansed and polished. I therefore hail asylums for idiot children as among the most blessed fruits of Christian civilisation. Though, strange to say, they are but commencing among us, yet I believe the day is near when they will be recognised as among the most needed, the most successful, and most blessed institutions of our country.

## STAFFA TOURISTS FORTY YEARS AGO.

UNTIL within the last forty years the West Highlands was a land of mystery to the London summer tourist. Dr Johnson had indeed penetrated those fastnesses, and returned in safety to London, not only without having been robbed, or obliged to wear a kilt and live on whisky and oatmeal porridge, but with a most flattering account of the people, and describing the clergy and gentry as polite, educated, and hospitable. Sir Joseph Banks and Mr Pennant had brought into notice, and admirably delineated, the marvellous Island of Staffa, not far from Inchkenneth and Iona, both of which islands were visited by Johnson, and excited his enthusiasm,—the one for its Laird, and the other for its memories of early piety. But when Scott adopted the Highlands as the subject of romantic story and song, investing its scenery, its feudal history, its chiefs, clans, old traditions, and wild superstitions, with all the charm of his genius, then began a new era of comfort in every spot which his magic wand had touched. The "Lord of the Isles," and the "Lady of the Lake," became the pioneers of the tourist. Good roads took the place of the old bridle-paths winding among the heather. Coaches-and-four bowled through wild passes where savage clans used to meet in deadly combat. Steamers foamed on every Loch and banished the water kelpies. Telescopes were substituted for second sight. Waiters with white neckcloths and white towels received the travellers, where red deer used to sleep undisturbed. The eagles were banished from the mountains, and "Boots" reigned in the valleys.

. Forty years ago steamers had not mingled their smoke with the mists of the hills, and the Highlands had not become common as Vauxhall to the

Londoners.  It was then a land of distance and
darkness.  No part of Europe is so unknown now to
the fireside traveller, as the Hebrides were then to
the English.  With the "Foreign Bradshaw" and
"Murray," any man now can so arrange his journey
as to fix the day on which he will arrive, and the
hour at which he will dine in any town from the
Baltic to the Mediterranean.  As he sits in his club
in London, he notes the minute when his train will
arrive at Moscow or Milan, and almost the day
when his steamer will land him at New York, and
when he can reach the Prairies of the far West,
or gaze on the Falls of Niagara or St Anthony.
The Hebrides are therefore now at his door.  He
dines one day in London, and sups the next
beneath the shadow of Ben Lomond or Ben
Cruachan.  But at the time I speak of, the journey northward to Glasgow by coach or post-
horses was tedious, tiresome, and expensive.
When the Highlands proper were entered upon,
at Dumbarton or Callender, then, between bad
roads and peat-reeked pothouses, rude boats without comfort, and a crew innocent of English, with
all the uncertainties of tides, squalls, heavy seas,

and heavy rain, a tour among the islands of Scotland was far more hazardous than one now to
India or America.

The continent of Europe was then still more
difficult of access, and during the wars of Na-
poleon, was well-nigh inaccessible.  Accordingly
such persons as loved adventure and had time
and money at their command, and who, above
all, could obtain good letters of introduction,
selected a Highland journey, with Staffa as its
grand termination.

Alas for the hospitable Highland mansion
which happened to be situated at a convenient
resting-place for the tourist *en route* to some spot
of interest!  There was then prevalent among
southern tourists a sort of romantic idea of the
unlimited extent of Highland hospitality, and of
the means at its command.  It was no unusual
occurrence for the traveller to land at any hour
of the day or night which winds, tides, or boatmen might determine; to walk up to the house
of the Highland gentleman; to get a dinner,
supper, and all, plentiful and comfortable; to retire to bed, without a thought where the family

had packed themselves (so that the travelling party might have accommodation); and finally to obtain next day, or, if it rained, days after, carts, horses, boats, men, with baskets of provisions, crammed with roast fowls, cold lamb, cold salmon, grouse, milk, brandy, sherry, and bottles of whisky. The potato digging, the hay cutting, or the reaping of crops might be put a stop to; what of that? they are *so* hospitable in the Highlands! And then these summer visitants bade farewell with shaking of hands and waving of handkerchiefs, and with the usual stereotyped hope expressed that, "should they ever come to England and visit Land's End, how glad," &c.—But the reception was nevertheless all put down to a *habit* of the country, a thing called Highland hospitality, something like speaking Gaelic, smoking tobacco, or wearing the kilt.

And I am compelled to acknowledge that the families who thus received and entertained strangers never looked on their doing so in that "light of common day" in which I cannot help placing these transactions. "What *can* the travellers do?" I remember well the lady of one

of those hospitable houses saying when a large
party of strangers had departed after a stay of
several days; "there are no inns where they can
put up, but those wretched holes. And then the
travellers are so nice! It is truly delightful to
meet with such well-bred, intelligent ladies and
gentlemen—I would put myself to much more
trouble to enjoy their society." And the young
ladies of the family would chime in and declare
that they had "never met sweeter girls than
those Smiths, especially Caroline, and that they
were so vexed when they went away,—and as for
the young men of the party——!" Here all the
ladies were unanimous. The host was equally
friendly—"I don't grudge my wine a bit," he
would say, "to Mr Smith. I never met a better
educated, scholarly man, nor one better informed."
This is really a true picture of the feelings at the
time with which those English travellers were
received; for very few penetrated those recesses
except the higher classes, or "well-to-do gentry,"
who had time and money at their disposal, and
who had sufficient culture to love scenery for its
own sake, to appreciate the manners of the coun-

try, and cheerfully to accommodate themselves to its inconveniences.

One may be surprised to know how comforts were extemporised in those out-of-the-way places. The process was a very simple one. Large stores of groceries, and all the materials required for every after-dinner luxury except the dessert, were obtained periodically from Greenock or Glasgow. Bread was the chief difficulty; as baking wheaten bread, strange to say, was an art never practised by Highland families. But they had all sorts of delicious hot *scones* made of flour, or barley-meal, in addition to crisp oatmeal cakes, while a loaf was brought from Oban by her Majesty's Post once or twice a week. Every other kind of food was abundant. As a Highland farmer once re-marked, in pointing to his plentiful board, "We growed all that on our ownselves!"

As the tourist voyages through the Sound of Mull he can hardly fail to notice Aros Castle— unless he be reading, as some do, amidst the noblest scenery, a green or yellow-backed shilling novel. Aros was the landing-place in those old days for parties going to visit Staffa. A narrow

isthmus of two or three miles of road here connects the Sound with an inland arm of the
sea, on the other side of Mull, which leads out
past Inchkenneth and Ulva, to the islands of
Staffa and Iona.   When these famous localities
had to be approached by boats from Oban, it
was necessary to take the safe and sheltered passage of the Sound, rather than to run the risk,
whether from dead calm or wild storm, of attempting to sail outside of Mull with a bare rock only
as the termination of the voyage.   And here I
am reminded—for all gossips, like Mrs Quickly,
are ever tempted to digress in the telling of their
story—of the "tricks upon travellers" which those
Highland boatmen were sometimes tempted to
perpetrate.   Between Oban and Mull there are
several bad "tideways" which, in certain combi-
nations of wind and tide, are apt to produce a
heavy sea of a most dangerous kind to all except
very skilled boatmen; and sometimes putting
even their skill to the severest test.   One of the
pilots of those famous wherries was nicknamed
"Daring Calum," on account of the almost reck-
less boldness with which he undertook to steer

his boat on the wildest days, when others, more prudent, would not venture to cross the stormy ferry to Mull. One of the fierce tideways on this passage was called "the dirks," from the figure of the waves which rose on every side, tossing their sharp heads in the sky. On one occasion when Calum was piloting a Staffa party through this wild and foaming tide, the spray of the waves flew over the bow and wet the passengers. A rival of Calum on board remarked in Gaelic to a companion, loud enough to be heard by Calum, "Bad steering that!" "Bad steering!" echoed Calum, with an angry growl; "there is no man living could carry a boat so dry through that wild sea; and if you think *you* can do it, come here and take the helm and try it!" The rival pilot thus challenged took the helm, and ordering the boat to be put about—after passing all the danger!—once more crossed the roaring tideway, which had thus necessarily to be crossed a third time before the boat could resume her voyage in the right direction! The poor passengers were of course ignorant of the cause of their prolonged misery amidst the salt sea foam. Nemesis at last overtook poor Calum;—for though he proved his superiority as a steersman on the occasion referred to, and survived his triumph thirty years, he was drowned at last.

Choosing the comparative safety of the inner passage, the travellers landed at Aros, crossed to the opposite side, and there took a boat—with four stout rowers, or a sail, in case of wind—for Staffa, which was thus reached in five or six hours.

The first time we visited the famous island was by this route; and though we have gone to it by steamer several times since then, yet the impression made by the first visit remains, and can never more be obliterated—neither, alas! can the fear be renewed. We had time and quiet to enjoy the scene, without the screaming of steam-whistles or the impatient wrath of steam-engines, threatening to burst unless passengers rush on board at the fixed hour.

It was a glorious summer morning. We started about daybreak, with four Highland boatmen, capital rowers, capital singers of boat songs, and crack men when sail had to be carried.

We swept along the shore, and had full time to see and enjoy all the glories of the beach, its huge boulders, its deep black water shadowed by the beetling cliffs—with all the magnificent outlines of bold rugged headlands, fantastic rocks and ever-varying "giant-snouted crags;" with echoing caves, and secluded bays—until we at last glided into the great ocean, with its skyline broken by the Treshinish isles, the Dutchman's cap, and the more distant Tyree. A long glassy swell heaved in from the Atlantic; flocks of all kinds of birds swam and dived, and screamed around us. At length came Staffa in solemn silence, revealing its own stately grandeur of pillared cave and precipice. Alone and undisturbed we listened to the music of the ocean in that marvellous temple not built with hands. There were no human beings there but the boatmen, and they seemed as natural to the island as the limpets on its rocks, or the brown tangle which waved among the waters that laved its sides. To see Staffa thus was like visiting a great cathedral for worship;—to see it with a steamboat company is like visiting the same cathedral desecrated by a public meeting!

But to return to Staffa tourists before steamboat days. There were four "hospitable houses" situated in this Mull transit, where persons with letters of introduction always put up. One was Mr Maxwell's, "the factor" or "chamberlain" for the Duke of Argyle, his house being close to the old castle of Aros. The other, about a mile off, was Mr Stewart's, the kind-hearted proprietor of Achadashenaig—a name which no Englishman ever pretended to pronounce correctly. On the other side of Mull, and beneath Benmore, was Colonel Campbell's of Knock—a brave and distinguished old officer; and then, six miles nearer Staffa, was the most frequented of all, Ulva House, the residence of Mr M'Donald, the laird of Staffa—the very impersonation of Highland hospitality.

There was one small inn on the Sound, "the Shore House," which received all extras, including the servants of those who were accommodated at Aros, and the neighbouring house of Acha—&c.

When the travelling season commenced, the telescopes of these houses were busy in reconnoitring the white sails of boats coming from Oban. There were three well-known "wherries," the "Iona," "Staffa," and "Fingal," whose rig was familiar from afar. "I think that is a Staffa party!" was a remark that roused the household, and caused a group to gather round the telescope, as the distant white speck was observed advancing towards the bay. By-and-by a flag was discovered fluttering from the peak. It was the sign of a party; but coming to which house? Aros, Acha, &c., or the inn?—or to cross the isthmus to Knock or Ulva? It was necessary to prepare for a possible invasion! The larder of Aros was therefore examined *in case;* bedrooms were put in order; innocent chickens, geese, ducks, or turkey poults killed; and preparations for every comfort set a-going. Mutton, lamb, fish, or game, were always ready. But the destination of the party could not possibly be discovered until at the door of Aros which was nearest the point, where all landed. Suddenly a group is seen ap-

proaching the door, near the old castle; pater-
familias and his wife leading; sons, daughters,
and servants following; with the luggage borne
on the shoulders of four boatmen. Then the
official rap at the door. Nancy, the girl, is
dressed in her best, and "looks both neat and
comely." Host and hostess, backed by the young
ladies of the family, are prepared with bow and
courtesy, smile and welcome, to read the letter
from the Duke of Argyle recommending Sir John
This, or my friend Lord That, to the kind attention of his Grace's viceroy; and soon all are
settled down in comfort to rest for a few days ere
they begin the voyage to Staffa under their hosts'
direction.

A pleasing remembrance of many of these
visitors remained for life in the memories of their
hosts, and in cases not a few, the visitors retained
a grateful and equally long remembrance of their
Highland friends. I remember well how the "factor" at Aros used to enumerate the names of
those who had impressed him by their manners,
their knowledge, their scholarship, or their wit.
He was himself an excellent classic, and the

visit of an Oxford or Cambridge man was always
a delight to him.    He had stories of many then
beginning their travels, whose names have since
become famous in the world.    But he frankly
confessed that Tom Sheridan, who accompanied
the Lord Lorne of the day, was out of sight the
pleasantest fellow he had ever met with.    The
visit was memorable from the number of bottles
of old port which were consumed, and the late
hours which for a series of nights were spent
amidst songs and shouts of laughter.    The factor
declared that he could not have survived another
week of Tom, whose stories and witticisms became a large literary property to him in after
years, and were often told after dinner to his
guests.

When Walter Scott was expected to visit Mull,
an intense anxiety was felt as to which of the
houses would have the privilege of entertaining
him.    Scott was then known as the poet, not as
the novelist ; and was touring it in the Highlands
with his young and most engaging wife.    The
factor, who was an enthusiast in ballad poetry,

Y

was sorely grieved when he saw the party pass his door on their way to Ulva House. But on Scott's return the factor had the happiness of having him under his roof for an evening. "Ha!" exclaimed Scott, on their meeting, "what puts a Maxwell and a Scott in this part of the world? We should meet, lad, on the Border!" That evening was also memorable in the history of Staffa parties.

I must not omit to record in passing the lines written by Scott, in the album of Ulva, on the Laird of Staffa—or "Staffa," as he was always called :—

> " Staffa ! king of all good fellows,
>   Well betide thy hills and valleys ;
>   Lakes and inlets, steeps and shallows ;
>   Mountains which the gray mist covers,
>   Where the chieftain spirit hovers,
>   Pausing as its pinions quiver,
>   Stretched to quit this land for ever !
>   May all kind influence rest above thee,
>   On all thou lov'st, and all who love thee !
>   For warmer heart 'twixt this and Jaffa,
>   Beats not than in the breast of Staffa !"

I quote from memory. But whoever possesses now that Ulva album must be able to select from its pages some memorial lines which would have some interest.*

Occasionally some rare specimens of the Cockney make their appearance in those parts. One instance of the credulity of the species may be mentioned, although to believe it seems to demand an almost equal amount of credulity in the reader. A London citizen presented himself at Aros. On entering the room where the family were assembled, he paused, and looked around him with an expression of wonder; then, apologising for his intrusion, he begged permission to return with his travelling companion, just for five minutes, to see the house. The landlady of "The Shore House," the small inn where the astonished visitor "put up," heard him say to his friend as he ad-

---

* The Ettrick Shepherd also left a memento in the album, but one less complimentary to the island than Scott's :—

> " I've roamed 'mong the peaks and the headlands of Mull,
> Her fields are neglected, uncultured, and weedy,
> Her bosom is dark, and her heaven is dull,—
> Her sons *may* be brave, but they're horribly (?) greedy."

An indignant native thus replies—

> " O Shepherd of Ettrick, why sorely complain,
> Though the boatmen were greedy of grog?
> The beauties of Staffa by this you proclaim
> Were but pearls thrown away on a *Hogg*."

dressed him in breathless haste, " I say, Dick, you must come with me instantly. I have got permission to bring you. We are quite mistaken about the people here, I assure you, — confoundedly mistaken! You will not believe me until you see it with your own eyes, but I was in a regular well-built gentleman's house, with carpets, furniture, a pianoforte, actually, and the girls dressed in nice white gowns!" It is a fact that these same travellers had brought red cloth, beads, and several articles of cutlery, to barter with the natives! They seemed to have consulted Cook's Voyages as the only reliable book of information how to deal with savages.

I have often to crave the reader's indulgence for inflicting my " auld-lang-syne" gossip on him. But these old travelling days belong to a past never to return ; and those old kind-hearted hosts who made the tour easy and agreeable to many a happy family, and to many an invalid in search of health, have all passed away, and have left no representatives in their once hospitable homes. I like to record their names even in the most evanescent form.

## THE CUSTOMS OF NEW YEAR'S EVE
## AND MORNING,

### AS NARRATED BY A HIGHLAND PIPER.*

ACCORDING to promise, I will give you a true account of the manner in which we used to part with the old year, and welcome the new, during my younger days in the family of Glendessarie. The last night of the year was, as you know, called *oidhche Challüinn*, (the night of

---

* This chapter is translated from the first Gaelic magazine ever published, which was conducted by my father, the late Dr Macleod, of Glasgow. The account of these Highland customs, though bearing the signature of "Finlay the Piper," was written by himself, and is now offered, along with a few illustrative notes, as a Reminiscence of the "Parish," and also as a characteristic specimen of the narratives of the Highland peasantry.

*Calluinn.**) They tell me that this word signifies *noise*, or *rattling;* and that the Highlanders so designated this night from the noisy mirth with which they celebrated it.

* The derivation of this word has sorely puzzled Celtic anti-quaries; and it is enough to show the straits to which they are reduced, to mention that some derive it from *Kalends*, and others from the name of the goddess Kalydon, said to have been worshipped by some tribes of Sclavonians on the shores of the Baltic. We consider the explanation given by the piper fully as good as either of these. -Let it be remembered, however, that the corresponding term *Hagmana*, used of old in England, (possibly still in some parts of it,) or *Hogmanay*, universally used in Scotland, is of equally uncertain origin—some deriving it from the Greek " *Hagia mēnē*," sacred month, while others resolve it into the French, *Homme est né*, "the man is born," referring of course to our Saviour's nativity. And we may remark, without going into anti-quarian dissertation, that, with the view of discovering the derivation of the word *Yule*, used in England and Scotland, almost every language from Hebrew to Danish has been questioned and tortured, all to little purpose.

The Gaelic term *Calluinn*, then, is not alone in the mystery of its origin. The *Cainneal*, or *Coinneal*, used to denote the first day of the year, has also exercised the ingenuity of linguists. Its simplest solution is, however, probably the nearest to the truth. It literally signifies candle, and in all likelihood refers to the illuminations customary at that joyous season.

*Nalluig*, or *Nollaig*, the Gaelic term for Christmas, is evidently of the same origin with the French *Noaille*, derived from *Natalis*.

We need say nothing about the Highlanders observing the season of the New Year as a festive and joyous one. Almost all nations, Pagan and Christian, have done so, visiting their friends, feasting on the best, and giving a liberal supply to their cattle as well. The

Well, my father was piper to Glendessarie, as was his father before him, and every son of mine has, as soon as weaned, taken to the pipe-chanter just as naturally as the young kid takes to scram-

piper giving a sheaf of corn to his cows reminds one of Burns's well-known lines to his old mare Maggie, on New Year's Day.

The expression of their joy through rhymes was also common to other nations as well as to the Highlanders. Abundant specimens both of French and English verses used on occasions are to be found in our older books, nor are we aware that the Gaelic rhymes deserve any special mention. We have heard many which were more doggerel —others, again, through which a vein of satirical humour ran, well fitted to rebuke any churlish tendency in those who were addressed; but the great majority of them, like the English ones, expressed kindly wishes towards the households visited, while they all craved a good *Calluinn* for the rhyming visitors.

The carrying about of the *hide*, beating on it with sticks, and surrounding the house three times, going always in the direction of the sun, or *Deas-iŭl*, is at least in modern times peculiar to the Highlanders. Till very recently it was generally observed, and is, we believe, in remote localities still practised. Some writers imagine that the thus walking around the house, clothed in the skin of a slaughtered animal, has reference to sacrificial and propitiatory rites. We learn, however, from "Brand's Popular Antiquities," edited by Ellis, that this is a remnant of the wild fantastic orgies of the old Roman Saturnalia, where men often disguised themselves in the skins of wild beasts, and abandoned themselves to the wildest enjoyments. Early Christian writers state that many of their flocks followed after these heathenish customs, saying expressively — "vestiuntur pellibus pecudum"—"they are clothed in the skins of cattle."

We read of slight traces of this strange transformation being discernible in Yorkshire till a comparatively recent date; but, like many

bling up the rocks. It was the habit of this family to gather for *Callüinn night* (New Year's Eve) all the tenantry on their lands, young and old, especially all the foster-fathers, mothers, brothers, and sisters, and according to wont, *Evan Bān maor* (Fair-haired Evan) the ground-officer, went round amongst them a few days before the time. " It is

other old customs, it found beyond the Grampian mountains a more lasting abode than anywhere else.

One other observance we mention which we believe was peculiar to the Highlands. The *Caisein üchd*, or the piece of skin covering the breast bone of sheep or cow—more especially the former, with its short curly wool—was kept as carefully as was the hide ; and on New Year's Eve, after being well singed in the fire, was applied to the nose of every one within the house, visitor or dweller. Thereafter it was carried to the byre, and the olfactories of the cattle also regaled with its fragrance. All we can say of this practice is, that it was observed with the view of conferring some benefit on man and beast. Pennant mentions that the cattle in the North Highlands were, on the evening in question, made to smell burnt juniper.

We gather from the old Statistical Account that in some parts of the Highlands *Hogmanay* is called *oidhche dar na Coille*—i.e., " The night of the fecundation of the trees," and that according to the direction of the wind on this night the character of the following season might be predicted. The fresh wind promised fish and milk. The south, warmth and general fruitfulness. The north, cold and shivering—literally, *skinning*. And the east wind, even as in the land of Pharaoh, the withering of the fruit.

For the principal statements in the foregoing long note, see " Brand's Popular Antiquities."

the wish of the family," says he, "that we should observe the *Callŭinn* as of old ; and see, my lads, that you have your *Camain* (shinties, or clubs) right and ready for New Year's Day." The piper set off in his full Highland garb about the height of the evening, (as the sun was beginning to decline.) We reached the great house ; and can I expect that my heart will ever be as light and joyous as it was on that night ? The young ladies of the family met us with bows of ribbon for the chanter of the pipe. The piper played a round on the green before the door, as the men gathered.

The time of *Callŭinn* came, when some one had to carry the dry cow hide on his back and run round the house, and every one that could tried to get a stroke at it with his stick. "Who will carry the *hide* this year?" says Evan Bān. "Who but Pāra Mōr?" (Big Patrick) says one. "Who but Broad John?" says another. "Out with the hide, Pāra Mōr," says Evan Bān ; "and you, Broad John, stand by his shoulder in case he may stumble." Pāra Mōr drew the hide about his head, taking a twist of the tail firmly around his fist.

"*Cothrom na Féinné*," (*i.e.*, fair play as among the Fingalians, or Fingalian justice,*) exclaimed he, as he drew near the door of the house where the Laird (*Fear a' bhaile*, the man of the place) was standing with his *Caman* (shinty) in his hand "*Callŭinn* here!" says he, giving the first rattle to the hide. Pāra Mōr set off, but swift of foot as he was, the men of the Glen kept at his heel, and you would think that every flail in the country was at work on the one threshing-floor, as every mother's son of them struck and rattled at him, shouting, "A *Callŭinn* here! The *Callŭinn* of the yellow sack of hide! Strike ye the skin! A *Callŭinn* here!" Three times they went *Deas-iul* (in a southerly direction, according to the course of the sun) round the house. "Blow up, piper,"

---

* We will not enter on the controversy as to whether "Fingal fought," or "Ossian sang." We must remark, however, that expressions like the above, referring to the belief in the existence of a band called Féinne or Fingahans, renowned for dauntless valour, high-souled honour, and unfailing constancy, are in daily use among the Highlanders from east to west, and from north to south.

We may add that the names of the principal heroes, and the scenes of their exploits, are familiar as household words among young and old.

(*Seid sŭas*) said Evan Bān, "and when the company are in order, let them assemble in the rent-room." My father played *Failt' a' Phrionnsa*, (the Prince's welcome;) for though there was not in the kingdom a man more leal and loyal to the family which then sat upon the throne, yet he loved to listen to this tune; and often have I seen him shedding tears on hearing that thrilling music which had stirred his forefathers to deeds of manliness on these renowned battle-fields, where alas! they lost their men and their estates.

We went into the chamber where the family and the neighbouring gentry were assembled. He himself, the graceful president of the feast, stood in the midst, and his mild, winsome lady by his side. The lovely young branches of the family were around them, though, woe's me! few of them are alive to-day. The Laird (good man) of *Corrie* was standing at the door to guard against any one slipping in without saying his *Callŭinn* rhyme, and John Bān, of the casks, (the butler,) beside him with a bottle in his hand. Every one had a rhyme that night except Lowland John and a young conceited fellow from the Glen, who had been for a year or two in Glasgow, and affected to have forgotten his native tongue, as well as the customs of his native land. John Bān dealt round the drink, and the bread and cheese, piled up plenteously, were distributed freely.

After a short time the songs began. He himself gave us an *iorram*, (boat song,) and well could he do it. Many a sweet song, lay, and ditty was sung, as well as those which were historical and commemorative. The fox-hunter gave us *Dan a' choin ghlais*, (the song of the gray dog,) and Angus of the Satires repeated a tale of the Fingalians. After the songs the dancing began, very different from the slow, soft, silken steps of the present day. First came in a smart dame, dressed like a housekeeper, with a bunch of keys jingling by her side; strong, sturdy, and active she looked. The woman sang *Port á Beul*, (*i.e.*, a tune from the mouth,) selecting *Cailleach an Dŭdain*, (the old wife of the mill-dust,) and it was she who capered and turned, and sprang nimbly. After this they danced the *Dŭbh-Lŭidncach*, (Black Sluggard.) But the best fun was when the "Goat Dance," "Weave the

Gown," (*Figh an Gŭn,*) and the Thorny Croft (*Croit am Droighin*) were danced.*

The time of parting at length came. The gentry

---

* We have preserved these names in the hope that some one more learned than we in Highland antiquities may explain them. The singing called *Port â Beul,* a tune from the mouth, we have ourselves heard, and heard with high pleasure. In the absence of musical instruments, persons trained to it imitate dancing-music with the voice, and when they sing in parts the imitation is remarkably happy. We have seen a company dancing for hours to this primitive music.

As to the dances, there are some of them we can give no account of. A poor remnant of the "Sword Dance" is still preserved among us, and may be often witnessed on the stage; sometimes on the decks of steamers, and even on the streets of our large towns, burlesqued by idle vagabonds who assuredly disgrace "the garb of Old Gaul," by exhibiting it in such contemptible performances. We learn from Brand, that among the Northern nations, and of old in England, the Sword Dance was practised on the most public and solemn occasions, and in a way that put the skill, the strength, and the nerve of the performers to a very severe test.

We know that in one or other of those mentioned in our text— the Thorny Croft—there was much pantomimic acting, as well as very dolorous recitative. A farmer, whose lot it was to be located on ground covered with thorns and briers, gives a woeful account of the hardship of his fate—with the view, we believe, of exciting the compassion of some fair spectator—and we believe there was a considerable amount of dramatic acting in all of them.

The *Dŭbh-Lŭidneach*—Black-Sluggard, or black clumsy one— we may observe, is the name by which the natives of Lochaber still designate the yacht in which Argyle sailed away on the day of the battle of Inverlochy—leaving his men to the fury of Montrose and the MacDonalds. Of the dance so called we can give no account.

gave us the welcome of the New Year with cordiality and kindliness, and we set off to our homes.
"My lads," says he himself, "be valiant on the
field to-morrow. The sea-board men (*Leththir—
i.e.*, Halfland) boast that they are to beat us Glen-
men at the shinty match this year." Thus we
passed the last night of the year at Glendessarie,
and neither I nor my father ever saw a quarrel,
or heard an improper word at such a gathering.
It is since the gentry have ceased thus to mingle
freely with the people that disgusting drunkenness
has become common in these black tippling-houses,
which prove the highway to almost every vice.
The people of each estate were as one family—the
knot of kindness tying every heart together, and
the friendly eye of the superiors was over us all.

I might here give many useful advices to our
lairds; but they do not understand Gaelic, and
they would not take the counsel of the piper, so I
must hasten to tell you about our way of passing
the first day of the New Year.

On this New Year's morn the sun was late of
showing his countenance; and after he came in
sight his appearance was pale and drowsy. The

mist was resting lazily on the hill-side; the crane
was rising slowly from the meadow; the belling of
the stag was heard on the mountain; the black-
cock was in the birch-wood, dressing his feathers,
while his sonsie mate—the gray-hen—was slowly
walking before him.

After I had saluted my family, and implored
the blessing of the Highest on their heads, I prepared the Christmas sheep,* (*Caora Nallaig,*) gave
a sheaf of corn to the cattle, as was customary, and
was getting myself in order, when in walked Pāra
Mōr, and my gossip Angus Ōg, (young Angus.)
They gave me the welcome of the New Year. I
returned it with equal heartiness. Then Pāra
Mōr produced a bottle from his pocket. "A
black-cock," says he, "whose gurgling voice (crowing, *Celticé, gŏgail*) is more musical than any roar
(*rāan*) that ever came out of the chanter of the
pipe." We tasted to one another, and then Mary,
my wife, set before us a small drop of the genuine
Ferintosh, which she had stored up long ago for
great occasions in the big chest.

It was my duty to gather the people together

* See note, p. 344.

this morning with the sound of the pipe. So we
set off, going from farm to farm up the Glen,
making the son of the cave of the rock (*i.e.*, echo)
answer to my music. I played "*A Mhnathan a'
Ghlinne so;*" * and if the pipe had been dry that
day it had ample means of quenching its thirst!
The company continually increased its numbers
until we came down by the other side of the Glen
to the ground-officer's house, where it was appointed for us to get our morning-meal. The
lady had sent a three-year-old wedder to his
house. We had a roebuck from the corrie of

---

* This still popular pipe tune, known, we believe, as Breadalbane's
March, is said to have been composed on the following occasion :—
The father of *John Glas*, *i.e.*, Gray John, of Breadalbane, to whom
frequent reference was made in the late case of disputed succession, was married to a daughter of the Earl of Caithness. The
promised dowry was not paid to him, and he, apparently content with his wife herself as his portion, lived and died in peace with
the Sinclairs. His son, John Glas, however, was of a different
mind. Collecting a hardy band of Campbells from the age of
thirty-five to that of fifty, he made a secret and sudden raid on the
land of the Sinclairs, gathered as much spoil as would cover the
amount of his mother's tocher, utterly defeated the Caithness-men,
who were unprepared for such an invasion, and, as he was leaving
their territory, early in the morning, he summoned the poor women
to arise, telling them that their cattle had been lifted, and their
husbands wounded.

yew-trees ; fish from the pool of whitings ; and
such quanties of cheese, butter, and solid oat-
cake, sent by the neighbours round about, as
would suffice for as many more—though we were
fifty men in number, besides women and children.
Grace was said by Lachlan of the Questions,
(*Lachum ceistear,*) the Bible reader. Evan Bān
well sustained the hospitable character of the
house which he represented. We had an ample
and a cheerful feast.

Breakfast over, I set off and played the tune of
the *Glasmheŭr*, while Red Ewen, the old soldier,
was marshalling the men. We reached *Guala-
nancärn,* (the shoulder of the cairns,) where the
gentry were to meet us ; and before we knew
where we were, who placed himself at our head
but our own young Donald, the heir of the family !
He had reached home that very morning, having
hastened on without sleep, or rest, all the way
from Dun-Edin, (Edinburgh.) Dear heart ! he
was the graceful sapling. I could not for a while
blow a breath into the pipe, " Play up, Finlay,"
says Pāra Mōr. " What sadness has seized you ? "
" Sadness ! " said I ; " very far is it from me." The

Z

people of the sea-board then came in view, and
*Alastair* Roy of the Bay at their head.   When the
two companies observed each other, they raised
a loud shout of mutual rejoicing.   We reached
the field, and many were the salutations between
friends and acquaintances exchanged there.

The sun at length shone forth brightly and
cheerfully.   On the eminences around the field
were the matrons, the maidens, and the children
of the district, high and low, all assembled to
witness the *Camanachd*, (shinty match.)   The goal
at each end of the large field was pointed out, and
the two leaders began to divide and choose each
his men.   "I claim you!" ('*Buailiah mi ort*,
literally, "I will strike on thee,") says young
Donald.   "I permit you," (*Leigidh mi leat*,) says
*Alastair* Roy of the Bay.   "If so," says young
Donald, "then Donald Bān, of Culloden, is mine."
This was by far the oldest man present, and you
would think his two eyes would start from his
head with delight as he stepped proudly forth, at
being the first chosen.

When the men were divided into two companies
—forty on each side—and refreshments set at

each goal, Alastair Roy flung his shinty high up in the air. "*Bas, no Cas*, Donald of the Glen," said he (*i.e.*, *Head*, or *Handle*.) "Handle, which will defy your handling till nightfall!" replies Donald. Alastair gained the throw, (toss,) and was about to strike the ball immediately, when the other exclaimed, "A truce, (*Deisdé;*) let the rules of the game be first proclaimed, so that there may be fairness, good-fellowship, and friendship observed among us, as was wont among our forefathers." On this Evan Bān stepped forth and proclaimed the laws, which forbade all quarrelling, swearing, drunkenness, and coarseness; all striking, tripping, or unfairness of any kind; and charged them to contend in a manful, but friendly spirit, without malice or grudge, as those from whom they were descended had been wont to do.

Alastair Roy, as he was entitled to do, gave the first stroke to the ball, and the contest began in earnest; but I have not language to describe it. The sea-board men gained the first game. But it was their only game. Young Donald and his men stripped to their work, and you would think

the day of *Blàr na Lèine* (Battle of the Shirt)*
had come again.    Broad John gave a tremendous
blow, which sent the ball far beyond the goal.
We thus gained the day, and we raised the shout

---

* This was a very fierce clan battle recorded in history, and
of which tradition preserves a very vivid remembrance.    Macdonald of Moidart married one of the Frasers of Lovat.    The
son and heir, Ronald, was brought up at Lovat, or Beaufort
Castle, and was known to his clansmen as *Raonull Gallda*, or
Ronald the Lowlander.    At his father's death, he came to take
possession ; but to the utter disgust of the people, he forbade the
killing of ox or sheep for the inauguration feast, saying that
poultry would be quite enough.    He was at once dubbed Ronald of the Hens, expelled the country with ignominy, and a
natural brother, John of Moidart, chosen as chief in his unworthy
stead.    The Frasers were far too powerful to allow such an affront
to pass.    They speedily mustered, and, to "make assurance doubly
sure," asked, and obtained the aid of some friendly clans in the
direction of Strathspey.    They invaded Moidart with a force which
it was vain for the Macdonalds to resist.    They therefore betook
themselves to the most inaccessible fastnesses, and made no show
of opposition.    But whenever the invading host departed, the
Moidart men followed carefully in their track for the southern end
of Loch Lochy ; the auxiliaries from the east struck off by the
Badenoch road, judging their friends quite secure at such a distance
from the land of Moidart.    At the north end of Loch Lochy, however, quite close to where the Caledonian Canal enters that Loch,
the Moidart men made a fierce onslaught on the Frasers, now left
alone.    Both parties, it is said, stripped to the waist, and on the
"lucus a non lucendo" principle, the battle was called the Battle
of the Shirt.    "Ronald of the Hens" was slain, and the Frasers were defeated with great slaughter.    History carries us thus
far ; but we see in a ballad published by Mrs Ogilvie on the sub-

of victory; but all was kindness and good feeling among us.

In the midst of our congratulations Pāra Mōr shouted out, "Shame on ye, young men! Don't you see these nice girls shivering with cold? Where are the dancers? Play up the reel of Tullochgorum, Finlay." The dancing began, and the sun was bending low towards the Western Ocean before we parted. There was many a shin and many a cheek of the colour of the *Blae-berries* (*i.e.*, black and blue) that day, but there was neither hate nor grumbling about these matters.

We returned to the house of nobleness, as on the preceding evening. Many a torch was on that night beaming brightly in the hall of hospitality, though dark and lonely in its state to-day. We passed the night amid music and enjoyment, and parted not until the breaking of the dawn guided us to our own homes.

And now you have some account of the manner

ject, that eighty of the Fraser widows were considerate enough to bear each a posthumous son, and these not only restored the weakened clan, but, as a matter of course, inflicted dread vengeance on the men of Moidart.

n which your ancestors were in the habit of passing New Year's Eve and New Year's Morn—*Calluinn* and *Cainneal*—in days not long gone by.

I know that people will not now believe me,
yet I maintain that many good results followed
from this friendly mingling of gentles and com-
mons. Our superiors were at that time acquainted with our language and our ways. The
highest of them was not ashamed to address us
by name, in our native tongue, at kirk or market.
There were kindness, friendship, and fosterage
between us; and while they were apples on the
topmost bough, we were all the fruit of the same
tree. We felt ourselves united to them, and in
honouring and defending them we respected and
benefited ourselves. But, except in the case of
the one family under whom I now am,

> " All this has passed as a dream,
>    Or the breaking of the bubble on the top of the wave."

Our superiors dwell not among us; they know
not our language, and cannot converse with
us; and even their servants many of our Lairds
scorn to take from among their own men. They
must have them from the Lowlands—spindle-

shanked creatures, with short breeches and white stockings, but without pith or courage enough to rescue the young heir of the family from the beak of the turkey-cock! Not so were thy men, Donald of the Glen, on the day when "thy king landed in Moidart!"

## *THE SPIRIT OF ELD.*[*]

IN the olden time, there lived at the back of Beinn nan Sian, a goat-herd, named Gorla of the Flocks, who had three sons and one daughter.

[*] Mr Campbell, in his very able preface to his interesting collection of popular Highland Tales, says, p. 20:—"Dr Macleod, the best of living Gaelic scholars, printed one old tale somewhat altered with a moral added in his 'Leabhar nan Cnoc,' in 1834; but even his efforts to preserve and use this lore were unsuccessful;" and at p. 28 the same accomplished writer says:—"The old spirit of popular romance is surely not an evil spirit to be exorcised, but rather a good genius to be controlled and directed. Surely stories in which a mother's blessing, well earned, leads to success; in which the poor rise to be princes, and the weak and courageous overcome giants, in which wisdom excels brute force—surely even such frivolities as these are better pastime than a solitary whisky bottle, or sleep in grim silence."

The following tale is that referred to in the above words. It is not an actual transcript of any individual tale, but it embodies "the spirit of romance," and presents an example of the general tone and teaching of the old Highland tale, most faithfully and vividly. In

The herding of the kids was intrusted to her, the Darling of the Golden Hair.   On one of the days when she was on the breast of the hill herding the kids, a fleecy wreath of mist, white as the snow one night old, twined round the shoulder of the hill, encircled the solitary darling, and she was seen no more.

At the end of a year and a day, Ardan, the eldest son of the herdsman spoke, saying :—

"A year past to-day, my sister, the Darling of the Golden Hair, departed, and it is a vow and a word to me that I will not rest, or stay, by night or by day, until I trace her out, or share her lot."

"If thou hast so vowed, my son," says the father, "I will not hinder thee; but it would have been becoming, ere the word had gone forth from thy

Gaelic it possesses all the freshness and gracefulness which the late Dr Macleod's intimate knowledge of the Highland character, or rather his own thoroughly Celtic heart and imagination, along with complete mastery of the language, enabled him to give.   Very much of its life-like character is necessarily lost in the translation into a foreign tongue; but imperfect as it is, it may prove interesting to the thinking English reader, as a specimen of the style of teaching which served to nourish and strengthen among the Highlanders those qualities which, even their enemies being judges, they possessed in a very eminent degree—reverence for parents, hospitality, fidelity, and fearlessness.

mouth, to have asked thy father's consent. Arise, wife; prepare a cake for thy eldest son. He is going on a long journey."

His mother arose, and baked two cakes, a large and a small one.

"Now, my son," says she, "whether wilt thou have the large cake with thy mother's displeasure for going away without leave, or the small one with her blessing?"

"Mine be the large cake," said he, "and keep the small one with thy blessing for those who prefer it."

He departed, and in the winking of an eye he was out of sight of his father's house. He plashed through every pool, strode over every knoll. He travelled swiftly without sparing of limb, or thew, or sinew. He would catch the swift March wind which was before; but the swift March wind which was after him could not catch him. At length hunger seized him. He sat on a gray stone to eat the large cake, and the black raven of the wilderness sat on a snout of rock above him.

"A bit, a bit for me, Son of Gorla of the Flocks," says the raven.

"Nor bit, nor sup shalt thou have from me, thou ugly, black, grim-eyed beast. It is little enough for myself," says the Son of Gorla.

When this was over the edge of his chest, he again stretched his limbs. The swift March wind before him he would catch, but the swift March wind after him could not catch him. The moss shook as he drew near it. The dew fell off the branchy brown heath. The moor-cock flew to his most distant retreat. The evening was begining to darken. The black gloomy clouds of night were coming, and the soft silken clouds of day were departing. The little bright-coloured birds were seeking rest, at the foot of each bush, or in the top of each branch, amid the most sheltered nooks which they could find ; but not so was the Son of Gorla.

At length he saw afar off a little house of light; but though it was a long way off, he was not long in reaching it. When he entered, he saw a powerful-looking, stout, old gray-headed man stretched on a long bench on one side of the fire, and on the other a handsome maiden combing her waving tresses of golden hair.

"Come forward, youngster," says the old man. "Thou art welcome: often has my bright lamp attracted the traveller of the mountains. Come forward. Warmth, and shelter, and whatever comfort is in the dwelling on the hill are thine. Sit down, and, if it be thy pleasure, let thy news be heard."

"I am a fellow in search of employment," says the herdsman's eldest son. "The bright lamp of thy dwelling drew me to seek warmth and shelter for the night."

"If thou remain with me for a twelvemonth to herd my three dun hornless cows thou 'lt receive thy reward, and shalt have no reason to complain."

"I would not so advise him," says the maiden.

"Advice unsought was never esteemed," says the Son of Gorla. "I accept thine offer, sir: in the dawn of the morning I am thy servant."

Before the belling of the deer in the forest the Maiden of the Golden Hair and the Silver Comb milked the three dun hornless cows. ."There they are to thee," says the old man; "take charge of them, follow them, do not turn or hinder them. They will seek their own pasture; allow them to travel as they choose; keep thou behind them, and whatever comes in thy way do not part with them. Let thine eye be on them, on them alone: and whatever else thou seest or hearest, give not an eye to it. This is thy duty; be faithful, be diligent, and trust my word; thy diligence shall not be without reward." He went in charge of the cattle, but he was not long away when he saw a golden cock and a silver hen running on the ground before him. He chased them: but though every now and then they were almost in his grasp, it defied him to lay hold of them. He returned from the vain pursuit, reached the place where the three dun cows were feeding, and began again to herd them; but he was not long after them when he saw a wand of gold, and a wand of silver, twisting and turning on the plain before him, and he immediately set off after them. "It cannot be but that these are easier to catch than were the birds which deceived me," he said; but though he chased them, still he could not catch them. He betook himself again to the herding, and saw a grove of trees on which grew every kind of fruit that he had ever seen, and twelve kinds which he had never seen. He began to fill himself with the fruits. The dun cows set their faces homewards, and he followed them.

The Maid of the Golden Hair milked them; but instead of milk there came only a thin watery ooze. The old man understood how the case stood.

"False and faithless fellow," said he, "thou hast broken thy promise." He raised his magic club, struck the young man, and made a stone pillar of him, which stood three days and three years in the dwelling of the hill as a memorial of breaking the word and covenant of engagement.

When another day and another year had passed, red *Ruais*, Gorla's second son, said, "There are two days and two years since my lovely sister departed, and a day and a year since my big brother went off. 'Tis a vow and a word to me to go in search of them, and to share their lot." Like as it happened to the elder brother it happened in every respect to the second, and a stone pillar he is in the end of the dwelling on the hill, as a memorial of falsehood and failure in covenant.

A year and a day after this, the youngest son, brown-haired, pleasant Covan, spoke :—

"There are now three days and three years since we lost my beautiful sister. My beloved brothers have gone in search of her. Now, father, if it please thee, permit me to go after them, and to share their lot, and let not my mother prevent me. I pray for your consent. Do not refuse me."

"My consent and my blessing thou shalt have, Covan; and thy mother will not hinder thee."

"Shall I," said the mother, "prepare the large cake without my blessing, or the small cake, with the wish of my heart, and the yearning of my soul?"

"Thy blessing, mother, give thou unto me, and much or little as may be given along with it, I am content. The possession of the whole world would be a poor inheritance with thy curse upon it. A mother's blessing 'tis I who will not despise."

Brown-haired Covan, the Son of Gorla, departed, and as his father and mother were disappearing in the mist, his heart was full. He travelled with speed; he reached the wood of roes. He sat under a tree to eat of the cake which his gentle mother had baked for him.

"A bit, a bit for me," says the black raven of

the wilderness. "Covan, give me a bit, for I am faint."

"Thou'lt get a bit, poor bird," says Covan. "It is likely thou art more needful than I. It will suffice for us both. There is a mother's blessing along with it."

He arose and went on his way. He took shelter with the old man, and went to herd the three dun cows. He saw the golden cock and the silver hen, but he turned away his eyes; he followed the cattle. He saw the wand of gold and the wand of silver; but he remembered his promise, and did not go after them. He reached the grove, and saw the fruit that was so fair to the eye; but he did not taste of it. The three dun cows passed the wood. They reached a wide moor where the heather was burning. They went towards it. The flames were spreading, threatening to consume them all; but the cows entered into the midst of them. He did not attempt to prevent them, for such was his promise. He followed them through the fire, and not one of the hairs of his head was singed. He saw after this a large river which was swollen with the flood of the mountains. Across it went the dun cows, after them fearlessly went Covan. A short while after this, on a green plain was seen a beautiful house of worship, sheltered from the wind, brightened by the sun, from which was heard the melody of sweet songs and of holy hymns. The cattle lay down on the ground, and brown-haired Covan went in to hear the tidings of good. He was not long listening to the message of gladness, when there rushed in a light youth with raised look and panting breath to tell him that the dun cows were in the corn-field, and to order him to drive them out.

"Depart from me," says Covan. "It were easier for you, my good fellow, to drive them out yourself, than to run thus with panting breath to tell me. I will listen to the pleasant words."

A very short time after this the same youth came back, excitement and wildness in his eye, his chest panting.

"Out, out, Son of Gorla of the Flocks, our dogs are chasing thy cows. If thou be not out immediately thou shalt not get another sight of them."

"Away, good fellow," said brown-haired Covan.

2 A

"It were easier for thee to stop thy dogs than to come thus panting to tell the tale to me."

When the worship was over, brown-haired Covan went out, and found the three dun cows reposing in the very place where he had left them. They rose, went on their journey homewards, and Covan followed them. He had not gone far when he came to a plain so bare that he could see the smallest pin on the very ground, and he noticed a mare with a young frisking foal pasturing there, both as fat as the seal of the great ocean. "This is wonderful," says brown-haired Covan. Very shortly after this he saw another plain, with rich abundant grass, where were a mare and a foal so very lean that a shoemaker's awl would not stand in their backs. After this was seen a fresh-water lake, to the upper end of which was travelling a numerous band of youths, bright and buoyant, fair and happy. They were going with joyful songs to the land of the Sun, to dwell under the shade of trees whose leaves were most fragrant. He heard the murmur of the brooks that flowed in the land of the Sun—the songs of the birds—the melody of strings which he knew not, and of musical instruments of which he had never heard. He perceived other bands of miserable persons, going to the lower end of the lake—to the land of Darkness. Horrible was the scream that they raised, woful was the sad wringing of their hands. Mist and dark clouds were over the land to which they were travelling, and Covan heard the muttering of thunder. "This is truly wonderful," he said; but he followed the three dun cows.

The night now threatened to be stormy, and he knew not of house or of shelter where to pass it. But there met him the Dog of *Maol-mòr*, and no sooner met, than this liberal giver of food invited him, not churlishly or grudgingly, but hospitably and heartily, to lay aside three-thirds of his weariness, and to pass the whole night with him. He was well and carefully tended by the Dog of *Maol-mòr* in a warm cave, where no water from above or below came near them,—if this would suffice him with sweet flesh of lamb, and of kid, without stint or scant, and in the morning abundance for the day's journey

"Now farewell to thee, Covan," says his host.

" Success to thee; wherever thou goest may happiness be always thy companion. I offered hospitality, and thou didst not spurn it. Thou didst pleasantly and cheerfully accept what I offered; thou didst pass the night in my cave; thou didst trust in me; thou hast made fast my friendship, and thou shalt not be deceived. Now attend to my words: if ever difficulty or danger overtake thee, whenever speed of foot and resolute action may deliver thee, think of the Dog of *Maol-mòr*, wish for him, and I will be by thy side."

He met with the like friendship and liberality on the following night from the renowned giver of food, the active, far-travelling black raven of *Corri-nan-creag*, on whom sleep never settled, nor sun ever rose, until he had provided what was enough for himself and for him who came and went. Short-hopping, wing-clapping, he led the way for Covan through the goats' track, to a hollow under a dry snout of rock, where he asked him to lay aside three-thirds of his weariness, and to pass the whole night with him. He was well cared for that night, if mutton and venison would suffice;

and on going away in the morning, he said to him,
" Covan, son of Gorla of the Flocks, take with thee
what thou needest. The stranger's portion I never
missed, and remember my words. If ever you
happen to be in peril or hardship, where a strong
wing, and courage which fails not, will avail thee,
remember me. Warm is thy breast, kind is thine
eye. Thou didst confide in me; thou hast ere
this fed the black raven of the wilderness. I am
thy friend—trust in me."

On the third night he met with companionship
and hospitality as good from the *Doran-donn*, the
sharp-eyed, the skilful, active seeker, who would
not be without food for man or boy while it was
to be found either on sea or land. Though in his
den were heard the mewing of wild cats and the
snarling of badgers, he led Covan—without awe, or
fear, or starting—firmly, steadily, straightly to the
mouth of a cairn, where he asked him to lay aside
three-thirds of his weariness, and to pass the whole
night with him. Well was he entertained that
night by *Doran-donn* of the stream—the constant
traveller—if fish of every kind better than another
would suffice, and a bed—dry, comfortable, and

soft—of the cast-wave of the highest spring-tide, and of the *dilse* of the farthest out shore.

"Rest for the night, Covan," said he. "Thou art most heartily welcome. Sleep soundly; the *Doran-donn* is a wakeful guard."

When day came Doran escorted Covan for a part of the way.

"Farewell, Covan," said he. "Thou hast made me thy friend; and if ever difficulty or danger overtake thee, in which he who can swim the stream and dive under the wave will avail thee, think of me,—I will be at thy side."

Covan went forward and found the three dun cows in the hollow where he had left them, and by the close of that same evening he and they reached the dwelling on the hill safe and sound. Welcome and kindness awaited him in the house when he entered, and he was entertained without stint or grudge. The aged man asked how it had fared with him since his departure, and he began to declare it. He praised him for not having meddled with anything which he had seen until he reached the house of the sweet hymns, because those were only a vain show to deceive him.

"I will, after this, open to thee the mystery of the matter, and explain the meaning of the sights which caused thy great wonder," says the old man. "Meantime, ask thy reward, and thou shalt have it."

"That will not be heavy on thee, I hope," says Covan, "and it will be abundant for me. Restore to me in life and health—as they were when they left my father's house — my beloved sister and brothers, and piece of gold or coin of silver Covan wishes not."

"High is thy demand, young man," said the aged. "There are difficulties between thee and thy request above what thou canst surmount."

"Name them," says Covan, "and let me encounter them as I best may."

"Hearken, then. In that lofty mountain there is a fleet roe of slenderest limb. Her like there is not. White-footed, side-spotted she is, and her antlers like the antlers of the deer. On the beautiful lake near the land of the Sun, there is a duck surpassing every duck—the green duck of the golden neck. In the dark pool of *Corri-Buy*, there is a salmon white-bellied, red-gilled, and his side like the silver of purest hue. So, bring home hither the spotted white-footed roe of the mountain, the beautiful duck of the golden neck, and the salmon which can be distinguished from every salmon,—then will I tell thee of the sister and brothers of thy love."

Off went brown-haired Covan. The Maid of the Golden Hair and the Silver Comb followed him.

"Take courage, Covan," says she; "thou hast the blessing of thy mother and the blessing of the poor. Thou hast stood to thy promise; thou hast rendered honour to the house of sweet hymns. Go, and remember my parting words. Never despair."

He sought the mountain; the roe was seen— her like was not on the mountain; but when he was on one summit the roe was on another, and it was as well for him to try to catch the restless clouds of the sky. He was on the point of despair when he remembered the words of the Maid of the Golden Hair: "Oh, that I now had the fleet-footed Dog of *Maol-mòr*," said he. He no sooner spoke the word than the good dog was by his side, and after taking a turn or two around the hill, he laid the spotted roe of the mountain at his feet.

Covan now betook himself to the lake, and saw the green duck of the golden neck flying above him. "Oh, that now I had the black raven of the wilderness, swiftest of wing, and sharpest of eye," says he. No sooner had he spoken thus, than he saw the black raven of the wilderness approaching the lake, and quickly he left the green duck of the golden neck by his side.

Then he reached the dark deep pool, and saw the silvery, beautiful salmon, swimming from bank to bank. "Oh, that I now had the *Doran-donn* that swims the streams and dives under the wave," says Covan. In the winking of an eye, who was sitting on the banks of the river, but *Doran-donn?* He looked in Covan's face with kindness — he quickly went out of sight, and from the dark deep pool he took the white-bellied salmon of brightest hue and laid it at his feet. Covan now turned homewards, and left the roe, the duck, and the salmon on the threshold of the dwelling on the hill.

"Success and gladness be with thee," said the aged man. "He never put his shoulder to it who did not throw the difficulty over. Come in, Covan; and when the Maid of the Golden Hair has milked the three dun cows, I will open the mystery of the matter to thee, and we will draw wisdom from the history, and the journey of Covan."

### THE MYSTERY OF THE TALE OPENED.

"Thou didst not leave the house of thy father and of thy mother without their consent: the blessing of father and mother was with thee, Covan. Thou didst not refuse a morsel to the hungry in his need: the blessing of the poor was with thee, Covan. Thou didst make an engagement, thou didst promise, and didst fulfil; and the reward of the true is with thee. Thou didst see the golden cock and the silver hen—the *glamour* which gold and silver cast on the sight: thou didst remember thy promise, and didst walk in the path of duty. Happiness attended thee, Covan. The tempter tried thee again with the wand of gold, and the wand of silver which appeared easier to grasp. Thou didst remember thy promise and didst follow the cattle. When he failed to lead thee astray by gold and silver, he tried to deceive thee with the fair fruit of the grove. He set before thee every fruit ever seen by thee, and twelve which had not been seen, but thou didst turn away from them. He then tried thy courage by means of the fire and the flood; but thou didst pass through them on the path of duty, and didst find that they were as nothing. Thou didst hear the voice of the holy hymns, and the sound of the sweet songs. Thou didst go in, doing well. But even thither the tempter followed thee. Good was thy answer to him. 'I will listen to the truth.' Thou didst see the bare pasture with the high-bounding steed and the frisking foal, glad in the midst of it. Thus often, Covan, is it in the world. There is scarcity in the house of hospitality; but peace, gladness, and increase are along with it. Thou didst see the abundant pasture, and every four-footed creature on it near dying from leanness. Thus, in the world, is the house of the penurious churl. There is abundance in it; but he has not the heart to

use it; there is want in the midst of plenty.
There is a worm gnawing every root, and every
flower is withered. Thou didst see the beautiful
lake, and didst hear the glad notes of the happy
bands who were travelling to the land of the Sun.
These are they who attended to my counsel, and
were wise in their day. Thou didst hear the
painful wailing of those who were going to the
land of Darkness. These were the people without understanding or wisdom, without truth or
faithfulness, who made light of every warning,
and now they lament miserably. Thou didst not
despise the kindness or hospitality of the poor.
Thou receivedst frankly what was offered thee in
friendship. Thou didst not shame the needy.
Thus thou didst bind their attachment to thee.
Thou didst stand to thy promise. Thou didst
follow the cattle. Thou hast earned thy reward.
I trusted to thy courage. Difficulties did not
deter thee. Putting thy shoulder to them, thou
didst overcome them. Thou didst never despair.
Thou didst also find that the Dog of *Maol-mòr*,
the Black Raven of the Wilderness, and the Brown
Doran of the Stream, were not without value.

"And now, Covan, Son of Gorla of the Flocks, hearken to me: 'Restore to me,' thou sayest, 'my beautiful sister and beloved brothers, whom thou hast under the power of witchcraft!' What is witchcraft, Covan? The false contrivance of the deceiver—the vain excuse of the coward—the bugbear of fools—the terror of the faint-hearted— what never was, is, nor will be. Against the dutiful and the upright there is neither witchcraft nor wile. Thy sister, the Darling of the Golden Hair, thou shalt get home with thee; but thy brothers, though they are alive, laziness and unfaithfulness have made wanderers without home or friend. Go thou to thy father's house, Covan, and treasure in thy heart what thou hast seen and heard."

"And who art thou that addressest me?" said Covan.

"I am the Spirit of Eld—the Voice of Age," says the old man. "Fare thee well, Covan. The blessing of the aged go ever with thee."

## THE EMIGRANT SHIP.*

RETURNING from Iona on the loveliest summer evening which I ever beheld, we reached
a safe and sheltered bay at the north end of the
Island of Mull. I never saw a harbour so well
defended from the violence of winds and waves.
A long narrow island encircled it seawards, spreading its friendly wings over every vessel that
comes to seek its covert from the storms of ocean,
or to await under its shelter for favourable weather
to double the great headland beyond. On the
right hand where we entered, the land rises up

* From the Gaelic of the late Rev. Dr Macleod of St Columba's,
Glasgow.

steep and abrupt from the shore. We sailed so close to the rocks, that the branches of the trees were bending over us. The fragrance of the birch was wafted on the breeze of summer, and a thousand little birds, with their sweet notes, were singing to us from amid the branches, bidding us welcome as we glided smoothly and gently past them. A glorious view presented itself to me wherever I turned my eye. I saw the lofty mountains of Ardnamurchan clothed in green to their very summits; Suanard, with its beautifully-outlined hills and knolls; the coast of Morven stretching away from us, rejoicing in the warmth of the summer evening.

When we neared the anchorage there was nothing to be seen but masts of ships, with their flags floating lazily in the gentle breeze—nor to be heard, except the sound of oars, and the murmur of brooks and streams, which, falling over many a rock, were pouring into the wide bay, now opening up before us. From side to side of the shore, on the one hand, there runs a street of white houses; and immediately behind them there rises up a steep and high bank, where the hazel,

the rowan, and the ash grow luxuriantly, and so
very close to the houses that the branches seem
to bend over their tops.   At the summit of this
lofty bank the other portion of the small town is
seen between you and the sky, presenting a view
striking for its beauty and singularity.

The bay, however, presented the most interesting sight.   There were in it scores of vessels of
different sizes ; many a small boat with its painted
green oars ;  the gay *birlinn* with its snow-white
sails, and the war-ship with its lofty masts and
royal flag.   But in the midst of them all I marked
one ship which was to me of surpassing interest.
Many little boats were pressing towards her, and
I noticed that she was preparing to unmoor.
There was one man in our boat who had joined
us at the back of Mull, and who had not during
the whole day once raised his head, but who now
was scanning this great ship with the keenest
anxiety.

"Do you know," I asked, "what this ship is ?"

"Alas!" said he, "'tis I who do know her.
Grieved am I to say that there are too many of
my acquaintances in her.   In her are my brothers,

and many of my dearest friends, departing on a long, mournful voyage for North America. And sad is it that I have not what would enable me to accompany them."

We pulled towards the vessel; for I confess I felt strongly desirous of seeing these warm-hearted men who, on this very day, were to bid a last farewell to the Highlands, in search of a country where they might find a permanent home for themselves and their families. It is impossible to convey to any one who was not present a true idea of the scene which presented itself on going on board. Never will it fade from my memory. They were here, young and old—from the infant to the patriarch. It was most overwhelming to witness the deep grief, the trouble of spirit, the anguish and brokenness of heart which deeply furrowed the countenances of the greater number of these men, here assembled from many an island and distant portion of the Hebrides.

I was, above all, struck with the appearance of one man, aged and blind, who was sitting apart, with three or four young boys clustered around him, each striving which could press most closely

2 B

to his breast.  His old arms were stretched over them ; his head was bent towards them ; his gray locks and their brown curly hair mingling, while his tears, in a heavy shower, were falling on them.  Sitting at his feet was a respectably dressed woman, sobbing in the anguish of bitter grief ; and I understood that a man who was walking backwards and forwards, with short steps and folded hands, was her husband.  His eye was restless and unsettled, and his troubled countenance told that his mind was far from peace.  I drew near to the old man, and in gentle language asked him if he, in the evening of his days, was about to leave his native land.

" Is it I, going over the ocean ?" said he.  " No! On no journey will I go, until the great journey begins which awaits us all ; and when that comes, who will bear my head to the burial ?  You are gone ; you are gone ; to-day I am left alone, blind and aged, without brother, or son, or support. To-day is the day of my desolation, God forgive me ! thou, Mary, my only child, with my fair and lovely grandchildren, art about to leave me !  I will return to-night to the old glen ; but it is a

strange hand that will lead me. You, my beloved
children, will not come out to meet the old man.
I will no more hear the prattle of your tongues
by the river-side, and no more shall I cry, as
I used to do, though I saw not the danger, 'Keep
back from the stream!' When I hear the barking
of the dogs, no more will my heart leap upwards,
saying, 'My children are coming.' Who now will
guide me to the shelter of the rock, or read to me
the holy book? And to-morrow night, when the
sun sinks in the west, where will you be, children
of my love? or who will raise the evening hymn
with me?"

"O father," said his daughter, creeping close
to him, "do not break my heart!"

"Art thou here, Mary?" said he. "Where is
thy hand? Come nearer to me. My delight of
all the women in the world. Sweet to me is thy
voice. Thou art parting with me. I do not blame
thee, neither do I complain. Thou hast my full
sanction. Thou hast the blessing of thy God.
As was thy mother before thee, be thou dutiful.
As for me, I will not long stand. To-day I am
stripped of my lovely branches, and light is the

breeze which will lay low my old head.   But while I live, God will uphold me!   He was ever with me in every trial, and He will not now forsake me. Blind though I be, yet blessed be His name! He enables me to see at His own right hand my best Friend, and in His countenance I can see gentleness and love.   At this very moment He gives me strength.   His promises come home to my heart.   Other trees may wither ; but the 'Tree of Life' fades not.   Are you all near me ?   Listen," said he, "we are now about to part.   You are going to a land far away; and probably before you reach it I shall be in the lofty land where the sun ever shines, and where, I trust, we shall all meet again ; and where there shall be no partings, nor removals.   No.   Remember the God of your fathers, and fall not away from any one good habit which you have learned.   Evening and morning, bend the knee.   Evening and morning, raise the hymn, as we were wont to do.   And you, my little children, who were as eyes and as a staff unto me—you, who I thought would place the sod over me—must I part with you ?   God be my helper ! "

I could not remain longer. The little boat which was to bear the old man to the shore had come to the side of the ship. Those who were waiting on him informed him of this. I fled; I could not witness the miserable separation.

In another part of the vessel there was a company of men, whom I understood from their dress and language to belong to the Northern Islands. They were keenly and anxiously watching a boat which was coming round the point, urged alike by sails and oars. Whenever they saw her making for the ship, they shouted out: "It is he himself! Blessings on his head!" There was one person among them who seemed more influential than the others. When he observed this boat, he went to the captain of the ship, and I observed that the sailors who were aloft among the masts and spars were ordered to descend, and that the preparations for immediate sailing were suspended. The boat approached. An aged, noble-looking man who was sitting in the stern rose up, and although his head was white as the snow, he ascended the side of the ship with a firm vigorous step, dispensing with any assistance.

The captain saluted him with the utmost respect. He looked around him, and quickly noticing the beloved group who had been watching for him, he walked towards them. "God be with you!" he said to them, as they all rose up, bonnet in hand, to do him reverence. He sat down among them. For a while he leaned his head on the staff which was in his hand, and I observed that great tears were rolling down his face—one of the most pleasant faces I had ever looked on. They all grouped around him, and some of the children sat at his feet. There was something in the appearance of this patriarchal man which could not fail to draw one towards him. Such goodness and gentleness surrounded him that the most timid would be enouraged to approach him; and, at the same time, such lofty command in his eye and brow as would cause the boldest to quail before him.

"You have come," said they, "according to your promise; you never neglected us in the day of our need. To-night we are to become wanderers over the face of the ocean, and before the sun will rise over those hills we shall be for ever out of their sight. We are objects of pity to-day—day of our ruin!"

"Let me not hear such language," said the minister. "Be manly; this is not the time for you to yield. Place your confidence in God: for it is not without His knowledge that you go on this journey. It is through His providence that all things are brought to pass: but you speak as if you were to travel beyond the bounds of the kingdom of the Almighty, and to go whither His Fatherly care could not extend unto you. Alas! is this all your faith?"

"That is all true," answered they; "but the sea —the great wide ocean?"

"The sea!" said he, "why should it cast down or disquiet you? Is not God present on the great ocean as on the land? Under the guidance of His wisdom, and the protection of His power, are you not as safe on the wide ocean as you ever were in the most sheltered glen? Does not the God who made the ocean go forth on its proud waves? Not one of them will rise against you without His knowledge. It is He who stills the raging of the sea. He goeth forth over the ocean in the chariots of the wind as surely as He is in the heavens above. Oh, ye of little faith, wherefore do ye doubt?"

"We are leaving our native land," said they.

"You are indeed leaving the place of your birth," he replied, "the island where you were nourished and reared. You are certainly going on a long journey, and it need not be concealed that there are hardships awaiting you, but these do not come unexpectedly on you: you may be prepared to meet them. And as to leaving our country, the children of men have no permanent hold of any country under the sun. We are all strangers and pilgrims; and it is not in this world that God gives any of us that home from which there is no departure."

"That is undoubtedly true," said they; "but we go as 'sheep without a shepherd'—without a guide to consult in our perplexities. Oh, if you had been going with us!"

"Silence!" said he. "Let me not hear such language. Are you going farther from God than you were before? Is it not the same Lord that opened your eyelids to-day and raised you from the slumber of the night, who rules on the other side of the world? Who stood by Abraham when he left his country and his kindred? Who showed himself to Jacob when he left his father's house, and slept in the open field? Be ashamed of yourselves for your want of trust. Did you say you were as 'sheep without a shepherd?' Is there any, even the youngest of your children, who cannot repeat these words: 'The Lord's my shepherd, I'll want not?' Has not the Great Shepherd of the sheep said: 'Fear not; for I am with thee. Be not dismayed: for I am thy God?' Has He not said: 'When thou passest through the waters I will be with thee; and through the rivers, they shall not overflow thee?' There are not, perhaps, houses of worship so accessible to you where you are going, as they were in your native land; nor are ministers of religion so numerous. But remember you the day of the Lord. Assemble yourselves under the shelter of the rock, or under the shade of the tree. Raise up together the songs of Zion, remembering that the gracious presence of God is not confined to any one place; that, by those who sincerely seek Him in the name of Christ, He is to be found on the peak of the highest mountain, in the strath of the deepest glen, or in the innermost shade of the forest, as well as in the midst of the great city, or in the most costly temple ever reared by man's hands. You are all able to read the Holy Word. Had it been otherwise, heavy indeed would be my heart, and very sad the parting. I know you have some Bibles with you; but you will to-day accept from me each a new Bible, one that is easily carried and handled; and you will not value them the less that your names are written in them by the hand which sprinkled the water of baptism on the most of you—which has often since been raised up to Heaven in prayers for you, and which will continue to be raised for you with good hope through Christ until death shall disable it. And you, my little children, the precious lambs of my flock, now about to leave me, I have brought for you also some slight memorials of my great love to you. May God bless you!"

"Oh," said they, "how thankful are we that we have seen you once more, and that we have again heard your voice!"

The people of the ship were now generally

gathering round this group, and even the sailors, though some of them did not understand his language, perceived that it was in matters pertaining to the soul he was engaged. There was so much earnestness, warmth, and kindliness in his appearance and voice, that they stood reverently still; and I saw several of them hiding the tears which rolled down those cheeks that had been hardened by many a storm.

The reverend man uncovered his head, and stood up. Every one perceived his purpose. Some kneeled down, and those who stood cast their eyes downwards, when in a clear strong voice he said, "Let us pray for the blessing of God." Hard indeed would be the heart which would not melt, and little to be envied the spirit which would not become solemnised while the earnest, warm-hearted prayer was being offered up by this good man, who was himself raised above the world. Many a poor faint-hearted one was encouraged. His words fell like the dew of the evening, and the weak, drooping branches were strengthened and refreshed.

While they were on their knees, I heard heavy sighings and sobbings, which they strove hard to smother. But when they rose up I saw through the mist of the bitter tears which they were now wiping off, the signs of fresh hope beaming from their eyes. He opened the Book of Psalms, and the most mournful, the most affecting in every way, yet at the same time the most joyful sacred song which I ever heard was raised by them all. The solemn sound reached every ship and boat in the harbour. Every oar rested. There was perfect silence; a holy calm as they sang a part of the 42d Psalm.

"O why art thou cast down, my soul?
Why, thus with grief opprest,
Art thou disquieted in me?
In God still hope and rest:
For yet I know I shall Him praise,
Who graciously to me
The health is of my countenance,
Yea, mine own God is He."

## THE STORY OF MARY OF UNNIMORE, AS TOLD BY HERSELF.*

THAT was the day of the sadness to many—the day on which Mac Cailein† (*Argyle*) parted with the estate of his ancestors in the place where I was reared.

The people of Unnimore thought that "flitting" would not come upon them while they lived. As long as they paid the rent, and that was not difficult to do, anxiety did not come near them ; and

* From the Gaelic of the late Dr Macleod, of St Columba's, Glasgow, illustrative of the poor Highlander in the great city.

† *Mac Cailein.* Sir Walter Scott, and after him Macaulay, writes Argyle's patronymic as *Mac Callum*, a mistake which sounds very offensive to a Celtic ear. Colin — Celtic *Cailein*—was the founder of the Argyle family.

a lease they asked not. It was there that the friendly neighbourhood was, though now only one smoke is to be seen, from the house of the Saxon shepherd.

When we got the "summons to quit," we thought it was only for getting an increase of rent, and this we willingly offered to give; but permission to stay we got not. The small cattle\* were sold, and at length it became necessary to part with the one cow. When shall I forget the plaintive wailing of the children deprived of the milk which was no more for them? When shall I forget the last sight I got of my pretty *cluster* of goats bleating on the *lip* of the rock, as if inviting me to milk them? But it was not allowed me to put a *cuarch* (pail) under them.

The day of "flitting" came. The officers of the law came along with it, and the shelter of a house, even for one night more, was not to be got. It was necessary to depart. The hissing of the fire

---

\* Cows forming the chief property of the Highlanders, known as *ni*, "substance," or "wealth," and furnishing epithets expressive of strong affection, the sheep were thought to be highly honoured by being styled "small cows," or "small cattle;" and here we are reminded of Isaiah xliii. 23, "The small cattle of thy burnt-offerings."

on the flag of the hearth as they were *drowning* it,
reached my heart.    We could not get even a bothy
in the country; therefore we had nothing for it but
to face the *land of strangers*, (Lowlands.)    The aged
woman, the mother of my husband, was then alive,
weak, and lame.    James carried her on his back in
a creel.    I followed him with little John, an infant
at my breast, and thou who art no more, Donald
beloved, a little *todd.er*, walking with thy sister by
my side.    Our neighbours carried the little furniture that remained to us, and showed every kindness which tender friendship could show.

On the day of our leaving Unnimore I thought
my heart would rend.    I would feel right if my
tears would flow; but no relief thus did I find.
We sat for a time on "Knock-nan-Carn" (Hill of
Cairns,) to take the last look at the place where
we had been brought up.    The houses were being
already stripped.    The bleat of the "big sheep"*

* The small cattle, (*meanbh-chro,*) the indigenous breed of sheep,
small in size, most delicate in flesh, and fine in wool, like the Shet-
land kind, housed every night, and milked every day, were favour-
ites with the people; but the large sheep that ranged the mountain
and the strath alike, and which have led to so many unhappy clearances, are to the common Celt objects of utter detestation.    The
"tooth of the big sheep" is "the root of all evil" in his estimation,

was on the mountain. The whistle of the Lowland shepherd and the bark of his dogs were on the brae. We were sorrowful, but thanks to Him who strengthened us, no imprecation or evil wish was heard from one of us. "There is no fear of us," says James. "The world is wide, and God will sustain us. I am here carrying my mother, and thou, Mary, with my young children, art walking with me on this sorrowful 'flitting;' yet we are as happy, and possibly as great objects of envy, as the owner of this estate who has driven us to the wandering."

What have you of it, but that we reached Glasgow, and through the letter of the saintly man who is now no more, my beloved minister, (little did I think that I would not again behold his noble countenance,) we got into a cotton work. Here James got good steady *earning*,* as did also the

and the "good time coming" is always associated with the extirpation of this accursed breed. We knew a minister who preached in Skye—a native not of the Highlands, however, but of the Lowlands—within the last thirty years; and who, wishing to present a very attractive picture of heaven, assured his hearers that "there would be no big sheep there."

* *Earning* is the Gaelic equivalent of employment. I suppose it may be inferred from this that the Highlander was often employed

children when they grew up. We were comfortable, and I hope that we were grateful. The old woman was still living, her intellect and memory as good as ever they had been. She knew so much of old Highland lore, that it was a relief to James, when he came home weary from the work, to sit down and converse with her.

We were able to do much justice (*give a good opportunity*) to the children. They read English and Gaelic equally well, and nothing did the old woman ever see that she valued like listening to thee, Donald, beloved, reading the Bible and other good books; and it is thou who could do that distinctly and sedately.

It pleased God to call the old woman away, and she fell into the quiet sleep of death, bequeathing her soul to the blessed Saviour who went to death for her. We missed her greatly. Instead of being thankful for the time that it had pleased God to spare her, we lamented for her beyond measure. God chastised us. My beautiful, splendid boy

without remuneration; and, beyond question, "remunerative work" would readily solve the difficulty as to the maintenance of the population of the Highlands.

took the infectious fever, which was at the time in the great city, and shortly after his father and his sister took it. It is He alone who enabled me to stand that has knowledge of what I endured at the time. Let men never say that there is not kindness in the Lowlanders. It is I who did not find them destitute of pity. Though the fear of the fever kept away the greater number of my acquaintance, God raised up friends who sustained me. A neighbour's wife, with whom I was but slightly acquainted, took the lassie from me, and I sent John to a friend's house to avoid the fever. My husband (*the man*)* and Donald were taken to the infirmary at the head of the town, and it was permitted to myself to follow them. Cheerless and heavy was my step after the carriage that conveyed them. I thought it could not be more sorrowful, though I were following them to the churchyard; but, oh! far asunder, as I have since felt, are the two things.

I heard so many stories of this nursing-house,

---

* The husband, styled in Scotch the "good-man," is in Gaelic styled simply the *man;* and, possibly, *the* man—the man, *par excellence*, is the most complimentary title that can be given.

that horror was on me for it; but it is I who did not need.   They were placed in a chamber which might suffice for a king, and a physician and a sick-nurse were as kind to them as if they had been their dearest on the face of the world.   Fifteen days after they went in—on the morning of the Communion-day—that pang entered my heart which has not left, and never will leave it.   From that time the world has lost for me much of its gladness.   Thou didst change, (*die*,) Donald, son of my love, who never saidst to father or mother, " It is ill."   But why should I complain?   He who called him to Himself had more right to him.   We must be resigned.

Donald departed: but thanks to the benign Father, all did not depart.   James recovered, and eight weeks after he had gone in we returned again to our home; but, oh! it was on that home that the change had come.   Donald was not.   It was he who used to read to us in the evening at the time of going to rest.   I noticed the sad cloud that was on the countenance of my husband as he said:—

" Wife, where is the Bible?   Bring it to myself to-night."

"Come here, John," said I, "and take the Bible."

"Oh! is it not right?" said James. "Thank God that you are spared!"

James had no strength for work. He was feeble and without courage. We had nothing but what John brought in from day, to day so that it was necessity to me to sell, little by little, what we could best spare of the furniture, hoping that better days would come. At length the rent was to be paid and nothing to meet it. James went out with Donald's watch, and the name of my darling cut on the back of it. He returned after paying the rent, and laid himself down on the bed without a word out of his head. But, as God brought it round, who came in that very evening but the minister, and that was the visit of blessedness to us. He held much discourse with us. He offered up a prayer which dropped on our hearts. Our courage rose greatly. His language was like the dew of the evening on the tender plants which were withering.

The health of James was improving, and he obtained some kind of night work during the year. But on a night of those nights at the beginning of winter five years ago, John came in and great grief was on his countenance, as if he had been weeping.

"What is the matter, my love?" I said.

"There is not much," he said. "Perhaps another place may open, though the work in which I am has stopped. The work-people have risen against the masters, demanding a heightening of wages, and threaten to burn the works if they will not yield. They have drawn out a writing, and they threaten evil to every one who will not put his hand to it."

James was stretched on the bed, but as soon as he heard this, he raised his head and said:

"I hope, John, that thou hast not put thy hand to that bad paper."

"Is it I, father?" said the poor lad. "Truly I have not put, and will not put."

"Thou never wilt, my brave boy. Be faithful and true, as were the men from whom thou hast come. Stand thou by thy king and the laws of thy country, and let there be to thee no companionship with those who seek to lawlessness. We have what will suffice us to-night, and put the

Sabbath past. When Monday comes, God will open another door. 'God comes in want, and there is no want when He comes.' Let us go to rest. Bring over the books, John, and let us give praise to God. To-night let us sing the 146th Psalm, and raise the tune together. Oft have I sung it in the great assembly, with many of those who are not now on the face of the world, and I never heard it that it did not give relief to my heart."

We went to church on the next day, and heard teaching that helped us to forget this poor world.

"Blessed," said James, as we returned home, "is the day of the Sabbath; it is God himself hath set it apart."

At the beginning of the week two men, whom we knew, came from the cotton-mill, asking James and my son to stand out with them, saying there was no good for them to continue separate; speaking much against the tyranny and covetousness of the great merchants, and very much about king and kingdom which I could not understand.

"Leave me," says James. "There is no use in your speaking further. I will not stand out, neither will I do injury to the kind man who has given me employment ever since I came to the place, and whom I found truly steadfast in every distress. Leave me; the blood of rebelliousness is not in my veins."

They told him it was in their power to help him—that they had money from England to aid those who would stand out with them, and as a proof of this they offered to leave a crown-piece with him.

" No," said James. " Not a penny of your money shall be left in this house—there is a curse along with it. I will not stand with you; no more will my son. I have only him. I saw his brother, my good and faithful son, borne to the grave without the power of my being under his head, and it was a hard trial; but I would choose to see him who is alive laid by his brother's side before seeing him in the midst of those who seek to bring confusion and bloodshed on the country. Take away your money. There is not a coin to-night in my house. I have not a single (*red*\*) penny on the face of the world; but on the day that I rise

---

\* A *red* penny, *i.e.*, a copper penny, the lowest coin contrasted with the *white* penny—the silver shilling. *White money* is the common expression for silver coin generally.

with you may I be without shelter for the night. Go," said he ; " but I beseech you give up your folly ; it will not prosper with you."

They gave a loud laugh, and went away ridiculing his language.

Day after day was passing, and employment was not to be found. Everything that could be sold was gone, except the two beds and a few small articles which were not worth the disposing of. James lost his cheerfulness entirely. He would not go over the door ; but kept rocking himself by the fireside, without a syllable from his head. We had new Bibles, which had belonged to Donald. I noticed my husband taking them now and then out from the place in which they were locked, and after gazing on them he would shed tears, start back with a heavy sigh, and replace them in the very spot where they had been.

" You will not sell these, father, while I am alive ?" said John.

" Truly, my son, I would not wish to part with them, if I were at all able to keep them."

That very evening John went out, and as he did

not return at the time of our usual going to rest,
we were under great anxiety (*many pangs*)* for
him.  When he came, there was a kind of flush
in his cheek, and a raised look in his countenance,
which caused us to wonder and to fear.

"Father," said he, "forgive me ; and thou,
mother of my love, do not thou condemn me.
You shall not sell the Bibles of Donald, nor yet
the bed on which you are lying.  There is what
will help you."

He took out ten gold coins, and he placed them
on the table.  His father started with horror, and
had there not been a support to his back he would
have been clean over on the floor.

"What is this that thou hast done, my son ?
What hast thou done ?  Has *God let thee com-
pletely off His hand ?*†  What, I say, has befallen
thee ?" (*has risen to thee.*)

"Nothing," said he, "but that I have joined
the army.  To-night I am a soldier belonging to

---

* *Iomaguin*, literally, "many pangs," or "shooting pains,"
translated by *anxiety*, is a most expressive word ; better than even
the Greek, which refers to being taken to pieces.

† *i.e.*, Abandoned thee.  The idea of being borne on the arm of
the Almighty is a fine one.

*Red* King George ;* and I trust I shall not bring shame on my ancestors or on my country."

James raised his eyes, and the blood which had forsaken his cheek returned.

" John, come near me. It might have been worse, my brave boy, much worse."

" Oh, it is good that it is not worse ; but wherefore did you not tell us what was in your intention ?"

" It is not customary with youth," said he, " to consult with their parents before they take the gold ? and good is it to the king that it is thus. I have enlisted with Allan of Errach,† (with the man of Errach,) and he promised to come to-morrow to make my excuse."

On the morrow Allan *Mòr* (great Allan) came, and when he understood who we were, he assisted us liberally. What is there to say but that he did not lose sight of John when he was under him ?

---

* Referring to the " Red Army," as the Highlanders always call the regular army.

† Allan Mòr of Errach, who raised the 79th Regiment, was one of the most popular Highland officers in the army. He was knighted for his gallantry, and has left descendants in very influential positions.

He advanced him step by step in the army. He is now on his way home with a pension from his king and country, which will keep him easy for life. He is quit of soldiering any more, and we look for his return home in the course of a month. James is now in good health. He has got an easy place from the humane men, who did not forsake him. My daughter is married to a prudent, industrious lad from the Highlands, and now, thanks to the Gracious One who sustained us, the voice of joy is to be heard among us. Hardship did meet us : but God blessed it for our good. He stood by us in every difficulty. Often does James, in the communing of the evening, go over everything that has befallen us, tracing as he best can the steps of the Lord's providence towards the good of our souls. " It is good for me that I have been afflicted," is his language, and of every cause of gladness the least is not that, according to every account, John remembers his God and loves his Saviour. He never parted with his brother's Bible. Often has it accompanied him on the day of battle, and been his pillow at night in a far distant land.

He has been writing to us that this very Bible has been blessed for good to several of his fellow-soldiers to whom he used to read it. And now have we not cause to be thankful? Oh, let people never lose their hope in God. Let neither hardships nor poverty compel them to break His law, nor to neglect His ordinances. The *higher the tempest strikes*, (the louder the tempest rages,) the closer may they flee to the shadow of the Great Rock in the weary land. Thou, Lord, hast said, and true are all Thy words, " Because he hath set his love upon me, therefore will I deliver him. I will set him on high, because he hath known my name ;" and it is we who have experienced that " faithful is He who hath promised."

## CONCLUSION.—THE COMMUNION SUNDAY.

ON a beautiful Sunday in July I once again sat down at the foot of the old Iona-cross in the churchyard of " the Parish." It was a day of perfect summer glory. Never did the familiar landscape appear more lovely to the eye or more soothing and sanctifying to the spirit. The Sound of Mull lay like a sea of glass, without even a breath of fitful air from the hills to ruffle its surface. White sails met their own shadows on the water ; becalmed vessels mingled with gray islets, rocky shores, and dark bays, diminishing in bulk from the large brigs and schooners at my feet to the snow-white specks which dotted the

blue of the sea and hills of Lorn. The precipice
of Unnimore, streaked with waterfalls, rose in the
clear air above the old Keep of Ardtornish. The
more distant castled promontory of Duart seemed
to meet Lismore. Aros Castle, with its ample
bay, closed the view in the opposite direction to
the west; while over all the landscape a Sabbath
stillness reigned, like an invisible mantle of love
let down from the cloudless heaven over the weary
world below.

It was a Communion Sunday in "the Parish."

Few of the people had as yet arrived, and the
churchyard was as silent as its graves. But soon
the roads and paths leading to the church from
the distant glens and nearer hamlets began to stir
with the assembling worshippers. A few boats
were seen crossing the Sound, crowded with people
coming to spend a day of holy peace. Shepherds
in their plaids; old men and old women, with the
young of the third generation accompanying them,
arrived in groups. Some had left home hours
ago. Old John Cameron, with fourscore-years-
and-ten to carry, had walked from Kinloch, ten
miles across the pathless hills. Other patriarchs,

with staff in hand, had come greater distances
Old women were dressed in their clean white
" mutches," with black ribands bound round their
heads ; and some of the more gentle-born had
rags of old decency—a black silk scarf, fastened
with an old silver brooch, or a primitive-shaped
bonnet—adornments never taken out of the large
wooden chest since they were made, half a century
ago, except on such occasions as the present, or
on the occasion of a family marriage feast, or a
funeral, when a bit of decayed crape was added.
And old men were there who had seen better
days, and had been " gentlemen tacksmen" in the
" good old times," when the Duke of Argyle was
laird. Now their clothes are threadbare ; the old
blue coat with metal buttons is almost bleached ;
the oddly shaped hat and silk neckerchief, both
black once, are very brown indeed ; and the
leather gloves, though rarely on, are yet worn out,
and cannot stand further mending. But these are
gentlemen nevertheless in every thought and feeling. And some respectable farmers from the " low
country," who occupy the lands of these old tacksmen, travelled in their gigs. Besides these, there

were one or two of the local gentry, and the assisting clergymen.

How quiet and reverent all the people look, as, with steps unheard on the greensward, they collect in groups and greet each other with so much warmth and cordiality! Many a hearty shake of the hand is given; and many a respectful bow, from old gray heads uncovered, is received and returned by their beloved Pastor, who moves about, conversing with them all.

No one can discover any other expression than that of the strictest decorum and sober thoughtfulness, among the hundreds who are here assembling for worship.

It has been the fashion indeed, of some people who know nothing about Scotland or her Church, to use Burns as an authority for calling such meetings "holy fairs." What they may have been in the days of the poet, or how much he may himself have contributed to profane them, I know not. But neither in Ayrshire nor anywhere else have I ever been doomed to behold so irreverent and wicked a spectacle as he portrays. The question was indeed asked by a comparative stranger, on the Communion Sunday I am describing, whether the fact of so many people coming from such great distances might not be a temptation to some to indulge overmuch when "taking refreshments." The reply by one who knew them well was, "No, sir, not one man will go home in a state unbecoming a Christian."

The sentiment of gratitude was, naturally enough, often repeated:—"Oh! thank God for such a fine day!" For weather is an element which necessarily enters into every calculation of times and seasons in the Highlands. If the day is stormy, the old and infirm cannot come up to this annual feast, nor can brother clergymen voyage from distant Island Parishes to assist at it. Why, in the time of the old minister, he had to send a man on horseback over moors, and across stormy arms of the sea, for sixty miles, to get the wheaten bread used at the Communion! And for this reason, while the Communion is dispensed in smaller parishes and in towns every six months, and sometimes every quarter, it has hitherto been only celebrated once a year in most Highland Parishes. At such seasons, however,

2 D

every man and woman who is able to appear partakes of the holy feast. No wonder, therefore, the people are grateful for their lovely summer day!

The previous Thursday had been, as usual, set apart for a day of fasting and prayer. Then the officiating clergy preached specially upon the Communion, and on the character required in those who intended to partake of it; and young persons, after instruction and examination, were for the first time formally admitted (as at confirmation in the Episcopal Church) into full membership.

The old bell, which it is said was once at Iona, began to ring over the silent fields, and the small church was soon filled with worshippers. The service in the church to-day was in English, and a wooden pulpit, or "tent," as it is called, (I remember when it was made of boat sails,) was, according to custom, erected near the old arch in the churchyard, where service was conducted in Gaelic. Thus the people were divided, and, while some entered the church, many more gathered round the tent, and seated themselves on the graves or on the old ruin.

The Communion service of the Church of Scotland is a very simple one, and may be briefly described. It is celebrated in the church, of course, after the service and prayers are ended. In most cases a long, narrow table, like a bench, covered with white cloth, occupies the whole length of the church, and the communicants are seated on each side of it. Sometimes, in addition to this, the ordinary seats are similarly covered. The presiding minister, after reading an account of the institution from the Gospels and Epistles, and giving a few words of suitable instruction, offers up what is called the consecration prayer, thus setting apart the bread and wine before him as symbols of the body and blood of Jesus. After this he takes the bread, and, breaking it, gives it to the communicants near him, saying, "This is my body broken for you, eat ye all of it." He afterwards hands to them the cup, saying, "This cup is the new testament in my blood, shed for the remission of the sins of many, drink ye all of it ; for as oft as ye eat this bread and drink this cup, ye do show forth the Lord's death until He come again." The bread and wine are then passed from the communicants to each other, assisted by the elders who are in attendance. In solemn silence the Lord is remembered, and by every true communicant is received as the living bread, the life of their souls, even as they receive into their bodies the bread and wine. During the silence of communion every head is bowed down, and many an eye and heart are filled, as the thoughts of Jesus at such a time mingle with those departed ones, with whom they enjoy, in and through Him, the communion of saints. Then follows an exhortation by the minister to faith and love and renewed obedience; and then the 103d Psalm is generally sung, and while singing it the worshippers retire from the table, which is soon filled with other communicants; and this is repeated several times, until the whole service is ended with prayer and praise.

Let no one thoughtlessly condemn these simple services because they are different in form from those he has been accustomed to. Each nation and church has its own peculiar customs, originating generally in circumstances which once made them natural, reasonable, or perhaps necessary. Although these originating causes have passed away, yet the peculiar forms remain, and become familiar to the people, and venerable, almost holy, from linking the past with the present. Acquaintance with other branches of the Christian Church; a knowledge of living men, and the spirit with which the truly good serve God according to the custom of their fathers; a dealing, too, with the realities of human life, and Christian experience, rather than with the ideal of what might, could, would, or should be, will tend to make us charitable in our judgments of those who receive good, and express their love to God, through outward forms very different from our own. Let us thank God when men see and are guided by true light, whatever may be the form or setting of the lens by which it is transmitted. Let us endeavour to penetrate beneath the variable, the temporary, and accidental, to the unchangeable, the eternal, and necessary; and then we shall bless God when among "different communions" and "different sacraments," we can discover earnest believing souls, who have communion with the same living Saviour, who receive with faith and love the same precious sacrifice to be their life. I have myself, with great thankfulness, been privileged to receive the sacrament from the hands of "priests and bishops" in the rural churches and hoary cathedrals of England, and to join in different parts of the world, east and west, with brethren of different names, but all having the same faith in the One Name, "of whom *the whole family* in heaven and earth is named." I am sure the "communion" in the Spirit was the same in all.

Close behind the churchyard wall I noticed a stone which marked the grave of an old devoted Wesleyan minister. He was a lonely man, without any "kindred dust" to lie with. It had been his wish to be buried here, beside a child whom he had greatly admired and loved. "In memory," so runs the inscription, "of Robert Harrison, missionary of the Lord, who died 29th January 1832. 'I have sinned; I have repented; I have believed; I love; and I rest in the hope that by the grace of God I shall rise and reign with my Redeemer throughout eternity.'" Beyond the churchyard are a few old trees surrounding a field where, according to tradition, once stood the "palace" of Bishop Maclean. The bishop himself lies under the old archway, near the grave of Flora Cameron. Was it "latitudinarianism" to believe, as I do, that could Wesleyan missionary and Episcopalian bishop have returned to earth, neither of them would have refused to remember Jesus with those Presbyterian worshippers on the ground of " schism ? "

When the service in the church was ended, I again sat down beside the old cross. The majority of the congregation had assembled around the tent in the churchyard near me. The officiating minister was engaged in prayer, in the midst of the living and the dead. The sound of his voice hardly disturbed the profound and solemn silence. One heard with singular distinctness the bleating of the lambs on the hills, the hum of the passing bee, the lark "singing like an angel in the clouds," with the wild cries coming from the distant sea of birds that flocked over their prey. Suddenly the sound of psalms arose from among the tombs. It was the thanksgiving and parting hymn :—

> " Salvation and immortal praise
>     To our victorious King !
>  Let heaven and earth, and rocks and seas,
>     With glad hosannas ring.
>  To Father, Son, and Holy Ghost,
>     The God whom we adore,
>  Be glory, as it was, and is,
>     And shall be evermore."

So sang those humble peasants, ere they parted to their distant homes,—some to meet again in communion here, some to meet at a nobler feast above. So sang they that noble hymn, among the graves of their kindred, with whose voices theirs had often mingled on the same spot, and with whose spirits they still united in remembering and praising the living Saviour.

Some, perhaps, there are who would have despised or pitied that hymn, because sung with so little art. But a hymn was once sung long ago, on an evening after the first Lord's Supper, by a few lowly men in an upper chamber in Jerusalem, and the listening angels never heard such music ascending to the ears of God from this jarring and discordant world! The humble Lord who sang that hymn, and who led that chorus of fishermen, will not despise the praises of peasant saints ; nor will the angels perceive the songs of the loving heart as ever out of harmony with the noblest chords struck from their own golden harps, or the noblest anthems sung within God's temple of the sky.

As I now write these lines where so many beloved faces pass before me, which made other years a continual benediction, and as I hear their familiar voices greet me as of yore, in tones which will never more be silent to me, but mingle with my holiest, happiest hours, I cannot conclude my reminiscences of this dear old parish, which I leave at early dawn, without expressing my deep gratitude to Almighty God for His gift, to me and to many, of those who once here lived, but who now live for evermore with Christ—enjoying an eternal Communion Sunday.

*Ballantyne & Company, Printers, Edinburgh.*

15 FE67